THE STRUGGLE
FOR THE
MEDITERRANEAN

By the same author

In English

I Chased a Ghost
Oleanders in the Wind
The Battle of Malta
The Ghosts of Malta
Industrial Relations in Malta
Britain and Malta – The Story of an Era
The Atlantis Inheritance
The Angel of Death
The Knights of Malta

In Maltese

It-Toroq Kollha Jwasslu għal Ruma *(All Roads lead to Rome)*
Taħt is-Sinjal ta' Taurus *(Under the Sign of Taurus)*
Ix-Xitan Wasal fit-Tlettax (The Devil came on the Thirteenth)
L-Aħħar Appuntament (The Last Appointment)

Bi-lingual

Malta – Know the country; Speak its language (A tourist booklet)

THE STRUGGLE FOR THE MEDITERRANEAN

by

JOSEPH ATTARD

THE STRUGGLE FOR THE MEDITERRANEAN

ISBN 99909-3-041-4

Printed & Published in 1995
Reprinted 1999
by Progress Press Co. Ltd.
341, St. Paul Street
Valletta – Malta

© 1995-1999 by Joseph Attard

All rights reserved. No part of this book may be reproduced, stored in a retrieval system, or transmitted in any form or by any means, electronic, electrostatic, magnetic tape, mechanical, photo-copying recording or otherwise, without permission in writing from the publishers.

Contents

	Foreword	vii
	Prologue	1
I	Confrontation	19
II	Brilliant Battles and Blunders	35
III	The Battle of Crete	53
IV	Mediterranean Crusades	70
V	Operation Crusader	86
VI	Towards a Climax	98
VII	The Turning Point	117
VIII	Operation Torch – The French Dilemma	136
IX	The Fight for Tunisia	149
X	Leap to Sicily and Italy	166
XI	Flare-Up in the Aegean	185
XII	The Battle for Rome – Forerunner of Overlord	204
XIII	The Winding-Up	229
	Bibliography	
	Index	

FOREWORD

I had always loved military history which I consider to have neither a beginning nor an end. Wars and their stories extend over a thousand years before our time, as they are also bound to be still with humanity for many more years to come, always finding writers to record them for posterity. But more than establishing facts, a writer of war history should help to rationalize their truths. And this is why, notwithstanding the several excellent books that have been written on the Second World War, I always felt the urge to write my own.

I could do this for two very good reasons. Firstly that I lived through the war, and also took part in it. Secondly that even in those early years I was already gifted with the aptitude for writing and research. The combination of these two factors then was at its best when I wrote my first war book *The Battle of Malta* which gave me much satisfaction with its run of success. But apart from that which was happening in Malta during 'those dramatic years, I could not help following also what was happening in other theatres of war. I noted everything. Then when time was ripe, all I had recorded was researched, cross checked and eventually collated to make it possible for me to write this work on the Struggle for the Mediterranean being published on the 50th Anniversary of the end of the war.

Much as I compiled all the material in this book myself, as always I was compelled to refer to a certain amount of authorative works. In particular to those by important leaders involved in the struggle like Sir Winston Churchill, Field Marshal Alexander, Admiral of the Fleet Sir Andrew Cunningham, and Field Marshal Kesselring. There was also reference made to works by war historians like Sir Basil Liddell-Hart (whom I followed since my youthful days), Major-General Playfair and Captain S.W. Roskill. However, a bibliography of the works I read for reference appears at the end. I want also to acknowledge with thanks the sources of the illustrations in this book. Particularly Mr. Griffith E. Fanthorpe who favoured me with pictures from his collection, most of them taken by himself during his naval war service in the Mediterranean. The map was as usual drawn by my son-in-law Mr. Costantino Consiglio.

The Struggle for the Mediterranean comprised a number of hard fought campaigns which made it the longest one of the war. Underlying the bitter fighting there were also the intense political struggles and piques which had begun long before the outbreak of hostilities. But in the final analysis the struggle's outcome depended on the courage and determination of the sailors, soldiers, airmen and merchant seamen of the belligerent nations, both victors and vanquished. It is to their memory, and particularly to those who perished that this book is dedicated.

MALTA
May, 1995

Joseph Attard

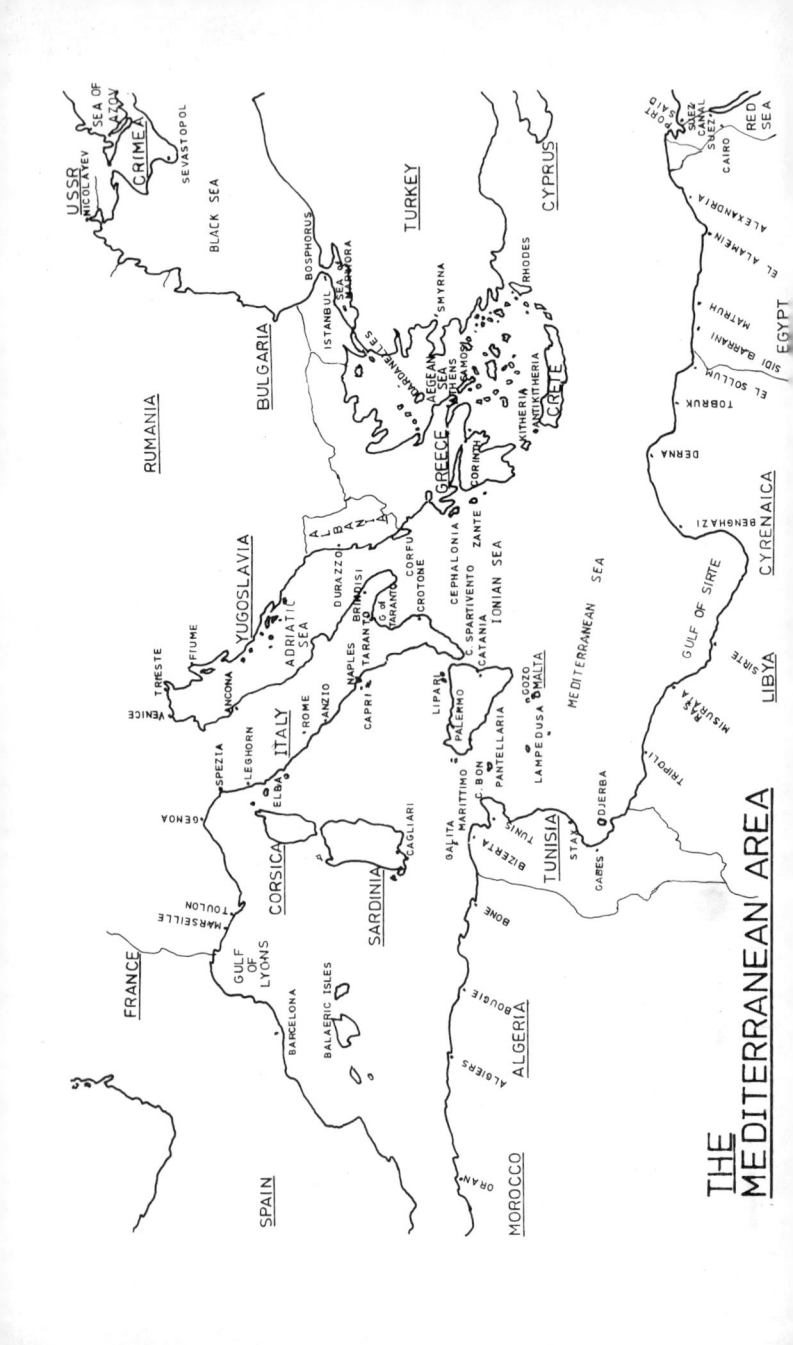

THE MEDITERRANEAN AREA

PROLOGUE

Since time immemorial the Mediterranean has been the core of the world. Culture and civilization emanated from the countries it washed. Generating commerce and many power games. This configuration of forces had reached a saturation point in the sixteenth century when, notwithstanding the domination by the Ottoman empire and Spain, there were several other powerful fleets plying this sea. France had a long coastline to guard, and Genoa controlled the Ligurian coast. Venice looked after the Aegean, but had also to protect Cyprus and Crete. It was at this time that Britain began casting eyes on this sea, no doubt attracted by the existing handsome prospects of trade.

What British intentions there were, however, had to stop in 1585 because of the war with Spain. It was only when James I began to reign that there was born again a British inclination to participate in this trade, and the English sovereign was soon enquiring into possibilities of breaking the endemic rule of the Mediterranean by Barbary corsairs. In 1620 Sir Robert Mansell sailed with a squadron into the Mediterranean with this purpose. But indeed his aim was more of an obsession to force an incursion into this sea. The use of Algiers as a base by the corsairs forced his hands to launch an attack on this port. But this was a failure and his squadron had to fall back, using Malaga as a base to recoup, as well as Gibraltar and Minorca as ports of call for replenishment. This was an arrangement which drove the point home that if Britain were to persist with naval operations in the Mediterranean, she had to have a secure base. It was this which prompted Captain Sir Henry Bruce to propose the capture of Gibraltar.

This plan did not materialize. But destiny smiled on Britain elsewhere, with a marriage of convenience between Charles II and the Infanta of Portugal in whose dowry there was included the turning of Tangier into a British possession. Only Spain intervened and threatened war again if this should come about. It was destiny again that made the governor of Tangier sally forth out of the town to engage Moorish raiders in one of their constant attacks and to be killed in the ensuing skirmish. With the leaderless Portugese appealing for British help it was easy for Lord Sandwich, the British admiral in the area to oblige, and on 16th January, 1662 to secure the first British foothold close to the Mediterranean. But as it was through Charles II that Britain begot Tangier, it had to be him to lose it after finding he could not hold to it because of financial implications. So British troops were pulled out on 5th March, 1684, and for the remaining 16 years Britain remained without a port in, or close to, the Mediterranean.

It had then to be a simple whim to make Gibraltar a British possession. One of those stray thoughts occurring to Sir George Rooks, a frustrated vice-admiral in search of something adventurous to do while patrolling the western Mediterranean with an Anglo-Dutch force, and which made him attack the Rock. On 21st July, 1702 he sailed into the Bay of Gibraltar and put ashore a force of 1800 men. Three days later, the small Spanish garrison capitulated and Gibraltar became British.

The acquisition of this first stronghold gave scope and impetus to Britain to strengthen her Mediterranean forces. Even while the Gibraltar garrison was in the meantime being called to fight off continuous attacks by French-aided Spanish forces, and sometimes being very close to capitulation only to be saved by timely reinforcements. It had also by now become similarly important to keep a watch on the French who were threatening the Western Mediterranean from their naval base at Toulon. So when hostilities with Spain finally came to an end, it was time for British confines to be pushed closer to the threatening French.

The British Secretary of State, conjointly with the Navy and the Army, was now thinking of Minorca, the second largest of the Balaeric Islands. It seems to have served his purpose that Admiral Leake, the Commander-in-Chief of the Mediterranean fleet was providentially engaged in capturing Sardinia for the Spanish claimant Charles III. So when Cagliari succumbed to his attack in August 1708, Malborough, the English commander of the forces of the Alliance, instructed Leake to attack Minorca which eventually fell to the British forces on 14th September, 1708. It was a hazardous move since, technically, it was occupied by a force fighting in the name of Charles III. But matters were clarified when the Treaty of Utrecht in 1713 confirmed Minorca as a British possession.

Britain had thus acquired two firm footholds in the Western Mediterranean. But in her characteristic way, during the lull that followed, she let down her guard. With Gibraltar full of intrigue there followed times when the British government was in two minds about holding to it as well as Minorca. And in the Seven year war that broke out with France in 1756, this island was lost to the French. Only, however, to be returned to the British fold at the end of the war in 1763.

This part of the Mediterranean had then become like a chessboard, with Britain, France and Spain moving their pieces intricately. Minorca was lost again to a combined Spanish and French attack in 1782. Then when things looked like quietening down, France broke the spell by declaring war on Britain in 1793. This made a further British base desirable and on 7th July, 1794 a British force under Major-General David Dundas captured the island of Corsica. This was another laurel to be achieved by the British navy which had now reached an unprecedented state of strength and efficiency, historically reflected in her able admiral Horatio Nelson.

As if to match him, there emerged out of the turmoil and bloodshed of the French revolution another stalwart on the enemy's side in the person of Napoleon Bonaparte. Following his successful crushing of a rising in Paris, and his victorious campaigns in Italy, he was being acclaimed as the greatest soldier of France. And he became an obvious choice to command a French armada that was now gathering at Toulon, Marseilles and Genoa posing a mysterious and deadly threat.

None knew of Bonaparte's intentions, and British precautions were taken only in the way of guessing them, as others were doing. An invasion of England was being mentioned, as well as a strike against Ireland or Portugal. But the French general's intentions were directed eastwards towards Egypt. Only that he did not want to move out as long as the British were close to strike. It was the Pitt government that played into his hands by deciding to evacuate Corsica. And as British forces were still in process of embarkation, Bonaparte's troops began moving in during October 1796.

The French armada moved out on 8th May 1798. A force of thirteen sail-of-the-line, eight frigates plus two Venetian 64 gun sips with six other frigates and smaller craft. Also 400 transports carrying some 36,000 troops. On 9th June they stopped on their way just off the island of Malta, which was to be the first prey.

The island had been in the hands of the Order of St John since 1530 and the Knights had embellished it beyond comprehension. But more than this they had turned it into a Christian stronghold using the latest techniques in military fortifications, all wrought with the finest examples of architecture. The Order had in its time become a strong naval power, and its warship construction was certainly in advance of its time. In the same tradition it had seen, as no other European power had, the approaching end of the oar-propelled galley and galleass, and this power was amply exploited and recorded for history in the Battle of Lepanto in 1571. The Order's troops, made up of Knights and the mercenaries they comandeered, had always excelled in strength and valour, and this too had been exemplified in the Siege of Malta of 1565. But by the time Napoleon had cast his eyes on Malta, the Order had deteriorated and the precision in atitude of the Knights had long succumbed to the inevitable change that so often takes place in human institutions. It was no surprise therefore that Napoleon's attack on 10th June, 1798 was successful, and the island became French.

This turn of events, however, did not let the Maltese stay idle. Their fervour for freedom and democracy soon planted the seed of rebellion, and on 2nd September, 1799 they rose against their rulers. Theirs was only a motley army, equipped with 3200 ill-gained muskets, pikes and cudgels. But the bearers were endowed with a lot of valour and determination, which weighed heavily against the French who were besieged in the capital city of Valletta. The Maltese, however, did not delude themselves in thinking that this situation could be maintained for long and they were soon seeking help in the way of arms, munitions and supplies. But until these could be obtained, the French had to be prevented from having similar replenishments and reinforcements. So it was decided to ask help from the British Navy to blockade the French. All this came at a time when Admiral Nelson, who commanded the British Mediterranean fleet was himself chasing Napoleon, now intent on his Egyptian campaign. Contact was made at Aboukir Bay, where Nelson engaged the French armada in one of the biggest battles of the Mediterranean. The French were defeated and Egypt was saved. But that wasn't the end, and Nelson could not see what lay ahead and what could be more profitable to the nation he served than the destruction and plundering of Napoleon's fleet. His first immediate thought was to withdraw to Naples and lick his wounds, for he had not escaped unscathed. It was while on his way there, after having traversed several hundreds of miles of ocean, tired and depressed, that he came across a small boat off Cape Passero on the southern tip of Sicily. His ship *Vanguard* was hailed by the men on the boat, who turned out to be Maltese carrying their nation's request for his help.

It might have been a strange request under normal circumstances, but Britain was still at war with France and Nelson could see that what he was being asked to do could get a very important acquisition to Britain. He agreed to help and until the necessary ships could be spared he arranged for a Portugese squadron to stand in for him. it was not long, however, when he had the necessary squadron available, which he despatched to Malta under the command of Captain Alexander Ball to take over. This was instrumental in bringing a French capitulation and a Maltese request to Britain to take Malta under her protection, thus adding this important stronghold as a British possession.

The 19th century then was characterised with a bigger British build up of strength in the Mediterranean against a scenario of minor struggles. There was the unfolding of a period of rapid technological change, with warships changing from sail to steam and improvement in guns and armour, which proved their effectiveness during the Crimean War of 1854-56. There were many lessons to be learned for posterity during this conflict. The way the harbour batteries at Sebastapol had mauled the Anglo-French fleets was an eye-opener for the future of coastal forts with the competence to outfight ships. While the use that was made of Malta as a rear base and to receive and care for the wounded drove in the point of the importance of having bases close to any theatre of operations in any future war. Indeed it was after the end of the Crimean conflict that there was an impetus to turn the island into the intended fortress and base in consonance with a new drive to modernise the Royal Navy she was to house and service. HMS *Warrior* was the first ship of the new era to be both steam-powered and armour plated. The *Royal Sovereign* was soon to be similarly equipped and with the added bonus of 9 ton guns mounted in double turrets. Now the race was on and throughout Europe there had began a feverish run to strengthen the power of coastal forts and warships. Speed became contagious and the drive was soon taking on the proportions of a great contest in which Britain could not afford to lag behind. Particularly now that there was the imminent opening of the Suez Canal which would revolutionalise her lines of communication to her Eastern empire and would therefore have to be secured.

It had now no longer become a question of acquiring more bases. In fact Britain had throughout this period shed covetous eyes on several naval stations which could afford anchorages for her expanding fleet. Corfu, Cyprus, Aden and even Sicilian ports were acquired without any strategic forethought. And all of them became temporary acquisitions, dropping off one after the other to leave Britain steadily and permanently placed with Gibraltar and Malta; but still desiring a closer base to the Suez Canal after this was opened in 1869.

There had to pass eleven years, however, before this British desire came out in the open. It had to be a mutiny in the Egyptian army in 1880 to spark it off. And just as the Liberals were returned to power, still carrying the reputation of not caring for their empire. Yet, Prime Minister Gladstone did not hesitate to act immediately to prevent Egypt from falling prey to anarchy with the risk of blocking the Suez Canal. The Mediterranean fleet was ordered to proceed from Malta to destroy the forts at Alexandria, while an army under Sir Garnet Wolseley crushed the mutineers. Coming as it fortuitously did, at a time when the whole world was astir, this intervention might have sparked a bigger conflict. But it didn't. And this enhanced Britain's position in the Mediterranean, which was only to be challenged after the onset of the twentieth century.

This time the challenger was Germany, who after British setbacks in the Boer War of 1899-1902, went all out to attain superiority over the British Navy. In reply to the super-battleship *Dreadnought* which could outrange and outsteam anything afloat, Germany began building her own. The British Government was now purturbed about the balance of power to be maintained and never ending arguments in Parliament were only resolved when Winston Churchill became First Lord of the Admiralty in 1912. But he did not give much importance to the Mediterranean. And his opinion prevailed to have the Mediterranean fleet denuded to strengthen the Home fleet. The 4th Battle squadron was moved from Malta to Gibraltar to be closer to Britain, and the Mediterranean fleet was left only with four armed cruisers and fifteen destroyers.

The Great War of 1914/18 was fouoght and won. Notwithstanding their supremacy the combined Anglo-French fleets suffered heavily when they tried to force the Dardanelles. And this was an occasion to emphasize the deadly menace of enemy submarines which on the other hand brought into use the system of convoys as well as the introduction of the first aircraft to support the navy.

It fell to Malta to be in the right position to house the first Royal Air Force squadrons which were to combat the 15 German U boats that infested the Mediterranean during the last years of the conflict. April 1918 saw the formation of the RAF Malta Group under the command of Colonel A.M. Longmore, which comprised No. 267 Seaplane Squadron of F2A flying boats and No. 268

Squadron equipped with Short Sunbeam 320 float planes. A local racecourse was then also turned into an airfield and equipped with two DM9 aircraft to operate when the rough sea made it impossible for seaplanes to take off. This marked the introduction of the Royal Air Force as the third armed service in the Mediterranean.

The war was followed by a lull to be characterized by a euphoria of sleepy contentment in British Mediterranean bases. The opposite was happening in Italy, however. With Mussolini and the Fascists in power, the Italian nation began moving forward in leaps and bounds, and had become more aggressive. A row and confrontation over Abyssinia pushed Britain out of the limelight, as well as those who were all out for peace. Then, in 1935, Italian troops marched into Abyssinia. It was Britain's turn now to be jolted into activity, since it became obvious that Italy had not only become the most powerful nation in the Mediterranean, but also a potential enemy. To strengthen this belief there was Mussolini joining Hitler and interfere in the Spanish Civil War in 1936 to enable Franco to overthrow Republican Spain. This immediately raised the spectre of a likely menace to the frontiers of France and Gibraltar in an eventual war. It also provided Italy with the right occasions to flout Britain's naval supremacy in the Mediterranean with her aircraft and submarines often attacking British shipping "by mistake" despite promises of non-intervention. There were now rising as well Italian claims for the Mediterranean as being an Italian sea, and also Malta as rightfully belonging to Italy because of her strains of race and culture. There were more than mere words behind these threats and this must have hastened Britain in concluding the Anglo Egyptian Treaty of 1936 and acquiring the use of Alexandria as a third naval base for her Mediterranean fleet.

This crisis was, however, not precipitated and indeed it seemed to fizzle out when Hitler moved to re-occupy the demilitarized zone of the Rhineland that same year. And no matter how many feelings of trepidation there were and deep-seated distrust of Germany's capacity to wage a major war, this move had the looks of a first step on the road to Armageddon. Those who did not agree had their answer in 1938 when the Germans moved into Austria. Now there could be no further doubts of Hitler's intentions and, however late, Britain began to prepare for war.

Even so, in the beginning of 1939 many still lulled themselves into the belief that these British rearmament measures would diminish the danger of the explosive situation. Indeed, with everyone being convinced that sea power would be the determining factor in any eventual war, a look at the naval forces of the nations involved in the fast deteriorating situation would have a very balanced position. The balance of naval power then stood as follows:

Category	Germany	France	Britain	Italy
Battleships	2*	6	12	6
Battlecruisers	2	–	3	–
Seaplane Carriers	–	1	2	1
Aircraft Carriers	–	1	7	–
Heavy Cruisers	4*	7	15	7
Light Cruisers	5	12	47	12
Destroyers	17	70	159	61
Escorts	8	–	38	83
Submarines	57	77	38	98

* Pre-dreadnoughts

Nothwithstanding the heartening outlook of naval statistics, however, one could not lose sight of the fact that the Italian navy could pose a powerful threat in the Mediterranean. And despite its numerical inferiority in capital ships it had more than enough submarines and light vessels to make the sea-route through the Mediterranean too precarious to use for British shipping. Both for naval operations and the carrying of reinforcements to the Middle and Far East, which would therefore have to be carried by the roundabout Cape route, down the coast of West Africa and up the East Coast into the Red Sea. There was some hope in the fact that Italy seemed to be lagging behind in Hitler's warmongering, and the British Government was now going out of its way to induce an atmosphere of trust and friendship towards Italy. Even while the British Prime Minister, Sir Neville Chamberlain was climaxing his government's efforts with Germany and amazing the world with his stand to block Hitler's movement by offering to support Poland if attacked, British warships of the Mediterranean fleet were still carrying out cruising activities in Italian ports. This could have served a secondary purpose of a show of force. Whatever it was, British hopes received a setback when on 9th April, 1939, which was Good Friday, Italian troops attacked Albania.

British efforts to maintain friendly relations with Italy continued, but it would have been folly to rest on hoping for positive results. So steps were taken to build up the Mediterranean command. On 9th May, 1939 Vice-Admiral Andrew B. Cunningham was appointed Commander-in-Chief of the Mediterranean Fleet and given the acting rank of Admiral. With his appointment there emerged the new Mediterranean fleet. In the 1st Battle Squadron there was allocated the battleship *Warspite* which was also the flagship, as well as the battleships *Barham, Malaya* and *Ramillies* with Vice Admiral Geoffrey Layton in *Barham*. The 1st Cruiser Squadron with Rear Admiral J.H.D. Cunningham in *Devonshire* had also the *Sussex* and

Shropshire. Then there was the 3rd Cruiser Squadron with Rear Admiral H.R. Moore in *Arethusa* accompanied by *Penelope* and two ships of the *Delhi* class. Three destroyer flotillas were under the command of Rear Admiral J.C. Tovey in the light cruiser *Galatea*. The aircraft carrier *Glorious,* a flotilla of submarines, and the depot ships *Woolwich* and *Maidstone* completed the array. The Commander-in-Chief's first job was to assess potentialities and pick on his more likely base. He found Alexandria to be poorly defended and was also too close for comfort to Italian occupied Libya. He found Malta to be a much better prospect, more amenable to defence and with refit facilities in her dockyard which were not available in Alexandria. The only snag was that the island was only sixty miles away from Sicily and easy prey to the Italian air-force. And to make matters worse, there were neither fighters on the island nor anti-aircraft guns. So rather than giving up his choice of Malta as a bad job he asked for guns and fighter aircraft to be supplied to the island.

The truth was that long before then Malta had been written off as indefensible by both the Army and the Royal Air Force because of her proximity to the Italian mainland. This was only rebutted by the Navy to no avail. And now there was Admiral Cunningham again trying to drive the point home. It had to be the Minister for War, Hore-Belisha, to bring this argument to a conclusion. As the summer months of 1939 were rolling on towards a climax and an impending war, he raised the point of Malta's defence in Parliament.

"If we were to give up the defence of Malta," he summed up, "it would mean giving up the challenge for supremacy in the Mediterranean. But if it is decided not to defend her then there is no point in leaving a garrison and equipment as we already have there, just to be overrun."

The Committee for Imperial Defence had then allocated 172 anti-aircraft guns for Malta, and what was more im portant, four fighter squadrons. It was also Hore-Belisha who realised the existing threat to Egypt and Alexandria by Italian forces in Libya and proposed the appointment of General Archibald Wavell as Commander-in-Chief Middle East in July 1939 which was readily agreed to. With this appointment the first steps were taken to strengthen British land forces in Egypt.

So all seemed set for the great showdown. It required only the conclusion of the different political ramifications that were going on to decide whether there would be a war or not. It seems that both Britain and Germany were dead intent in concluding some agreement with Russia. As usual British negotiators proceeded with wariness and delay, and this might have encouraged the Germans to exploit the situation, quicken their pace and press their suit. In contrast to British hesitation Hitler conceded Stalin's exacting conditions and on 23rd August Ribbentrop flew to Moscow to sign the German-Russian pact, under which Poland was to be partitioned between Germany and Russia. All was set down for war. And there was only one exception as to whether Italy would join Germany. On this point hung Britain's fate in the Mediterranean.

It is no secret that British hopes were for a neutral Italy, and no efforts were spared to have this.

The climax to an explosive situation was reached on Friday, 1st September, 1939 when the German armies invaded Poland. On Sunday, the 3rd, Britain declared war on Germany in fulfillment of her guarantee to Poland. Six hours later France joined Britain. But Italy chose to sit on the fence and remain neutral. Nobody could say for how long. But what time she were to remain out of the conflict was to be of a respite to British interests in the Mediterranean.

* * *

On a quantitative reckoning it appeared in those first days from the onset of war that the Allies were strong enough to contain German attacks wherever they came from. Between them, Poland and France could muster the equivalent of 130 divisions against a German total of 98, and of which 36 were virtually untrained. The numerical superiority of the Luftwaffe over allied airforces was not great as was generally imagined, while there was a distinct allied advantage in naval power. Yet, the expected surge by the Allies did not materialise. And while a strange lassitude seemed to blanket the western front with Germany giving justified cause for the Americans to describe the situation as a "phoney war", the German war machine of combined armoured and air forces was unleashed on Poland.

There were those who explained the Allies attitude as being tactical. Others thought it could be an overture for peace. But in the meantime German panzers were running havoc with the ill prepared Polish army. In a matter of days Kluge's forces had reached the Lower Vistula, while an army under Kuchler pressed hard from East Prussia. The crossings to the Warta were forced by Reichenan, and List's forces were soon isolating Cracow. These were four crack armies all supported by heavy air attacks which coined the new term of 'Blitzkrieg' for the world and posterity. Then on 17th September, with the Polish forces in general retreat Russian armies crossed Poland's eastern border to sound the death knell to the heroic nation. The garrison at Warsaw held till the 28th, but by 5th October, 1939 the last Polish forces had surrendered.

An expected French offensive had by then still not materialised. Now it seemed that the fall of Poland would have it countermanded rather than hastened. It was now the turn of the German navy to take the limelight. There had already been the first ,merchant ships falling prey to German U boats during the first days of fighting. No doubt highlighted by the sinking of the *Athenia* on the evening of

September 3. But there was a harder blow when U boat 29 sank the aircraft carrier *Courageous* off the Western Approaches to the British Isles on 17th September. This set the admiralty in a bustle to withdraw aircraft carriers from submarine hunting. Now in mid-October, U boat 47 penetrated the fleet anchorage at Scapa Flow and sank the battle-ship *Royal Oak*. Losses in British merchant shipping had by now reached 114 ships and over 420,000 tons.

Apart from the U Boats roaming all over the Atlantic there was also the added threat by the pocket battleships *Admiral Graf Spee* and *Deutschland*, both let loose for specialised attacks on British shipping. And this soon raised the need for more naval ships to hunt the enemy and to be put into convoy service. The navy was already extended enough in the Atlantic and Home waters which necessitated the calling of more warships. Most of these had to come from the Mediterranean. Admiral Cunningham was first deprived of his 1st Cruiser Squadron. Then he had soon to give up a number of his destroyers. The aircraft carrier *Glorious* followed, and before he knew it there was also the pride of his fleet *Warspite* being taken as well for Atlantic service. And so the admiral was even deprived of his flagship. A similar situation prevailed in the Far East where the admiralty preyed on the 5th Cruiser Squadron, leaving only a few submarines and the sloop *Bideford* to watch Japanese ports which still housed a number of German ships, amongst them five believed to be potential raiders.

But our concern is with the Mediterranean with a still neutral Italy now brushing up her forces. In contrast with the depleted British fleet, the Italians had two new battleships due for commission. Their air-force was now boasting the latest Macchi fighters which were to take over from the older Fiat CR42. The army was steadily being built up, and if any proof was needed of the proportions reached this could be found in Libya and Italian East Africa where Italian forces amounted to some 500,000 men. Since the appointment of General Wavell as Commander-in-Chief,

British forces in Egypt were being strengthened but they could be considered to be not more than a handful when compared with the Italians.

There was also the question of Malta which was the only naval base with refit facilities. Following the British Government's decision to allow four fighter squadrons for her defence, the three available airfields were brought up to scratch, and there was even Air Commodore Maynard posted there as Air Officer Commanding. But the island was still without a single fighter plane. As if to confuse further an already desperate situation a fully trained anti-aircraft regiment from the Royal Malta Artillery was taken away from the island and sent to Egypt.

It was only in March 1940 when the Mediterranean situation had become more threatening that there was a change of wind, and things began moving. The 4th and 8th submarine flotillas with their depot ship *Medway* were the torch bearers to the now obvious potential theatre of war. Admiral Cunningham was given back the *Warspite* and with her also another battleship the *Ramillies*. Other units continued to trickle in, amongst them the cruisers *Sydney* and *Leander*. Now Cunningham could carry on with his plans of co-ordinating with the French to share responsibilities for the Mediterranean, while they had to be responsible for the Western part, where they had allocated three battleships and four cruisers besides a number of destroyers and smaller vessels. Malta too now began receiving anti-aircraft guns and additional infantry. Her population was being instructed in air-raid precautions and the first primitive shelters were being built. But there was still no sign of any aircraft in her airfields. And there was not a more frustrated man than Air Commodore Maynard.

As fate would have it on 9th April the Germans invaded Norway and several waships were hastily called to that theatre of operations. The aircraft carrier *Furious* was bundled out of Clyde without having time to take on her aircraft. The *Glorious* was similarly called with haste from Malta, leaving four crates of aircraft spares behind. The Air Officer Commanding Maynard lost no time in signalling Cunningham asking to take them over. Permission was granted, and in the following weeks he had assembled three Gladiator fighters out of those spares which gave him something to fight with should Italy come into the war before he had his promised fighters.

But she did not. Not even after Norway was lost to the Allies and the Germans were left in complete control on 2nd May. There seemed to be something else Mussolini was waiting for before he would jump. Then on 10th May the Germans launched their offensive on the Western Front and broke through the Allied lines. It seems that all knew that this was going to have far-reaching effects and that the course of the war was going to be changed. On that same day Air Chief Marshal Longmore who had commanded the first Royal Air Force units in the Mediterranean in 1918, was appointed to take command of the Royal Air Force in the Middle East. But a more important appointment was that of Winston Churchill who on that day became Prime Minister of Great Britain in place of Neville Chamberlain.

The German breakthrough in France was no fluke. Within a week their panzers reached the Channel coast, cutting off the Allied armies in Belgium. The French army was beaten back in disarray and the British Expeditionary Force in Belgium withdrew to Dunkirk and on 25th May made a getaway for home. The mortal blow to France was delivered on 5th June with the launching of a fresh German offensive. The French collapsed, and three days later General Weygand was advising his Government to ask for an armistice.

This was what Mussolini had been waiting for. On 10th June, 1940 he brought Italy into the war. Britain's struggle for the Mediterranean had taken new dimensions.

CHAPTER 1

CONFRONTATION

Nothwithstanding the many hopes and endeavours made to keep Italy out of the war there had been no illusions about the final outcome. What bad blood or pique there might have lain hidden beneath the relations between the two nations, owed their beginning to as far back as 1935. Since then the accent had been on the respective navies. The Italians riding the waves of reputation with their modern and biggest fleet in the Mediterranean wanting to emphasize their assertion of *Mare Nostrum* making the Mediterranean their own sea; the British from their end going all out to break this myth and maintain their traditional naval superiority, also in this part of the world. It was no wonder, therefore, that the Italian declaration of war did not catch Admiral Cunningham, unawares, and he had well in time rebuilt his forces for the expected confrontation.

Amassed around him and his flagship *Warspite* there were three other battleships, *Ramillies*, *Malaya* and *Royal Sovereign*, and the 7th Cruiser squadron composed of *Orion*, *Neptune*, *Sydney*, *Liverpool* and *Gloucester*, as well as the 3rd Cruiser squadron made up of *Capetown*, *Caledon*, *Calypso* and *Delhi*. He had twenty five destroyers, and the submarines *Olympus*, *Odin*, *Orpheus*, *Otis*, *Phoenix*, *Proteus*, *Pandora*, *Parthian*, *Grampus* and *Rorqual*. Furthermore, there were expected to join him later the *Regulus*, *Regent*, *Rainbow* and `Perseus* still on passage from the Far East.

The same could not be said of Lieutenant-General William Dobbie, the governor of Malta, with the island being caught like a sitting duck awaiting the Italian onslaught. On learning of Italy's entry in the war he had spoken to the people of Malta, appealing to them to rely on God to help them. It was indeed the only source of help he could bank upon. There were not as yet enough anti-aircraft guns to go about, and Vice-Admiral William T.R. Ford had only four ships at his disposal. The monitor *Terror*, two gunboats *Aphis* and *Cicala*, all of them retained to support anti-aircraft defences with their guns, and the old minesweeper *Fermoy* whose only contribution was to carry out a daily sweep. The biggest problem, however, belonged to Air Commodore Maynard, the Air Officer Commanding, having to face the might of the *Regia Aeronautica* with only his three made up Gladiators which, in frustration, he aptly called *Faith*, *Hope* and *Charity* after the three virtues on which rests the catholic religion. The least he could do was to hope for more time and reinforcements, but there was no reprieve. At 7 a.m. on the following morning of 11th June, the Italians launched the first of their systematic air attacks on the island.

In Egypt General Wavell was caught in a similar quandary. When Italy's entry into the war became imminent in May he had been promised more troops in the way of reinforcements. But they had not reached him, and now he was caught with only 36,000 British, New Zealand and Indian troops to face an overwhelmingly superior Italian build up of 280,000 men under Marshal Graziani. There was also the additional discomfort of knowing he could not hope for much air support from the 200 odd aircraft Air Marshal Longmore had at his disposal, in contrast with an enemy potential of 1,500 machines. It goes to Wavell's merit, however, that none of this made him lose heart, and rather than remaining passive, he detached forward part of an incomplete armoured division he had, to begin a series of harassing raids on Italian advanced posts. Longmore too used some of his Blenheims and Wellingtons to begin a series of attacks on the enemy's rear supply dumps.

It might have been considered to be a mild beginning. But all the same it was wrought with a very serious preoccupation, this time particularly for Cunningham, because of the imminent collapse of France. The French navy had been allotted an important part to play in being responsible for the Western Mediterranean. If France were to fall and her navy withdrawn, then this would tilt the balance against the British fleet. There could even be worse if the French ships were to join the enemy. It was known that Winston Churchill was doing his best to make the French continue the fight, in the same way as Polish, Dutch and Norwegian warships had done. But there was also the strong feeling that Hitler was bound to use this matter as a pawn in any armistice negotiations.

Even so, this did not detract Cunningham from emulating his counterpart on the Western Desert front and go on some sort of an offensive. The main object in his operation orders had been laid down as the disruption of enemy seaborne communications to North Africa. And in this respect he had already deployed his submarines. But now on the first day of war he had set out in *Warspite*, accompanied by *Malaya, Eagle,* and the 7th Cruiser squadron with 9 destroyers, intending to make a sweep to the North West of Crete, hoping as well that in the offing he might meet some enemy patrols. But in this he was disappointed, and he met neither ships nor aircraft. His sweep would have looked like being a normal peacetime cruise had not the destroyer *Decoy* detected a lurking enemy submarine which she attacked. The following day looked like bringing a repetition. Only that the 3rd Cruiser squadron had in the meantime moved to the South West of Crete, where one of the cruisers, *Calypso* was torpedoed and sunk by an enemy submarine. This was what

Cunningham believed then to have been his first casualty.

The truth was, however, that British submarines were having a much worse time elsewhere. The *Grampus* after laying mines off Augusta in Sicily was detected and attacked by depth charges by the Italian torpedo boats *Circa* and *Cleo*, and eventually sunk. *Odin* too, while at its billet in the Gulf of Taranto was sunk by the enemy destroyer *Strale*. Off Tobruk another Italian destroyer, the *Tribune* did away with HMS *Orpheus*. This was without a doubt an auspicious start for the Italian navy bringing to the fore the high efficiency of its submarine direction finding apparatus. Fortunately the news of these distressing losses was somehow balanced by what was happening in the Western Desert. During one of the raids programmed by Wavell, a mobile column under Brigadier J.A.C. Caunter struck at Fort Capuzzo which instead of proving to be the strong vanguard protecting the approach to more important positions, was captured without any stiff resistance being offered. This easy conquest might have led Cunningham to follow up with a naval bombardment of the next important port of Bardia as if to soften it up. This attack was carried out on 20th June, and more than an operational success it was a morale booster for the British admiral since he had included in his squadron the French battleship *Lorraine* and the cruisers *Suffrein*, *Duguay* and *Trouin*. And this when the French government was on the verge of concluding an armistice.

An enthusiastic Cunningham now intended to use the French ships again in his first attempt to induce the Italian main fleet to give battle, which was considered necessary if he were to establish British sea power in the Mediterranean. His plan was to go as close as he could to the Italian mainland under the guise of a sweep off Southern Italy. Then he would bombard Augusta in Sicily and move right into the Straits of Messina. It was an audacious plan had it been carried out. But on 22nd June, France agreed to an armistice, so the plan was cancelled.

Confrontation

The British Commander-in-Chief now had to face the more troublesome situation he had feared. Indeed, seeing that his cajoling of the French government did not bear results, Winston Churchill now issued specific orders to the Royal Navy with regard to French warships. These were to be given the choice to continue fighting alongside Britain against Germany and Italy, or to accept internment or repatriation of their crews. If none of these alternatives was accepted then the British navy would use force to prevent them falling into enemy hands.

Cunningham had the uncomfortable task of transmitting these offers to Admiral Godfroy who commanded the French elements in Alexandria, and who was a personal friend of his. But the Frenchman would not commit himself. It seemed as if he wanted to wait and see what was being done by his compatriot Admiral Gensoul who commanded the most powerful units of the French fleet at Mers-el-Kebir in Oran. The task of approaching this admiral fell to Admiral Somerville who had now entered the Mediterranean with his Force H comprising the battle-cruiser *Hood*, the battleships *Valiant* and *Resolution*, and the aircraft carrier *Ark Royal*. There were some tense negotiations, but finally the Frenchman rejected the British offers. So without much ado Somerville ordered his ships to open fire on the French. With the first salvo from her 16" guns the *Hood* blew up the battleship *Bretagne*. The rest of his force followed suit and damaged the battleship *Provence* which had to be beached, and disabled another battleship, the *Dunkerque*, as well as the destroyer *Mogador*. Another battleship, the *Strasbourg*, with four des troyers managed to get away in the heat of the skirmish and made their way to Toulon. On learning of this action which showed Britain's determination not to compromise her sea superiority, Admiral Godfroy allowed himself to be persuaded, and agreed to disarm his ships in Alexandria. Then France capitulated on 24th June.

Responsibility for the Western Mediterranean was now

taken over by Admiral Somerville and his Force H. They were based at Gibraltar to be on hand when needed, both in the Mediterranean and the Atlantic. But the new situation must have pressed on Cunningham the more urgent need of getting to grips with the main Italian fleet. There was some promising information reaching him about three Italian destroyers having been located making their way to Italy from Libya, and not wanting to discard the possibility of their being the advance party of a bigger squadron, he ordered one of his own consisting of two battleships, an aircraft carrier, cruisers and desroyers to give chase. The enemy was sighted on 28th June about 75 miles off Cape Matapan, but the Italian ships made use of their superior speed to escape a fight. Nonetheless, the cruisers opened fire at long range and managed to hit and sink one of the destroyers, the *Espero*, before the other two got away.

A better chance for the desired engagement came to Cunningham on 8th July. It was started by a signal reporting the sighting of an Italian fleet with at least two battleships some 100 miles off Benghazi. Now Cunningham set out with *Warspite*, *Malaya* and *Royal Sovereign*, together with a Cruiser squadron and destroyers dead intent to engage the enemy whose movements were being given to him by reconaissance aircraft. The enemy was sighted off Calabria on the following day, and indeed there were the Italian battleships *Cavour* and *Giulio Cesare* accompanied by twelve cruisers and some destroyers. The British ships engaged the enemy, and the Italians replied. Cunningham had occasion later to report in his memoirs how much he was impressed with the accurate firing of the Italian warships which continually straddled the British ships. A second and perhaps a more important point which impressed itself upon him during this battle concerned the shortcomings of his battleships the *Malaya* and the *Royal Sovereign* whose firing never crossed the target. It was in fact his flagship the *Warspite* which saved the day after scoring a direct hit on the Italian flagship and put her on fire. This seemed to take all the fight out of the italians who dispersed behind a smoke screen and withdrew from the battle taking advantage of their superior speed.

It was a battle which was broken when it began to be interesting. But it did not give the desired conclusion, neither to Cunningham nor to the Admiralty in England. The Commmander-in-Chief now learned his lessons and tried to remedy the weak points he had noticed in his fleet in this which was his first confrontation with the enemy. This was in the form of a request to the Admiralty to send him 8" gun cruisers with a harder hitting power and longer range. There was also noticed the vulnerability of his fleet to aerial attack and this could be remedied by the addition of an aircraft carrier with an armoured deck and fighters, as well as an anti-aircraft cruiser.

This kind of confrontation could not be said to have similarily prevailed in Malta. The Italian air-force had continued its bombing of the island without respite, But strangely enough what anti-aircraft guns there were, together with the three Gladiators managed to contain the enemy onslaught. Air Commodore Maynard had also managed to procure two Hurricane fighters originally intended for Egypt which supplianted his defence. By 27th June the Italians had lost twelve planes over Malta to one Hurricane. The Maltese people too had by then become more confident and at home with the air attacks, and the local authorities had managed to get themselves organized to meet the situation. So much so that the war was being looked at as some adventure, however crude, that had to be seen through. The news of Cunningham's encounter with the Italian fleet on 9th July was received with much celebrations, but there was still further scope for more felicitations when on the 15th there were the first ships laden with food, guns and ammunition reaching the island. Then on 2nd August there were twelve Hurricane fighters flown to Malta from the aircraft carrier *Argus*. This was a positive move. All were convinced that the new aircraft would turn the tide of battle with the Italian air-force, but the most significant meaning to be registered was that the long existing belief that Malta was untenable had disappeared.

August was in itself a significant month for war in the Mediterranean in more ways than one. For Cunningham it began bringing him some harassing moments with an increase in activity by Italian aircraft. They were not only shadowing very closely all fleet movements from Alexandria and bringing in the bombers when there was a target to attack, but were also proving murderous to British reconaissance flying boats which were heftier and slower. The answer to these problems would have been long range fighters. But with the Battle of Britain having just started no such aircraft could be spared for the Mediterranean Command. To make up for this however, Cunningham's request of the previous month to strengthen his fleet was met. There was the aircraft carrier *Illustrious* sent to him, complete as he had suggested with an armoured deck and eight-gun Fulmar fighters, together with two anti-aircraft cruisers, the *Calcutta* and the *Coventry*. The still prevailing lull in the Western Desert did not deceive Wavell, and he now found time to go to England to make his case for reinforcements to be sent to his command before an Italian offensive might be launched. But the biggest problem lay with the British war leaders who had not yet recovered from the blow received with the fall of France and the loss of her colonies. In particular there had been Syria with her strategic position and her oil, as well as the fear for the 500 miles of the Iraq to Haifa oil pipeline which ran through that country. Matters had somehow cooled down when there had not been any of the feared developments. But when in August the Haifa refinery was attacked by Italian aircraft which set fire to storage tanks destroying several thousand tons of crude oil, the problem erupted again. If the flow of oil were to be stopped it would create serious complications not only for the Mediterranean theatre of operations, but also to Britain itself who was receiving part of this oil, which was being shipped around the Cape from Suez.

There had been ardent hopes when France fell that General Mittelhauser the military commander in Syria would decide to fight on. But after the commander of all French African Forces General Nogues had sided with Vichy and the armistice, Mittelhauser followed him.

There would, however, have been more concern had it been known that at the same time a German Intelligence agent Gerhard Westrick, posing as an influential trade official was using his influence in the United States to have that country keep out of the war, and also to slow supplies to Britain. This question of American supplies could not be taken lightly, and there was another ill wind blowing. This time it came from an American, Big Bill Donovan, who was subsequently to set up the OSS which after the war became the Central Intelligence Agency. He was now engaged on a tour of Europe trying to assess for the benefit of the American people the intensity of a prevailing belief in the continent that Britain was a spent force. And he was soon conveying the notion to Winston Churchill that this was indeed the general idea that had gone rampant all over Europe. His conclusion then, was that something should be done to disprove such belief to the American people if supplies were to continue to flow across the Atlantic.

It might have been a mildly put threat, but it was very heavy in meaning. It could be simply coined that Britain was being pressed to produce some substantial military venture if she were to be able to continue the war with American help. But coming so soon after the fiasco of the Norwegian campaign, and with a Britain extending herself, first with her armies driven out of France, and now fighting off the Luftwaffe's offensive for dear life, there was certainly no promising field where to generate such a venture. It needed no saying that what little strength could be recouped had to be husbanded for the imminent German invasion of the homeland which Hitler was known to have planned. It was to be expected that Churchill would look for such a possible field in the Mediterranean. But even there, the situation presented a very dismal picture, with Admiral Cunningham still looking for an enemy phantom fleet and Wavell sitting down waiting for an Italian offensive that would not come. Even Malta that had promised so much with her superb resistance was now enjoying a lull from Italian attacks. It seemed as if the war in the Mediterranean had come to a standstill. There was a spark of activity on 13th September when the Italians began moving in the Western Desert. But after advancing fifty miles towards the British position at Mersa Metruh they stopped, and showed no further intentions to continue and engage Wavell's forces. It appeared as if they too preferred to resign to simple confrontation rather than giving battle.

Admiral Cunningham must here be given the credit of making ample use of this lull in activity. It gave him the opportunity to organise his first important convoy to Malta with the dual purpose of taking there much needed supplies and also to test enemy reaction, now that he had the *Illustrious* to provide continual air cover to his ships. Indeed the convoy, consisting of three merchantmen and a tanker with a powerful escorting squadron ran into heavy enemy air attacks on coming within range of enemy aircraft operating from Rhodes. For the first time, Fulmar fighters from *Illustrious* went into action against the enemy, but Cunningham also retailiated by havng other aircraft from *Illustrious* and *Eagle* bombard the enemy airfields. And as if this was not enough he detached the cruiser *Sydney* and some destroyers to shell the airfield as well. One of the ships in the convoy, the *Cornwall*, was hit and set on fire, and had to be left behind. With its wireless and two guns out of action its eventual loss was a foregone conclusion. But its skipper, Captain Petty remained with his ship and the crew to fight the fire. When they had the situation under control the intrepid captain steered the ship by the propellors and made his way to Malta alone and unaided,

Confrontation 29

reaching his destination two days after the rest of the convoy.

No doubt encouraged by the success of this operation Cunningham soon enough found occasion to make another run to Malta, this time carrying a reinforcement of 2,000 badly needed troops, in the cruisers *Liverpool* and *Gloucester*. As fate would have it, whilst on his way an aircraft from *Illustrious* sighted an Italian force with four battleships amongst them the *Littorio* and *Vittorio Veneto* some 120 miles away. It was another occasion which had been eluding him for so long, but if he were to grasp this opportunity it meant he would have to delay his mission to Malta, and also risk the precious forces being carried in the warships. His was a dilemma requiring the consideration of priorities. So he decided to give up this chance and press on with carrying troops to the bealeagered island.

It seems that his decision did not find support with the British High Command for they were soon hinting more openly that he had done very little if indeed anything to try and engage the Italian fleet.

With a Winston Churchill now getting more tense and anxious to escape from the vice in which Donovan had gripped him, Cunningham realised it might after all pay him better to put everything aside and concentrate on getting to grips with the Italian fleet. He had already been playing with the idea of delivering an aerial attack on the enemy in his lair. But he had been discouraged from thinking further about it first because of the lack of aircraft to do it, and secondly by the fact that it had never been done before. Now his first difficulty seemed to have been solved with the availability of *Illustrious* and its Swordfish torpedo bombers with which to mount an attack. As for the second difficulty he was now finding support in Rear Admiral A.L.St.G. Lyster who had arrived with *Illustrious* to take command of the carrier force, and who suggested the mounting of such an attack on the Italian fleet in the harbour of Taranto.

When the idea was mentioned to Sir Dudley Pound, the First Lord of the Admiralty, he disagreed with it. More than this he expressed the view that if such a fallacious attempt were to be made it would very likely be like the last feeble blow of a dying fleet. It was a bitter reply which Cunningham did not merit. But it helped to make him more determined to carry on and put his plan into operation. Only that before he could give this matter further thought there was a development which was to have long reaching repercussions on the Mediterranean situation. On 29th October, Italy attacked Greece.

There had long been bad blood between these two countries over the Aegean Islands, and Mussolini had been provoking the Greeks since he had annexed Albania in 1939. The Italian dictator was known to be vain and bombastic, but he had always been in two minds about adding another front. And on this he was more than once warned by Hitler himself not to undertake any further military ventures. It seems, however, that his vanity and bombasticity took the better of him when he might have felt eclipsed by the growth of German strength, and thought of cutting a figure for himself. And his foolishness was his undoing.

Instead of the easy victory he must have expected, Mussolini found a hard nut to crack in Greece. Despite their superiority in air, artillery and tanks his troops were halted after two days, during which they had only advanced six miles. Then the under-equipped Greek troops counter-attacked, and they were soon driving their enemy far back into Albanian territory. With a bitter winter setting on them, both armies ran out of steam in the mountainous terrain along the Albanian frontier. The Greeks being ready to endure what suffering there lay in store as long as they kept the enemy out of their homeland. The Italians on the other hand not wanting to swallow their pride and withdraw. Both of them, however, knew they could not face the prospects of a hard long campaign. And it was a checkmate which gave no positive hopes to anyone.

But it gave an idea to Winston Churchill.

Britain had guaranteed the independence of Greece as far back as April 1939, but as he himself found scope to confirm later in his *History of the Second World War*, Churchill was not being deluded by this guarantee in considering help to be given to Greece in what could be described as her hour of need. His, was a visioin of a Balkan Front comprising Yugoslavia, Greece and Turkey which would either discourage Hitler from dabbling in the Balkans, or if he did, then to involve him in another major front in that theatre. His innermost feeling, however, must have been that here was the chance to create the military venture he wanted in answer to Donovan's threat.

It must be said that although the British were cognisant of the plight of Greece and what it could lead to, they were divided on the matter of intervention. The Secretary of State for War Anthony Eden happened to be in the Middle East with General Wavell when Greece was invaded, and being well aware of the situation in that theatre of operations and also, one should say, of Churchill's likely whim, he lost no time in cabling him his opinion. "There should be no troops spared if the Greeks sought them," he told him, "as this would forestall our plans for offensive operations against the Italians in North Africa." Then apparently on second thoughts he added that if after all was said and done it was decided to send help, this should not be more than one brigade. On the other extreme there was Air Chief Marshal Sir Arthur Longmore, the Air Officer Commanding Middle East who on his own initiative despatched five squadrons of aircraft to Greece which he could ill afford. This decision was endorsed by Winston Churchill, but who could only reply to Eden in a simple sentence that something had to be done. Then at this first stage British aid was limited to the occupation of Crete and the island of Lemnos which in fact were to prove to be more advantageous to the British with their respective refuelling base and airfields, than to the Greeks.

The ironic part of this story was that the Greek dictator General Metaxas refused to be drawn into accepting any British intervention. He was convinced that until then the Germans had no belligerent intentions against Greece or any other Balkan country. But if he were to accept British forces then these would more likely bring the Germans, who would not be held back with what the British were likely to send him. This seems to indicate that rather than not wanting assistance, Metaxas wanted it only on the condition that it would be substantial which he knew the British could not afford. Any doubts he might have had about this were proved when the five squadrons sent by Longmore were quickly used up, and there was an urgent request for more which was refused.

* * *

It was in a way fortunate that there was this deadlock in Greece which brought to the surface an initial reluctance by the British to intervene any further. It fitted with Cunningham's advanced plans for his attack on Taranto which he could now put into operation, after having to put it off several times. It was code-named *Operation Judgement* and was scheduled for the night of 11th November. Because of some minor damage the aircraft carrier *Eagle* could not take part. So rather than putting the operation off for another time Cunninghm transferred what aircraft he needed from that carrier to *Illustrious*. Then this left Alexandria accompanied by *Warspite*, *Valiant*, *Malaya*, and *Ramillies* together with destroyers on 6th November. Four days later there was a rendezvous with the cruisers which had converged from somewhere else to make the battle fleet, which was positioned west of the Ionian Islands. Their presence there was by no means a secret any longer for they were located, and they were soon being attacked by Italian aircraft. However, the Fulmars from *Illustrious*, and the anti-aircraft cruisers beat all attacks off, and there were no casualties amongst the fleet.

While all this was going on, reconaissance aircraft from Malta were flying over Taranto, taking pictures to ensure that the main Ialian battle fleet was there. Cunningham's next step was to move his fleet to about 110 miles from the target, but in the meantime he despatched a plane to Malta to get the recce pictures taken of the harbour. In this last part of the operation there were no mishaps, and as Cunningham reached his position on the night of 11th November, the aircraft was back with pictures taken on that same day which showed that there were five battleships in Taranto. So the Admiral launched his attack.

A pathfinder squadron first flew over the harbour dropping flares and bombs on the side of the Mar Grande. The bombs were intended to shake up defences and also to disguise the real purpose of the attack. The flares were dropped in a pattern which would show the target ships in silhouette, even though it was a moonlit night. And they worked admirably. The first wave of twelve Swordfish torpedo bombers went in, dived low and let go their torpedoes. They were followed by another wave also of twelve aircraft which again went straight for their target. The battleship *Cavour* which was the pride of the Italian navy was sunk, while two others were so badly damaged that as recce pictures showed on the following day, they had to be beached. Two cruisers had also been hit by bombs. The British suffered the loss of two Swordfish aircraft and their crews.

The success of this attack can be realised better when it is considered that it was the first of its kind to be carried out. There had never been any torpedo attack from the air against battleships in a heavily defended harbour like Taranto. Moreover, it was always considered impossible to launch aerial torpedoes in water where the depth was less than 75 feet. – which was the average in Taranto. As this would make the torpedo 'porpoise' and more likely to hit the bottom rather than the target. But the British planes went down so low that they could eliminate this handicap with their torpedoes running horizontally to their targets. The technical details of this attack were later to be studied by both Americans and the Japanese who emulated them in their attack on Pearl Harbour. The aerial torpedo had overnight become the most devastating weapon to be used against ships, anytime and anywhere. This was to revolutionize naval warfare and the role of aircraft carriers.

But the significance of this brilliant achievement was being reflected more in the Mediterranean. It signified to all that Admiral Cunningham had not only achieved his principal goal – of hitting at the Italian main fleet, but that he could now reach the enemy wherever he was to be found. And this augured well for his other scope of disrupting communications between Italy and North Africa which he had by now not been able to do. Now submarines were going to Malta more often. Not just for replenishments and refits but in a silent endeavour to make her their base again, as all could feel the imminent change of tide. The Royal Air Force too had swollen to respectable proportions in the island's airfields. Not just in Hurricanes for defence, but in Blenheims and Wellingtons for bombardment, as well as Swordfish for torpedo attacks. What final stores and equipment were required to make them operational had all arrived with two convoys of six ships which reached Malta on 28th November.

In the Western Desert things were ticking too. Wavell had waited too long. But he had in the meantime received reinforcements which made him play with the idea of a frontal attack on the enemy. He had hesitated, but now with him too there was a feeling of the change that was coming.

It wasn't a change in fighting or tactics, but something which Cunningham's success seems to have signified to all the Mediterranean command. That the time of confrontation was over. And it was now expedient to get on with the fight.

CHAPTER II

BRILLIANT BATTLES AND BLUNDERS

Much as British military commanders were now more concerned with escalating fighting in their particular sectors, Winston Churchill was pressing with his whim for an operation in Greece. He was aware that his strategists did not see Greece as a potential theatre of operations. But for him this had become like an obsession. Or maybe a pressing crusade.

The British Cabinet discussed the matter on 26th November, and tried to look at it against the background of what strategic alternatives there were available to the Germans. This boiled down to exploring possibilities of a German invasion of Greece through Bulgaria and Yugoslavia. Such a possibility was then ruled out since it was felt that a new front in the Balkans would run counter to German interests. The Cabinet moreover felt that Germany might attack Greece only in *caso extremis* to remove any eventual British threat to her Rumanian oil supply.

This was correct reasoning. And it was soon being proved by diplomatic moves that were initiated by the Germans through Admiral Canaris. He was proposing German assistance to Greece in negotiating a cease-fire with Italy which would also include territorial concessions in Albania. The obvious aim was to keep Greece quiet and neutral which goes to indicate that Germany had as yet no aggressive intentions against her. This would have in a way favoured Britain as well by enabling her to concentrate her fighting elsewhere. But if on the other hand she were to be involved, her forces in Greece would certainly constitute a threat to Rumanian oil, with her bombers being within comfortable range to bomb oil production and transport facilities in Ploesti. Then what? But it seems that the Cabinet did not discuss this part of the matter concerning Germany's likely reaction to invade Greece, and what British chances there were to beat back such an invasion.

Oil was indeed a vital problem for Germany. Both in conserving it in Rumania for her use, and in disrupting its flow from Iran and Iraq to Britain. While the Germans could take care of the first contingency they had left the second one to Italy with her proposed occupation of Egypt which, however, was already raising German doubts about the italians' ability to carry out their assignment.

Then as if to confirm their fears, General Wavell struck at the Italian Army in the Western Desert on 7th December, 1940.

British forces set forth from Mersa Metruh. General Wavell had, however, changed his plan at the last moment. And rather than launching a frontal attack he had on the suggestion of one of his staff officers, Brigadier Dorman-Smith, changed this to a more modest attempt of penetrating the enemy lines in between one of the many fortified camps the enemy had established. Then he intended to take the enemy from the rear. There was an element of caution in this plan which ensured that the British forces would only have to engage one camp at a time rather than the whole of the Italian forces that were in that area which amounted to 80,000 men. The British force numbered 30,000 men with 120 tanks and was under the command of General Richard O'Connor.

It took the attackers twenty four hours to cover the seventy mile approach to the enemy. Having started under the cover of night they similarly reached a position level with the Italian lines on the night of the 8th. Then they pressed stealthily through between two camps without being detected, and waited.

At first dawn on the 9th, the 7th Royal Tank Regiment, followed by the 4th Indian Division under General Beresford-Peirce swerved to the right and took one of the camps from the back. It was Nibeiwa Camp with 4,000 Italians who were caught napping and were soon captured at the price of only a few British casualties. Fired by this unexpected success General O'Connor continued with his run and by the end of the day had stormed two further camps. Next in line were other positions, clustered together and forming part of the ensemble of Sidi-Barrani. This time O'Connor had to contend with a sandstorm and also an alerted enemy which momentarily halted his advance. He made up for this by taking forward two additional tank regiments from the 7th Armoured Division and on his next assault he cut through the enemy lines like a tin-opener. Before the day of the 10th came to an end, the greater part of Sidi-Barrani was occupied with the Italians being in full retreat. O'Connor had anticipated this. So much so, that he had despatched a brigade from the 7th Armoured Division right on to the coast to intercept the retreating enemy forces, which in fact it did and captured. This meant another 14,000 prisoners with 88 guns.

It was then unbelievable as it is still now, how such a success could have been achieved in a matter of two days' fighting. O'Connor's biggest problem now was that concerning the 40,000 prisoners he had taken which outnumbered his whole army. This, however, did not cool his enthusiasm, and he was game to attain more. But before he could continue with his advance, the higher commanders in the rear recalled the 4th Indian Division which they intended to transfer to the Sudan. With the Indians being a key element in his army, O'Connor therefore could not resume operations. Truly enough he was promised to have the Indians replaced by the 6th Australian Division from Palestine. But one here cannot help asking why whoever had been behind this change could not have sent the Australians to Sudan and left the Indian Division with O'Connor not to hold his advance. It is of course a question which was never answered. So while a scattered and panic striken Italian army was retreating fast, leaving important positions and equipment for easy taking, O'Connor had to sit down and wait until the Australian Division would arrive to join him.

In Malta, by contrast, there was no such folly being enacted. Short work was being done of converting old destroyer torpedoes for use by submarines. And these were losing no time in moving out to look for enemy shipping crossing to North Africa and bringing the first results. The bombers too were not having any idle time in the island's airfields and they began a round the clock bombing of Sicilian airfields at Cermisso, Augusta and Catania as well as harbour installations with whatever ships happened to be there, thus substantially cutting off the lines of supply to the Italian forces in North Africa.

If this situation worried Mussolini it was not less of a preoccupation to Hitler. More than ever before the question of Middle East oil supplies came to the fore which made him think of helping the Italians in some way. His generals, von Brauchitsch, Halder and von Thoma were openly all against sending any German troops to North Africa but then they also made quite clear their feelings about the Italians' inability to fight. But Hitler could not remain adamant. There was also worrying him the likelihood that should Italy lose North Africa, Britain might hold a pistol to her head which could make the Italians change sides with the obvious results. So, ignoring all Italian rejections of his help, Hitler ordered the Luftwaffe to Sicily from where it would be able to help with keeping clear Italian supply lines to North Africa.

The entry of the Germans into the Mediterranean

should have warned Winston Churchill of what he could expect, if he persisted with his intended crusade in Greece. But he would not budge, and the only obstacle which prevented him from having his way was General Metaxas, the equally stubborn Greek dictator, who would not be drawn to accept British help lest this would serve to attract the Germans without providing the means to resist them. The year 1940 closed with a meeting of the Cabinet to discuss this question again, and rather than temporizing Churchill now appeared determined to have another try to persuading the Greek dictator. This time, however, he would entrust the matter to Wavell.

With the 7th Australian Division having reached him, O'Connor put aside all thoughts of the Italians having had time to recoup during his three weeks' standstill, and launched another offensive on 3rd January, 1941. Indeed he needn't have worried. The Australians, under Major General I.G. Mackay, were thrown in the assault on Bardia, as before, spearheaded by the 7th Tank Regiment and the previous story began to repeat itself. The enemy defence collapsed and the whole of the Italian garrison consisting of 45,000 men surrendered with all its equipment of 462 guns and 129 tanks. It was an occasion for rejoicing, with another page to be written in the annals of British military history. But O'Connor was not all that happy, because what reinforcements he had asked for, and which had been promised, had not reached him. Although he did not know it then, this devolved from Churchill, now intent on husbanding forces to send to Greece. On 8th January he was given the Cabinet's approval to have Wavell increase the British offer to a full-scale commitment when he would be meeting Metaxas in a few days time. The shadow of the Churchillian Greek escapade had thus involved the North African campaign.

One commander-in-chief who was as yet not caught in this shadow was Admiral Cunningham who on 10th January, left Alexandria with his battle fleet in an attempt to complete a repetition of Operation 'Hats of the previous September. Again, this was intended to rendezvous two convoys from the East and West in the central Mediterranean with one of them going to Malta. The combined convoys consisted of fourteen ships, but the more glamorous element was their escort. Cunningham had his flagship *Warspite*, as well as the battleships *Valiant* and *Barham* which had replaced the *Malaya* and *Ramillies*. There were the aircraft carriers *Eagle* and *Illustrious*, as well as the cruisers *Orion*, *York*, *Ajax*, *Perth*, *Calcutta*, *Gloucester* and *Southampton*, together with sixteen destroyers. The escort for the Western convoy was provided by Admiral Somerville with his Forces H and F from Gibraltar. Flying his flag on the battleship *Renown*, he had with him the battleship *Malaya*, and the aircraft carrier *Ark Royal*, the cruiser *Bonaventure* and eleven destroyers.

The passage of both forces past the respective Italian hornets nests of Rhodes and Sardinia, was relatively quiet. But this was because it was the Luftwaffe they had to face this time which had transferred its Fliegerkorps X to Sicily, and was now following the progress of the two convoys, and waiting to strike when they reached the desired spot. This, the Germans did when the combined convoys were near Pantalleria, some 80 miles away from Malta. The first wave of German attackers was met by the Fulmars from *Illustrious*, and this might have been the reason why the enemy seemed to unleash its fury on the aircraft carrier. The ship met the attack with a fantastic fortitude. It launched what Fulmar and Swordfish aircraft she had for Malta to clear her decks. Then she faced the enemy with her guns together with those of the ships around her. The carrier was hit by several bombs and badly crippled, but continued with the fight. When their fuel and ammunition was running out, the Fulmars flew to Malta for re-fuelling and re-arming, and returned to fight for their ship which in the meantime continued with her progress to Malta, however slowed down. Two further attacks turned her trip to the island into a running battle, but she made port on the night of the 10th, now finding protection of the Malta defences, for her and for the convoy ships she had valiantly escorted there.

Her arrival now posed a problem to the Malta dockyard which had to race against time to make her seaworthy before the Germans got to her again. As Hitler had promised that Grand Harbour of Malta should be the ship's grave.

In the following days as the *Illustrious* waited for her death knell in Malta, a worried Wavell was waiting for a different kind of catastrophe in Cairo. He knew that if eventually there were to be sent any forces to Greece they would have to be found from his army. And he had no doubt that, notwithstanding the successes he had achieved, this would jeopardize his position in the Western Desert. He had already explained the situation to Churchill, but it was to no avail. Then as if to humour him, he had also sent to the Greeks 180,000 pairs of boots and 350,000 pairs of socks. But now he had to go to Metaxas himself with a fresh offer and attempt.

He was in Athens with the Greek dictator on 15th January, and even though against his convictions, he obeyed orders and tried to persuade Metaxas to accept aid in the form of troops, anti-aircraft units and tanks. But he breathed a sigh of relief when even this offer was refused. Faith played him an ace then when he received the news that, notwithstanding his lack of reinforcements, General O'Connor had captured Tobruk with another 30,000 prisoners, 236 guns and 87 tanks. If after this refusal the Greek obsession were to fizzle out and he would be able to give O'Connor what reinforcements he needed, he knew he would soon conquer Tripolitania and indeed the whole of North Africa. There was still hope.

But the news on the morrow weren't what he had hoped for. He was ordered to meet Metaxas again in four days' time, and now to increase the British offer by four divisions. In the meantime he learned that the Luftwaffe had attacked *Illustrious* in Malta and was keeping a constant bombardment of the island as if to obliterate it for ever. It was as if the world was going mad around him. But Wavell did not lose his head. He met Metaxas again on the 20th as ordered, enough to have another refusal. Then he flew back to Cairo and pressed O'Connor to push on. The gallant general complied, notwithstanding his depleted forces. His next objective was Derna, but finding that the Italians were there in strength he decided to skip that until he could have his reinforcements.

Then fate struck when on 27th January, General Metaxas had a stroke and died.

There was also the news on 3rd February that the Italians were abandoning the Benghazi corner. And this made O'Connor go on the chase. But as his wise dispositions were reaching Wavell there was not the expected exultation. The Commander-in-Chief knew that Metaxas had been the only stumbling block to the Greek escapade and now that he was gone, his replacement Koryzis and King George of Greece might well be amenable to Churchill's pressure. He found consolation in the escalating fighting which he knew was mounting towards a climax. O'Connor had despatched his 4th Armoured Brigade under Brigadier Caunter and the 11th Hussars with their armoured cars after the enemy, but was soon making a faster deployment of motorized infantry to run ahead of the main forces and reach Beda Fomm where they could block the enemy's route of retreat beyond Benghazi. With only two days' rations and just enough petrol, these forces had embarked on one of the most breathless races in military history. But Wavell knew he was running another race himself with his Prime Minister.

As one day followed another, there were always hot news coming in. Caunter's tanks broke up the first columns of Italian artillery and transport; then his 29 tanks were locked in a deadly battle with 100 of the enemy cruiser tanks. The British infantry was soon involved in fierce fighting in what has gone to be recorded as the Battle of Beda Fomm. Sweet relief followed with a British victory which rendered 20,000 more prisoners, 216 guns and 120 tanks for good measure. But it had also opened a clear passage through the Agheila bottleneck, and an open road to Tripoli. It was any general's wild dream. But not to Wavell.

On that day of 12th February, Winston Churchill had sent Anthony Eden, now Secretary of State for Foreign Affairs and General Dill, the Commander-in-Chief of the General Staff to Cairo with specific instructions authorized by the Cabinet, to make a further approach to the new Greek authorities. It was a near miss for them since their flying boat ran out of petrol on its way to Gibraltar. And this might have delayed their mission. But Churchill was taking no chances. He had on the same day sent a telegram to Wavell congratulating him on the fall of Benghazi. but also containing the dreaded thunderclap that he was to halt his advance and hold only to Cyrenaica, retaining only a small garrison. There was a similar order for the forces in East Africa. What troops were thus withdrawn from both fronts were to be held in readiness to form part of an expeditionary force that was to be sent to Greece.

* * *

It became evident to all that notwithstanding that there remained about 100,000 Italian troops in Libya, their hold in that country was spent. But more than to anyone else this was of direct interest to the Germans who immediately felt the need to take over if they were to keep alight their ever existing aim of eventually stopping the oil flow from the Middle East to Britain. Their first move in taking some 200 aircraft of the Luftwaffe to Sicily had already paid dividends. Not only in harassing British naval movements in the Mediterranean, but also to bomb Malta which stood in their way to North Africa. Now Hitler decided to send over the first land forces which were to make a beginning in building up the Afrika Korps. On 6th February, as the Italians were being routed in the Battle of Beda Fomm, Hitler called Lieutenant-General Erwin Rommel to Berlin and entrusted him with this new assignment. Five days later Rommel was in Rome from where he flew to Tripoli. There were sent to him a reconnaissance battalion and an anti-tank battalion. Two divisions, the 5th Light and the 15th Panzer had to be sent later in mid-April and the end of May respectively. In the meantime the Luftwaffe continued to attack Malta without interruption during February in an attempt to subdue her. Aircraft and submarines from the island had until then sunk 34 Italian ships on their way to North Africa, with a total tonnage of 120,193.

There was no British reaction to this move. "No large scale German intervention in Libya is to be anticipated" the War Cabinet Planning Section had said. But Wavell was not so sanguine in his appraisal. After all he did no longer have the experienced troops to set his mind at ease. The 7th Armoured Division had been withdrawn while the 6th Australian Division was all ready for despatch to Greece. The 2nd Armoured Division and the 9th Australian Division he was given in their place were both inexperienced and short of equipment and training. General O'Connor too had been given a rest, and in his place there was placed General Neame, still an untried commander. The month of March was then highlighted by the transport of the British Expeditionary Force to Greece, a concotion of 60,000 men under General Wilson.

From its very first moment of arrival in Athens, there was reflected the kind of charade the whole thing was thought to be. The British and Commonwealth troops arrived in Athens when Greece was not at war with Germany, so it was the easiest of things for military attaches from the German Embassy to be stationed on the wharves watching the troops arrive, counting them, and noting their equipment. The Germans must have been more amazed with their inadequacy for the task they had

Brilliant Battles and Blunders

been assigned. But the real difficulties began to appear as the army tried to settle down. Means of transport were negligible. The Greek army used bullock-cart and mule, which were scarcely suited for a modern army. Even so when two ship-loads of pack-mules were sent, one of them was sunk, and the other arrived too late to be of any value. It seems that no serious thought had been given to systems of rationing and supply which soon became a nightmare to Brigadier Brunskill who was responsible for it. The only accurate map he could obtain to arrange supply arrangements had to be borrowed from a Greek colonel. But then grain and meat could not be procured, as all resources had been taken to meet Greek military needs. There were a hundred and one things that any normal army needs but which could not be made available in Greece, and much time which could have been usefully spent in training had to be used up trying to bring some organisation which never materialised. It seemed as if Churchill's crusade became entangled in the web he had refused to foresee.

Maybe the only person who got some satisfaction from the Greek escapade was Admiral Cunningham because it afforded him the chance to engage the Italian fleet as he had always wished. Since there wasn't likely to be a better occasion for the Italians to venture out than now when the British were transporting troops and stores to Greece.

If there was any indication of this wanted, it was found in the persistence with which the Mediterranean fleet was being watched, and this being considerably intensified during the month of March. But the beginning came in the form of a message from Malta to Admiral Cunningham reporting that three Italian cruisers and destroyers were sighted by reconnaissaance aircraft heading in a direction towards Crete. This made it obvious to the admiral that the Italians were probably going to join some heavier ships, possibly a battle-fleet.

On 27th March then, there was considerable wireless

activity detected from Italian ships at sea. By now Cunningham's main battle-fleet was safe and snug in Alexandria, while there was only one convoy at sea on its way to Greece. The Admiral issued instructions to this convoy to proceed on its way until it became dark. Then it was to reverse its course. He turned then to find ways and means how to hide his intentions with regard to moving his main fleet from harbour.

He had always suspected that the Japanese consul in Alexandria might have been reporting fleet movements from that port to the Axis powers. So on this day Cunningham made it a point to play golf with the Japanese gentleman who was his acquaintance, as if to make it obvious he had no pressing operations on his mind. Moreover, when the usual Italian reconaissance aircraft flew over Alexandria harbour at noon they could report that the British main fleet was there. But no sooner had Cunningham returned to his flagship *Warspite* at dusk, that he left harbour, followed by the battleships *Valiant* and *Barham*, the aircraft carrier *Formidable* and the destroyers *Jervis*, *Janus*, *Nubian*, *Mohawk*, *Stuart*, *Greyhound*, *Griffin*, *Hotspur* and *Havock*. In the meantime Vice-Admiral Pridham-Wippell in the cruiser *Orion*, accompanied by the cruisers *Perth* and *Gloucester*, as well as the destroyers *Flex*, *Hasty*, *Hereward* and *Vendetta* was asked to cut short his patrol in the Aegean and rendezvous with the battle-fleet south west of Gavodo Island on the morrow.

Early the following morning, however, Pridham-Wippell reported to Cunningham the sighting of three enemy heavy cruisers with destroyers northward of him. These were probably the same ships that had been sighted by the recce from Malta, and very likely still on their way to join others. Pridham-Wippell was game to engage them, but then he had to consider that the three enemy cruisers were 8" gun ships and superior to his own. So rather than attacking, he thought of a stratagem to draw them

Brilliant Battles and Blunders

towards Cunningham's battle-fleet which he knew was drawing close. When he let his squadron to be seen by the Italians, these began to follow him as if they were walking into the trap he had laid for them. When they were 13 miles behind him the enemy cruisers opened fire which seemed to be reaching the cruiser *Gloucester* at the back. She replied with her 6" guns, but no hits were made by either side. Then suddenly the Italians gave up the chase and scurried away.

Hardly had he lost them that Pridham-Wippell sighted the Italian battleship *Vittorio Veneto*. It must have then occurred to him that while he was trying to hoodwink the enemy ships and take them to Cunningham's battle-fleet, they had all the time been driving him towards theirs. Whatever it was, he was not allowed to think about it since the Italian flagship opened fire on his squadron when it was still sixteen miles away. This was too far for him, and he had to get closer if he were to reply. So he ordered his cruisers to make smoke and run at the Italian dreadnought. But no sooner had they done this that they were being uncomfortably straddled by her 15" shells. Cunningham from his part was soon making the necessary dispositions to relieve the cruiser squadron in her ordeal, and ordered *Formidable* to launch an air strike against the Italian battleship, while he steered his fleet at full speed towards the scene of battle. Half an hour later it was reported to him that the Italian battleship was hit with a torpedo which had certainly handicapped her speed, and this made Cunningham certain he would now overtake her to engage. However, he was soon being flooded by reports from different sources of enemy cruiser groups in the vicinity, and the situation became so confused that he could not say whether all of them were reporting the same ships or not. It was only about 6 p.m. that he could establish that he was about 45 miles away from the *Vittorio Veneto*, but now it was also time for him to decide whether to ignore the Italian cruisers and risk having them attack Pridham-Wippell's lighter ships while he would continue after the battleship. His decision was to send eight destroyers to attack the enemy cruisers where they found them, while he would continue in pursuit of his main prey, the *Vittorio Veneto.*

At 9 p.m. he had still not sighted her. And it was at that time that Pridham-Wippell reported that his radar had located a heavy ship lying stopped some 6 miles from his position. Cunningham couldn't check this as the *Warspite* had no radar, but it looked obvious to anyone that this ship must have only been the battleship that was his prey, since she was the only ship reported hit until now. So he altered course to close on the indicated location.

An hour and a half later he was quickly summoned on the bridge to identify two silhouettes seen in the darkness which could have easily been heavy cruisers. And so they were. So without thinking any further of his other prey, Cunningham decided to engage this new element of the enemy. With her first salvo the *Warspite* riddled one of the enemy ships at point blank range. It happened to be the Italian heavy cruiser *Zara,* that got the works and was immediately shattered by the *Warspite's* 15" shells. The *Valiant* too had opened fire on the other cruiser which was the *Fiume,* and similarly sank her. Between them the *Barham* and the destroyers took what Italian destroyers had joined the battle out of darkness and sank two of them before they withdrew.

The British Admiral must have realised by now that what time he had spent in this battle must have decreased if not lost him altogether what chances he had to overtake the *Vittorio Veneto,* thinking all the time that Pridham-Wippell's message must have referred to one of the sunken cruisers after all. So he signalled his ships which were not engaging the enemy to return for fresh dispositions for dawn which was now approaching. This was not meant for Pridham-Wippell who was still looking for the Italian battleship, but he thought otherwise and began making his

Brilliant Battles and Blunders 49

way back. Hopes were then raised again when one of the returning destroyers, the *Havock* reported sighting the enemy stopped battleship. This sent Cunningham again with haste for the killing. Only that on the way, the message was corrected to say that the enemy ship was not the wanted battleship, but another cruiser. This time there was no mistake since the destroyer *Jervis* had already drawn alongside the enemy. And indeed, the captain was then signalling the admiral whether he should board the enemy ship and take it pirate-like or what? He was asked to take the crew away and then to sink the ship by torpedoes. The Italian cruiser was the *Pola* which had been hit by a torpedo from the *Formidable's* aircraft.

This battle was fought off Cape Matapan, hence earning its name for history as the Battle of Matapan. Indeed the Italian flagship had got away. But the enemy had in this first engagement at close quarters with the British Mediterranean Fleet, paid with three heavy cruisers *Zara*, *Fiume* and *Pola*, as well as the two destroyers *Alfieri* and *Carducci*. British losses were of one aircraft from *Formidable*, with its two man crew.

What of British prestige was shed by this victory was, however, soon being overshadowed by more than humiliating events elsewhere. In North Africa an under-strength Rommel created a fictitious picture of his forces by building a number of dummy tanks mounted on Volkswagen cheap cars. And the British seemed to have been taken in by this trick. Then when the German general received his first tank regiment on 11th March he moved this together with two new Italian divisions to the Agheila bottleneck which he occupied without difficulty. Until now this had been his only object, to pave the way until he would have received all his forces in April and May. But seeing there was no worthwhile resistance from the British he moved on with only fifty tanks and the Italian troops but with a much more magnified impression he had given Wavell. So much so, that British forces in Benghazi fell back in confusion and evacuated the place. As if this was not enough, Wavell had, on realizing the emergency recalled back General O'Connor and sent him hastily to advise the inexperienced General Neame. Then, both of them being in an unescorted car ran straight into the back of a German spearhead group and were captured.

However palpitating hearts must have lain more with Greece, where the combined British and Commonwealth forces were trying to make some order out of the confusion that reigned there. Many of them were given a false introduction in the way of landing them at the Piraeus with time for a stroll to the old ruins of Athens and a look at the Acropolis. They were even given a chance to visit the brothels, get a good feed and then get drunk. But after that, it had to be dry rations for them, with bully beef, biscuits, cheese and water to be consumed as they were transported to the lines they were to defend, by whatever means came to hand. Some went by rail, others by truck. But the crux of the matter was that on reaching destination they found that they were expected to create defensive positions from almost nothing. In the position on the Aliakmon they found only trees which had to be cut down about knee high to give a field of fire and support. The stubs were then used as posts for the barbed wire entanglements. They had to leave gaps for some villages which would have to be evacuated in the eventuality of attack. These would no doubt have to be mined in time. Oh yes, they had some mines but not enough detonators. Over and above this they had to dig themselves in, repair roads, shift crumbling Greek soil to make slit trenches and gun emplacements, and all this in cold weather.

It was simply madness to think of these being preparations to meet a German attack on Greece. As far as 13th December, 1940 Hitler had drawn attention to the arrival of British aircraft in that country which would produce the feared threat to the Ploesti oil installations. And as a precautionary move he had ordered the deployment of

German divisions in that area which would be able to move through Bulgaria and attack Greece to prevent Greek airfields from falling into British hands. The intention was to mount this German build up to 24 armoured divisions. Now that things had reached this stage the Germans had also built their air-force for the Balkan campaign to some 1200 front line aircraft. Against this massive array Air-Vice Marshal J.H. D'Albiac, Air Officer commanding in Greece could only muster a total strength of 200 aircraft with only 80 being asolutely serviceable. The hopelessness of this situation was then amply reflected on the administrative side. All liaison with the Greeks had to be conducted through a British Military Mission situated in cities and in Pireaus. Petty jealousies and feuds arose between this Mission and Wilson's headquarters, which was also inadequately staffed, and handicapped by being an eight hour journey away from Athens, and badly served by telephone communication.

There might have been a belief of some advantage having been gained through roping in Yugoslavia with the British/Greek side. Indeed this country had resisted all British approaches for an alliance, while it had also delayed its response to similar German feelers. But notwithstanding the wish of the government of Belgrade to remain sitting on the fence, it had succumbed to sign a pact with Germany on 25th March. On the following day, however, a clandestine pro-Allied group under the leadership of air-force general Simovic, which had already been deeply involved with Colonel Bill Donovan, the same person who had pumped Churchill into the Greek venture, turned the tables on the Yugoslav government. They sent the Regent packing and the President Minister was forced to resign at gunpoint. Then they replaced the government by a Serbian junta. Winston Churchill no doubt thinking this was a stroke of good luck to an otherwise dismal outlook of the Greek venture quickly sent General Dill to Belgrade for talks. But his reply to him after more than a harassing experience was far from being encouraging. The

Yugoslavs were confused, he told him. Besides it was still the new junta's intention to keep the country neutral.

It is not known how much of this reached Hitler. But it is certain that he was enraged on learning of the coup, only a day after he had succeeded in having the Yugoslavs on his side. So on 27th March he issued his directives which were not for a normal invasion of Yugoslavia, but for an attack intended to destroy that country, both militarily and nationally. This was delivered without any warning on 6th April, catching the well equipped Yugoslav defences unawares as well as the population of which 17,000 lay dead among the rubble after three days of aerial bomardment.

At the same time the German army played up to Winston Churchill's frivolous tickling. Two army groups moved south and east. One group under General von Weich, composed of two panzer, one motorised, one mountain and six infantry divisions moved into Yugoslavia and towards Greece from the north. Another group under General von List composed of five panzer, two motorized, three mountain and eight infantry divisions, as well as an SS Adolf Hitler division went in from the east.

British and Commonwealth troops in Greece were doomed before actual fighting had started. Churchill's balkan military venture was shown for what it was, as another blunder.

CHAPTER III

THE BATTLE OF CRETE

With its strategic importance in the Mediterranean, the island of Crete had drawn the Axis attention well before Italy invaded Greece. But what plans Hitler and Mussolini generated for that part of the Mediterranean were overtaken by the events which have until now taken up this narrative. Crete fell into Britain's lap when after the first Greek request for aid in October 1940 there was a small British force despatched to the island. And one might have expected that this would develop into something more substantial to turn the place into the potential base it promised to be. But there was nothing of the sort being done.

It is true that topographically the island did not present an easy task. In fact with a very long coastline, few roads and a continuous mountain range from tip to tip it required a herculean effort to turn it into the kind of base one would have liked it to be. But there was both time and scope to make a start in November 1940 after the British had moved in. Yet, whatever improvements one could think of making, seemed to fail in finding the necessary determination to have them carried out. It will suffice to say that after the first British Commander, Brigadier Tithbury took over, the command of the island changed four times in six months leaving no time to any of the five officers who shared it to think and plan in terms of defence. It was only after the despatch of substantial British forces in Greece in March 1941 that Major General

E.C. Weston of the Royal Marines who was the latest commander raised the question of the island's vulnerability to an airborne attack. And this had set the British thinking.

Now, what sluggish preparations had been started were quickened. Suda Bay was upgraded to a naval base, given an anti-submarine boom defence, provided with lighters for oiling, and a few soldiers were posted there for garrison duties. But Suda Bay did not make Crete, and the little that was done there, was from the very start further belittled by the magnitude of what was realised to be still required elsewhere. And as if to start the series of mishaps that were to follow, on the morning of 26th March some elements of the Italian underwater force, Decima Flotilla Mas penetrated the newly laid boom at Suda Bay and seriously damaged Cunningham's only 8" gun cruiser *York* which had to be beached, as well as the tanker *Pericles*.

There is no doubt that there was too much reliance being laid on the Mediterranean fleet to defend the island in the eventuality of invasion. And after the way Admiral Cunningham had driven the Italians off the seas, none had any doubt that he could do it. But there was now the more threatening problem from the air. Not only for consideration of the airborne attack as Weston had mentioned, but also as an eventual way of a German strike against the British fleet. There had long been five sites earmarked for use as airfields in Crete, but none of them had been given enough attention because of shortage of construction equipment. Weston found only nine aircraft dispersal pens at Heraklion, but none at the other localities. What little facilities existed to transform a landing strip into an airfield could be found only at Heraklion, Retimo and Maleme. But again the three of them were not suitable to take anything more than light aircraft. Yet, this did not diminish their possibility of being ideal sites for landing airborne troops.

Now that the British had officially taken over the island

there was more reason to wonder why the situation was allowed to linger in such a desolate manner. There were not even the necessary means of coordination for defence against air attacks, and when an air-raid warning unit was sited above Suda Bay in December, this was until May 1941 connected to the operations centre at Canea with only a single telephone line. This proved to be vulnerable to weather conditions, and one could easily understand how much more it would be to eventual air attacks. The only anti-aircraft defences Weston found in the island consisted of ten heavy guns and 20 Bofors apart from a few 2" pom-poms. It was a situation enough to send him crazy.

Respite came only when the evacuation of Greece started, and troops were being taken to Crete. Some of them were intended to be further transhipped to Alexandria. But Weston was told he could expect some 25,000 men to be retained in the island for its defence. This obviously meant that Crete was now in the front line.

* * *

If this reinforcement might have caused any positive reaction with Weston and his superiors it would have been immediately erased had they known of what Hitler was preparing for Crete, and of the directive he had issued to General Karl Student.

In contrast with the scanty British preparations that were now being hastened, those by the Germans had been going on very much longer. General Student had been building up his airborne force, the 7th Fliegerdivision since 1938. He had meticulously selected and trained his men and moulded them into a force of shock troops that could be utilized at a moment's notice, sustaining all dangers and mocking even death for the fanatical love of the fatherland. That his force had reached the optimum state of efficiency could be seen from the roles already played in the capture of Narvik in Norway, Rotterdam and The Hague in Holland, as well as in the several battles in Belgium. There had even been the last dress rehearsal in

Greece, when these paratroops captured the important Corinth Canal Bridge. Now they were launching their first large-scale attack on enemy territory from the air. This operation was expected to determine the force's future as well as that of its commander General Student, who was allotting for its execution a parachute division, a glider regiment and the 5th Mountain Division under General Lohr. The plan was for the first elements of the force to neutralize anti-aircraft defences. Then the bulk would attack the three airfields at Heraklion, Retimo and Maleme simultaneously, as well as Suda Bay. Whichever airfield were to be captured first, would then receive reinforcements by transport aircraft, while heavy equipment, artillery and even more troops were to be sent by sea.

Considering that the whole operation involved the transfer of some 30,000 men with their equipment from Germany and Rumania to their take off point in Greece. And also that these required not less than 4,000 vehicles for the first stage of their trip, then 493 transport aircraft for their second, it was indeed to be a gigantic operation. But the orderly way in which these preparations were set about, reflected German determination for the operation's success. Student had everything planned to the minutest detail, and he was more than convinced of a successful conclusion.

But there were two things he did not know. Firstly, that between them, British, Commonwealth and Greek forces in Crete had swelled to the respectable number of 42,000 men. The second and more important thing was that through the new invention *Ultra*, the secret system of cracking German military codes, details of the intended invasion were already known to the British, even to the exact date and time of launching. Had Student been aware of this he would have doubtlessly cancelled the invasion. On the other hand, this raises the obvious question as to how and why the British lost Crete even when they possessed numerically superior forces than the enemy, and the advantage of this advance information? The answer

The Battle of Crete

can be found in the dramatic story of the battle that was to follow.

The defence of the island was the responsibility of General Wavell, but he detailed General Bernard Freyberg to take command. A tough New Zealander with a Victoria Cross from the 1914/18 war, Freyberg was a seasoned campaigner and a good choice. But he had still to shape his 42,000 men into an army when he took over. He had to clothe them, feed them and what was more important, equip them adequately from the mixture of equipment that had been salvaged from the Greek operation. He could no doubt rely on British and Commonwealth troops, but there were also 11,000 Greeks in his army, with nothing known of their potential. Although he was convinced that the British Navy would certainly provide the necessary defence from any seaborne attack, he knew he had no airforce to rely upon. All he found in Crete were six Hurricane fighters and seventeen obsolete Fulmars and Gladiators. These could not be expected to stand a chance against the 430 bombers and 180 fighters that the Germans were likely to throw at him. There was also the headache to get more supplies of food and stores to last him through the battle. Not only for his troops but also for the civilian population of 400,000 as well as 15,000 Italian prisoners of war that were in Crete. His, was without any doubt a mammoth task to be undertaken. But the worst was that he had no time to do it. Three weeks was all he had, during which he was to be continualy pestered by German air-raids.

General Freyberg did not mince words in his first message to Wavell after assessing the situation. The gist of it was that what forces he had were considered inadequate to meet the envisaged attack, and that unless he was given more aircraft and the navy made available to deal with any seaborne attack, there was no hope. He concluded by suggesting that the holding of Crete should be reconsidered.

Wavell passed that message to England with his own comments which could not have been much different, since he was not anxious to defend Crete. However, it goes to his merit that after receiving Churchill's reply expressing his determination to hold to Crete, Wavell transmitted this to Freyberg in a more reassuring tone trying to mitigate expectations, and promising more artillery, as well as assuring Freyberg of the navy's help. He didn't mention anything about the air-force. He couldn't, since what aircraft were available were tied up in Egypt, where Rommel was at the door of the Nile Delta and the Suez Canal. Then as if to complicate matters further Air Chief Marshal Longmore, the Air Officer Commanding was recalled to England. So the only tangible assurance that reached Freyberg concerned the navy's co-operation.

In the meantime Admiral Cunningham had his problems, too, and much as he was determined to give his contribution, was caught in a quandary. With Malta now gaining more importance in intercepting German supplies to Rommel he had despatched six destroyers from England, *Kelly, Kipling, Kelvin, Kashmir, Jackal* and *Jersey*, all under the command of Captain Lord Louis Mountbatten, to replace the *Jervis, Janus* and *Nubian* which returned to Alexandria. But Malta had also to be replenished, and two convoys of essential supplies and 24,000 tons of oil-fuel were being despatched. These coincided with another convoy of 5 ships which was leaving England with tank reinforcements for the Desert army. This convoy, code-named Operation Tiger was to be escorted by Admiral Somerville's Force H as far as the Sicilian Narrows, from where Cunningham had to take over. It was fortunate that he had an idea of the date of the invasion. As it was, he could just make it. And he did. He also got a bonus when the Germans delayed their attack by a few days. This gave him time to redeploy his fleet now reinforced with the battleship *Queen Elizabeth*, and the cruisers *Niaide* and *Fiji*. Now he had Vice-Admiral Pridham-Wippell hoist his flag in *Queen Elizabeth*, while he gave *Warspite* to Rear-Admiral Rawlings, and each of them was allotted a battle squadron. This enabled him to

The Battle of Crete

stay back for co-ordinating efforts. The Germans escalated their air attacks on Crete on 15th May, and much as it was desired to have the *Formidable* assist with her aircraft, she couldn't do it, because the casualties incurred while escorting the convoys to Malta and Tiger to Alexandria, had left her with only four serviceable aircraft. She was not expected to become operational before the 25th May. Then five days before that date, the Germans launched their attack on Crete.

The morning dawned fine and sunny, and when the alarm was sounded there was nothing to show it was not another air-raid like the others Crete had been having daily for the last five days. But it was not long when on the horizon there appeared the deadly cloud made up of 280 bombers, 150 Stukas and 180 fighters. Following close behind there were 500 transport aircraft and about 70 gliders towed by JU 52s.

The German attack was directed against four objectives. At the town of Canea and Suda, the main port of supply; Maleme airfield, the Akrotiri peninsula overlooking Suda, and a point between Maleme and Kastelli to cut communication between the two. But apparently the plan did not take into consideration certain difficulties. For one, with so many aircraft close to each other there were several collisions which forced other transport planes to drop their paratroopers away from their destined locations. To make up for this there were the wrongly sited anti-aircraft guns which could not fire on the low flying German aircraft. There were also guns which had fired incessantly for the three previous days and now had strangely enough remained silent. But, notwithstanding all this, the German attack met with stiff resistance which showed them how wrong they had been in expecting the British forces in Crete to have been only in the strength of one division besides remnants of the forces that had fought in Greece.

In at least two of the intended objectives the German attacks were abortive. In Akrotiri it was repulsed by

British forces, while in Kastelli the Germans were mauled by local makeshift troops who when running out of ammunition clubbed or stabbed the paratroopers to death. The German forces intended for Canea who found themselves spread out to Galatas had to contend with three battalions of the 4th Brigade of a New Zealand Division which quickly mounted up to some five thousand men and pinned down the attackers. The Germans had taken some useful positions, but by late afternoon they had suffered heavy casualties and found themselves under a heavy bombardment from artillery which the British had moved up. The only relief for the Germans came at Maleme and Pirgos where they had landed over two thousand men and where they found the British and Commonwealth troops badly placed. But the attack was all the same contained. By noon, having received no news, Student sent an aircraft to Maleme to investigate, but as it reached the airfield it was met with heavy machine gun fire which showed that the place was still in Allied hands. Indeed, later in the afternoon Student received the news that the attack on Canea had been beaten back with heavy casualties while the situation at Maleme was far from being that he had expected. This made him launch his second wave later on, this time intended for Retimo and Heraklion. At the first objective 1,500 Germans found 1,200 battle-hardened Australians waiting for them plus Cretan police and levies, while at the second 2,800 infantrymen and three Greek battalions brought appalling slaughter to the 2,000 German paratroopers that landed there. As the first day came to a close, the German invaders were beaten on all fronts.

There were also good news from Admiral Cunningham whose fleet had moved to the North of Crete where it met only six Italian motor torpedo boats which retired quickly after being engaged. Seeing that there was no scope to remain there, the fleet was ordered to move to the south.

The first swing in the battle came on the following day,

the 21st. And as fate would have it, what misunderstandings occurred had to be at Maleme, which the enemy considered the most important for his plans. There was a British move afoot to try and sweep back what Germans had held to their sporadic positions in the Maleme area. It was decided to use some of the few light tanks that were available. But since these had been sparsely distributed there were only two that could be used, as had been allotted to each airfield. The plan was for the two tanks to move forward on the enemy in single file about 30 yards apart, with an infantry platoon to follow. And so they did. But no sooner had they come within range of the enemy that the second tank turned back because it was realised that the amunition it had did not fit the machine-guns, and the turret had jammed. The other tank continued and was soon firing merrily which shook the Germans since they had not expected tanks. Then suddenly the vehicle stopped as its turret also jammed, while its engine failed. The Germans around lost no time in crowding the tank to capture its crew and catching the following platoon in a withering fire. Only three British soldiers returned unscathed to their lines out of the lot.

It was now time for Brigadier Hargest, the commander in the area to send reinforcements, but there were misunderstandings between him and Colonel Andrew. What with radios going out of order and messages having to be sent by runner, reinforcements never reached their destination, thus creating a chance for the enemy to improve his position at Maleme. Getting to know he had now more than a toehold in the airfield, Student immediately ordered his own reinforcements. 6 JUs with supplies and ammunition, and 350 paratroopers. Further troops were sent in later with the result that while in the morning there had only been a small battered and exhausted German unit in the airfield, by nightfall there were one thousand fresh paratroopers spoiling for a fight and to get complete control of the airfield. The situation was such that even the British felt that a counter attack had become imperative, and they were soon moving into position to launch it. It had by now become dark. Then the sound of heavy gunfire began to be heard away at sea. The sky was filled with a red glow, and Germans and British knew that the expected seaborne invasion must have started and that the Royal Navy had gone into action. Neither knew what was going to be the outcome, but both were aware that whatever this would be, it would affect either one side or the other. So while the Germans waited in hope, the British somehow postponed their counterattack.

It was indeed the British Navy that was running the show out at sea. Since the early morning of the 21st two squadrons under Rear-Admirals King and Glennie had been under air attack as they moved to their new position in the South of Crete. The cruiser *Ajax* was damaged while the destroyer *Juno* was hit by Italian bombers and sunk. The crews must have breathed a sigh of relief when darkness fell expecting some respite and a much needed rest after a whole day's gruelling. But at 11.30 p.m. the men in Rear-Admiral Glennie's squadron were called to action stations. An enemy convoy was located some eighteen miles north of Canea. The squadron, consisting of the cruisers *Dido*, *Orion* and *Ajax*, with the destroyers *Kimberley*, *Hasty* and *Hereward*, proceeded to intercept. The convoy indeed consisted of a number of caiques packed with German troops and several small ships, escorted by torpedo boats. And the British ships were charging into the enemy group ramming many of them and firing at the others. One of the escorting torpedo boats was also sunk. That action which lasted more than two hours must have cost the Germans some 4,000 troops who were drowned. With the first dawn then it was the turn of Rear Admiral King's squadron consisting of the cruisers *Naiade* and *Perth*, the anti-aircraft cruisers *Calcutta* and *Carisle* with destroyers *Kingston*, *Kandahar* and *Nubian* to go into action. In their case they were subjected to heavy enemy aerial attacks. But later they began sighting caiques. First one which was quickly sunk, then a small ship also carrying German troops which was similarly dealt with. An hour later another convoy was encountered which tried to escape behind a smoke screen laid by an escorting torpedo boat. The cruisers shot up the torpedo boat while the destroyers went rampant amongst the caiques behind the screen. A few more thousands of German troops must have perished with this action, and never reached Crete where they were intended for.

When the expected reinforcements reached Hargest after a nine hour journey and continually harassed by German aircraft, the much awaited counter attack was launched, and without going into detail of the many shortcomings that were evident it will suffice to say that it failed to move the Germans from Maleme. It now became more a battle of tactics with Student throwing in all his reserves at Maleme and ignoring all other sectors where his troops were hard pressed. He was banking on having the airfield all to himself where he could land enough reinforcements to consolidate the whole campaign. He was so determined that he ordered his troop carriers to land at Maleme even when the airfield was still under bombardment by the withdrawing British forces artillery. Some of his transport planes were hit, and troops were killed. But those who weren't, still swelled his ranks enough to make him order them to infiltrate through the hills towards Canea. And although still uncertain of the fate of his men elsewhere he was already considering that once he had conquered Maleme he would have won the battle of Crete. And he was not far wrong, for on the following day which was the third of this campaign, Freyberg found himself in a dilemma.

But the 22nd May was the Royal Navy day. Air General Freiherr von Richthofen, a nephew of the 1914/18 air ace, and now commanding Luftflotte VIII which was covering the Crete campaign turned his attention to the British Navy. In his airfields he had 228 bombers, and 205 Stuka dive bombers. He had also some 230 fighters, with no fear of any British aircraft to stand in his way. And the order went out to his pilots to seek ships of the British navy and destroy them. The first prey was Rear-Admiral King's squadron. They caught up with it and followed up with a furious three and a half hour attack damaging the cruisers *Naiade* and *Calcutta*. Then when Rear-Admiral Glennie joined up with his squadron, the Germans continued with their attacks on the whole fleet. In the afternoon it was first the turn of the destroyer *Greyhound* to go. Hit by two bombs it sank in 15 minutes. Then the cruiser *Gloucester* was hit and set on fire which destroyed her. The cruiser *Fiji* followed and was also lost. Even the battleships *Warspite* and *Valiant* did not escape unscathed. They were both hit, but not extensively damaged.

As the day drew to a close reinforcements reached the fleet in the form of the 5th Destroyer Flotilla under the command of Captain Lord Louis Mountbatten which had been recalled from Malta. It had an easy night as it moved to a position north west of Canea and Maleme. But in the following morning it also came under heavy aerial attacks. The *Kashmir* was sunk in two minutes. Half an hour later it was the turn of the *Kelly* with Lord Mountbatten aboard who was one of the survivors to be machine-gunned by German aircraft as they were in the sea awaiting rescue by the *Kipling*.

In the meantime as the fleet was being decimated, General Freyberg was still with his dilemma as to whether he should launch another counter attack on Maleme or not. It may have been out of character for this general to have to dwell so long on such an important decision. But it seems that this was due to a divergence of opinion with his subordinate generals. In fact even though he finished by ordering the counter-attack, General Puttick, his subordinate was two hours later proposing that it should not be carried out as he felt this would be pushing more men forward into a position in which they might be cut off and lost. As an alternative, Puttick suggested to have the 5th Brigade which was fighting forward pulled back and

The Battle of Crete

strengthen the rear lines. And with him agreed also General I.M.D.G. Stewart. Tactically this meant a withdrawal which might indeed have strengthened the indicated lines, but it was certainly going to remove what remaining difficulties the Germans were facing in landing more reinforcements. It was a question worth deliberating upon, but Freyberg agreed to let his subordinate generals have their way. And as night fell to bring the May 23 to an end, instead, of the proposed counter-attack, the 5th Brigade was carrying out the withdrawal which as things turned out, was the first step to a retreat.

One here cannot help having a look as well at the battle of words and orders that was going on in the triangle of leadership. Freyberg was by now asking for reinforcements and stores from Wavell to which he was not receiving the response he wanted. Not much could be spared, and even so, the navy was no longer in a position to guarantee delivery after its bad mauling. Wavell was in turn informing Winston Churchill of everything, and the Prime Minister was now pressing Freyberg to win the battle. On that very day of May 23rd he was asking Wavell to send supplies and tanks to Freyberg and to keep them flowing every night, as if neither caring whether he could spare them or considering his responsibilities in regard to Rommell still knocking at the doors of Egypt. Nonetheless Wavell compromised and with the help of Air Chief Marshal Tedder who had replaced Longmore as Air Officer Commanding Middle East, had bombers sent to attack Maleme airfield. But when it came to sending 12 Hurricane fighters for aerial defence, only seven of them reached Crete, and again 4 of these were so badly damaged that they had to return to Egypt leaving only three which were also destroyed before they could go into action. An attempt was also made to land No. 8 Commando to help in the fighting but notwithstanding naval efforts only 200 men could be put ashore. The destroyers *Jaguar* and *Defender*, however, managed to land badly needed ammunition.

The Germans were believed to have 15,500 men in Crete at this time. Of these there had been 3,340 casualties. They were holding Maleme, and were now advancing towards Galatas which like Heraklion and Suda was strongly held by British and Commonwealth forces. It had beome amply clear by now too that what had jeopardised the situation for the British was the lack of air power, which had left the Luftwaffe in complete control of the air and to do as it willed both with Allied land forces and the Royal Navy. And it needed no saying that no amount of troops, valour and determination were going to save the situation, unless there was to be air support.

On 25th May Vice-Admiral Pridham-Wippell sailed with *Queen Elizabeth, Barham* and 8 destroyers to attack Scarpanto airfield in the Dodecanese Islands from where German aircraft were flying for their attacks. But this time he took the *Formidable* with him, now that the carrier had built up her fighter force to eight Fulmars. He obtained the surprise he wanted and the carrier's aircraft destroyed several German planes found in the airfield. But this was not enough. The more so that the operation was carried out at a sacrifice in that the squadron was attacked by the Germans about twenty times on its way back. The Fulmars gave combat to the enemy hordes and shot down many of his planes. But this did not prevent the *Formidable* from being hit twice and badly damaged, and the destroyer *Nubian* to have her stern blown off.

Freyberg's forces were in the meantime trying to contain a fierce German attack on their Stalos-Galatos line which was the last stage before Canea and Suda Bay. Both sides were aware that this could well be the last battle for Crete. For some time German aircraft did not join in battle, and the British lines were held with several German attacks being repulsed. It was only when the Stukas and Messerchmitts appeared on the scene that the situation changed. British and Commonwealth troops

The Battle of Crete

began falling like kingpins under the enemy dive bombing and strafing, leaving wide open gaps for the enemy to penetrate. Now nothing could hold the Germans. It fell to the New Zealanders to stop them temporarily by resorting to their preferred way of fighting with the bayonet. They charged the Germans with bloodcurdling shouts and battle cries and made them stop and even withdraw. This was no doubt heroism of the highest order but the gained respite was very brief. They were hardly left time to turn and care for their wounded and to reform their lines when the enemy attacked again. Now the Germans found a disintegrated Allied line to face them.

General Freyberg saw his front crumbling down, and he certainly found no consolation in his subordinate generals. General Pullick, with his communications broken down was falling back. General Weston, on the other hand, realizing his appalling casualties, was suggesting surrender. To make matters worse there was now also General Scoular reporting how his Greek troops were disintegrating after fighting off what German troops had landed from the sea, and he was attributing this to the foodstuffs and other stores that his troops had been deprived of. There was nowhere else Freyberg could look for relief and he reached the conclusion that his position became hopeless by the end of the day of 26th May. So he cabled Wavell and suggested evacuation.

More than ever before now it became apparent how the British Cabinet must have been out of touch with the real situation. The reply given to a disturbed Wavell asking for authority to evacuate Crete came from Winston Churchill saying that Crete was to be held at all costs, and that he (Wavell) was to hurl all possible aid to Freyberg. This was the limit, for an exasperated Wavell now having received further information from Freyberg saying that the hard-pressed British front had shrinked back to Suda, while the force at Retimo was reported to have been cut off. There was also the worsening of the situation at Heraklion with

Britiish forces there being surrounded. There was now no alternative to evacuation,

It was to be the second operation of its kind within a month. Only that to carry it out Admiral Cunningham now had a depleted fleet. Also that although the episode of Crete could be considered as closed, the battle was not yet over. And the Germans were expected to try their damnedest to kill or capture as many Allied troops before these could embark; and they would also try to sink as many ships in the process. And the Luftwaffe was as powerful and unrestrained as before. None more than Cunningham knew this, as he knew as well of other obstacles he had to overome in that unlike what happened in Greece, the forces to be evacuated were dispersed and lacking coordination. There was also the matter of not knowing how many of them there were, and so he could not plan. Nonetheless he ordered every available ship of his fleet to the task.

To help things out Wavell provided Cunningham with Major General J.E. Evetts to act as liaison officer between them. Air Chief Marshall Tedder also provided some fighters with long range tanks to provide cover for ships engaged in the evacuation, and this, was as was done in Greece, to be undertaken during the night. In the meantime, General Weston was detailed to fight a rearguard action while the rest of the forces were to embark.

The operation got under way on the night of May 28th-29th. The cruisers *Dido* and *Ajax*, with the destroyers *Decoy, Jackal, Imperial, Hotspur, Kimberley* and *Hereward* having to wait some 90 miles away from Crete awaiting darkness to fall. Even so they were attacked by a now desperate German airforce, and the *Ajax* had a near miss which started a fire. The cruiser was therefore ordered to return to Alexandria. The rest closed on Heraklion when it was dark and by 3 a.m. of the following day had embarked 4,000 men.

Mishaps were of course calculated risks, and there was

one when the destroyer *Imperial* had a failing steering gear. But Rear Admiral Rawlings lost no time in dilly-dallying. He took the crew off the ship then had the destroyer sunk by torpedoes. The situation had become hectic and it was better to lose one ship than have the rest delayed and subjected to attacks while they were carrying the troops. Even so the *Imperial* mishap delayed him enough as to be caught still on his way at sunrise, and was attacked. Now the destroyer *Hereward* was hit, and its captain rather than delaying the progress of the other ships to safety made back for Crete and was sunk. His crew and the troops he was carrying were subsequently rescued by Italian torpedo boats and taken prisoners.

The same story repeated itself right to the 31st May, with naval squadrons approaching Crete during the night, embark troops, and then run the gauntlet to Alexandria. The Luftwaffe too kept up its appointments, and several ships were hit and damaged during the crossing, while the cruiser *Calcutta* was sunk. But by 1st June, 16,500 British and Commonwealth troops had been evacuated. This was not all, and 5,000 more had to be left behind. Stores were left for those who did not want to obey the instructions given to them to surrender to the enemy.

The Battle of Crete was over. It had been a bitter fight which cost Britain heavy losses in men, warships and also prestige. What remained to be seen was whether any lessons were learned which could avoid what mistakes might have contributed to them. In the meantime, however, the war had to go on.

CHAPTER IV

MEDITERRANEAN CRUSADES

Opinions varied on what the debacle of Crete had got for the Germans and lost to Britain. But one outcome that could not be denied was the way in which it had thrown into sharp relief the British situation in the Mediterranean.

With the Luftwaffe now established in Crete and within range of the Middle East oilfields, there was again the dreaded speculation of the disruption of British oil supplies. In fact this did not materialise because of a new apprehensive Hitler following the outcome of the Crete campaign. Much as this had proved to him the tactical advantages of an airborne invasion it had cost him too much. The losses of 6,580 in dead, missing and wounded was considered to have been a very high price for such a small operation. And he was certainly not going to embark on anything similar. Particularly now that he wanted to clear the decks for the invasion of Russia. Therefore he was soon curbing the whims of an enthusiastic General Student who was already thinking of a similar operation against Suez as a means of getting to the Middle East oilfields. If there was indeed to be a thrust with this aim, Hitler decided, it would have to be made by General Rommel from North Africa.

It could then be said that the collapse of Crete was not

Mediterranean Crusades

disastrous to Britain as much in its loss, as that it had followed on the heels of three other disasters in Dunkirk, Norway and Greece. And in a way it was fortunate that it now appeared that the next important situation to be considered would have to be that of Egypt and North Africa. The British High Command had not got over Wavell's delusory winter success in capturing Cyrenaica only to lose it again to Rommel in ten days. And now as if to rekindle dying embers there was Rommel again counter attacking to re-occupy Halfaya Pass and make Brigadier Gott withdraw to his original position. The next move came from Winston Churchill himself, now in an uncontrollable mood and not trusting anybody, to order an operation, and lay down its plans himself. He had it all set down with what forces to be used, and the scope, which was that of driving Rommel out of North Africa. He had it all planned in detail, right to its code-name of Operation Battleaxe.

It had a simple plan starting with an assault by the 4th Indian Division and the 4th Armoured Brigade on the Halfaya-Sollum-Capuzzo area. Then the rest of the 7th Armoured Division would drive to Tobruk to link with the garrison there, and together they would then advance westwards. Considering the numerical superiority the British had over Rommel both in troops and tanks now brought by the convoy Tiger, this did not seem impossible. "Our first object," the Chiefs of Staff told Wavell, "must be to gain a decisive military success in the western desert and to destroy the enemy armoured forces." With this operation being his baby, Churchill did not fail to add his personal note emphasizing the numerical superiority held over the enemy. Wavell still thought it was too ambitious, and he told Churchill so. "I think it right to inform you," he told him, "that the measure of success which will result from this operation is in my opinion doubtful." What must have been in Wavell's mind was the vulnerability in both protection and speed British tanks and armoured cars had when compared with those of the Germans. He had then concluded his reply by saying that in spite of numerical superiority, he was still not going to accept battle with confidence. This must have certainly not improved the bad impression the general had made with the Prime Minister. But Wavell complied to the letter with his orders, and directed General Beresford-Peirce to carry out the operation. Before it would be launched, however, there was another offensive to be planned and undertaken in Syria where there had been too many indications of German penetration. This could easily threaten the Haifa oil fuel flow more than the North African situation and had to be straightened out. The only way to do it was to forestall it and for which he needed troops which he could ill afford with Operation Battleaxe in the offing. With a little effort he was able to scrape a small force which was placed under General Sir Henry Maitland Wilson. The lion's share of the operation, however, fell on the Navy which managed to scrape the cruisers *Phoebe* and *Ajax*, with the destroyers *Kandahar*, *Kimberley*, *Jackal* and *Janus* under Vice-Admiral E.L.S. King to try and neutralise French military resistance.

This operation was launched on 8th June, but it soon became apparent that the French were not taking things lightly. Reinforcements were needed, and rather than touching again the forces alerted for the imminent Operation Battleaxe, Wavell had resort to recall troops which had been sent to Iraq to quell a German inspired revolt. Then leaving operations in Syria to take their course he launched Battleaxe on 14th June.

General Beresford-Peirce was experienced in desert warfare, and he had already showed his mettle at the head of the 4th Indian Division on the first occasion when the Italians were driven out of Cyrenaica. But in Rommel the British had a different enemy who could not be gauged by anything or anyone they had met before then. And they were soon to find this out for themselves.

The offensive got going by three separate columns, with the right one making first contact with the enemy in the

Mediterranean Crusades

early hours of the 15th June. The first British mistake was to hold back their tanks until the artillery would have enough light to open up and this took away what element of surprise there might have been. But then there was a different kind of surprise awaiting them round the corner When the time came to launch the tanks into action against the Halfaya Pass the commander had only a short time to wait for the result of this first impact. It came when he heard his tank commander's voice on the radio shouting: "They are tearing my tanks to bits."

What had gone wrong? It is not known whether the British knew that most of the German anti-tank guns were still the old 37mm type of five years before the war, and could do nothing against the British Matilda tanks. Even what replacements Rommel had received in the 50mm type were not expected to penetrate the armour of British tanks. Then what was tearing the Matildas to pieces? It was of course Rommel, who being aware of his limitations in anti-tank weapons had improvised by using 88mm anti-aircraft guns for this purpose. Indeed he had only eight of these guns which he mounted in two groups of four where he expected the attack and made mincemeat of anything that approached his ingenious 'tank traps'. Of the first thirteen Matildas that led the attack, only one survived.

The centre column pushed towards Fort Capuzzo, finding no obstacles to the Matildas, and captured its objective. But when the left column was ordered to swerve right to outflank the enemy it ran into Rommel's anti-tank gun traps. By nightfall while the German commander had kept all his tanks intact, the British had lost more than half of their force. It soon transpired that Rommel had used that tactic to delay the British attack until he could bring up his panzer regiment from the rear. When this turned up to the attack, British troops managed to contain it, until they found the German 5th Light Division which had been investing Tobruk now on their flank. Rommel had moved it right through the night to converge on the spot with the panzers. In contrast with Wavell's preference to go and play golf with his deputy when the attack was launched, Rommel was on the 16th writing to his wife. "To-day – it's 2.30 a.m. now – will see the decision. It's going to be a hard fight, so you'll understand that I cannot sleep." By nightfall of the second day the British began falling back, and on the morning of the third day it was realized that Rommel had started a new move intended to cut their lines in two. This he did after having on the 17th intercepted a message from the commander of the 7th Armoured Division to Beresford-Peirce which outlined the critical British situation. Ironically enough this message which signified the loss of the battle, reached Beresford-Peirce when Wavell was present, after having first flown up from Cairo on his first visit to the Battleaxe front. There was now no alternative left to him but to order his forces to withdraw to their original position.

It had been more a battle of tactics than anything else, and with very few casualties. The British had lost 91 tanks against the Germans' twelve. But it had also shown some of the qualities of the German general the British had set upon to drive out of North Africa. Instead it was him who had nullified their offensive, and leaving no doubt that Operation Battleaxe had failed. Four days later there was Churchill's reaction when he removed General Wavell from the Middle East command, and had him exchange positions with General Sir Claude Auchinleck, who had been the Commander-in-Chief in India. Even this move did not detract any of the dismal gloom that had fallen over the Middle East in those days. There was also the Syrian operation which was not getting the expected results and was giving Admiral Cunningham a hectic time. The cruiser *Phoebe* which was acting as flagship for the operation had just been missed by a French torpedo, while the French flotilla leaders *Valmy* and *Guepard* had caught the destroyer *Janus* off Sidon and straddled her with gunfire hitting her three times. When she was brought to a stop

Mediterranean Crusades

she would have fallen prey to them hadn't the desroyers *Jackal, Hotspur* and *Isis* arrived on the scene which made the French ships run away at full speed. Two days later, however, the *Isis* was caught with another destroyer the *Ilex* and bombed. They were both severely damaged, which deprived the Mediterranean fleet of their services as well.

It must be remembered that a number of important warships had by then left to be repaired somewhere away from the battle area. The *Warspite* had gone to the United States, and the *Barham* to South Africa. The *Formidable* too was waiting to be taken to the United States, while the cruiser *Orion* was intended for the United Kingdom. Moreover, the escalated bombing of Alexandria by long range bombers from Crete did certainly not help this situation. The only respite that came in those days was the news of the German invasion of Russia on 22nd June. There was hope this might make the Germans relax their activity.

Spring had merged into summer and with the longer days it was becoming unbearable to wait for developments. The Syrian operation had become like a never ending crusade, with another imminently building up to re-supply Malta. It was true that with the invasion of Russia a number of the Luftwaffe squadrons in Sicily were taken to that new front and thus decreasing in number and intensity the air raids on Malta. But on the other hand, with Rommel's recent burst of successful activity it had become more important for the island to maintain and possibly increase her interventions of his supplies from Italy. And this had increased the need for stores and supplies being sent more often. This had become more difficult with Cunningham's depleted fleet, and the admiral had resorted to send supplies by submarines, using the big minelayers *Cachalot, Rorqual, Thrasher* and *Clyde*, which activity was soon being called the 'Magic Carpet Run.' But these stalwarts of the deep could never carry enough, and time was still drawing close to when there would have to be a proper convoy for Malta despite the lack of an escort aircraft carrier and other risks that would have to be faced. This too now had become like another crusade to be undertaken.

It was fortunate that the tide began turning in Syria. Fleet Air Arm aircraft from Cyprus attacked and sank the French flotilla leader *Chevalier Paul*. On 22nd June then, a similar warship was bombed and damaged in Beirut harbour. This spate of British activity seemed to shake up the French. The third and remaining ship of their naval squadron in Syria, the *Guepard*, then tried to put to sea and was soon engaged by British cruisers which put her out of action.There only remained the submarine *Surcouf*, and this too soon met its doom by torpedoes from the British submarine *Parthian*. This last encounter wiped out all the French naval forces in Syria. On 10th July, General Dentz asked for an armistice, and the Syrian crusade came to a successful end.

The time was now ripe to think of another convoy for Malta. But much as he wanted to, Admiral Cunningham could not lay hands on enough warships to escort it. So he had a *stratagem* worked out. If a convoy could be sent from England and escorted by Admiral Somerville's Force H, he could send out a squadron from Alexandria to hoodwink the enemy in thinking this would be escorting the convoy from the Sicilian narrows to the Middle East. This was bound to reduce the risk of attacks on the convoy between Gibraltar and Malta. His suggestion was agreed to and code-named Operation Substance. The convoy was formed up in England. It had seven large ships laden with much needed supplies, to be escorted by Force H. But Admiral Somerville was taking no chances. He proceeded in his flagship, the battle-cruiser *Renown* and the aircraft-carrier *Ark Royal* together with his cruisers and destroyers. Then for good measure he also added the battleship *Nelson*. Unfortunately one of the ships went aground at Gibraltar and could not continue, but the remaining six

Mediterranean Crusades

and their escort proceeded to run the gauntlet. Admiral Cunningham sent his squadron out towards Sicily, and on his orders British submarines began sending fake wireless messages to put the stratagem across. There was an indication that the ruse might be working when Cunningham's squadron was besieged by reconaissance aircraft as if to watch out for its rendezvous with the convoy. This was supported by the fact that the convoy was indeed having a relatively easy passage. But in the early hours of 24th July, when it was only a few miles away from Malta, the convoy was located by a force of Italian E Boats of La Decima Flotilla Mas which had long been training and preparing for a seaborne attack on Malta's Grand Harbour. They had put off the attack on 28th June because of rough seas. Now on their second attempt they had met this convoy, and no doubt, one look at the escort made them turn back without letting the British squadron see them. As things turned out it did not worry them having had to cancel their operation, because the fact that they knew there was going to be a convoy in harbour strengthened the scope for their attack. In fact the convoy reached Malta later on 24th July. La Decima Flotilla Mas then delivered its attack in the early hours of the 26th.

This kind of attack had been in Italian minds since the creation of the human torpedo in 1935. With Italian eyes already shed on Malta, and the strained relations that existed with Britain in those days had made the newly invented human torpedo a likely weapon of vengeance to be used against the British Navy. It had of course been much developed since then, and the specialist Italian unit was also eventually equipped with *barchini* which were small boats carrying an explosive charge through most of their length, leaving space only for the motor at the back and its pilot with an ejector seat to shoot himself away to safety before the moment of impact and explosion. This unit had already been successful in putting three human torpedoes past the boom defence in Suda Bay, in Crete two months before, where they had sunk the cruiser *York* and a tanker. But Malta was different and their attempt was therefore more elaborate. They were using three human torpedoes, eleven barchini and two bigger E Boats. The plan was for one of the torpedoes with its crew of two to undertake a suicide assignment to blow up a viaduct which held the harbour's boom defence in place, and thus open an entrance into the harbour for the *barchini*.

It was no doubt a good and audacious plan, that must have been worked out by men who had long been tense and eager for this operation. But Maltese gunners of the 1st Coast Regiment of the Royal Malta Artillery were not less frustrated with the lack of targets for their guns. And this occasion gave them the chance they had been waiting for. Having detected the raiders by radar they expected the attack. When this came, nine of the thirteen surface elements were destroyed by the Maltese gunners in as many minutes, three more were destroyed by Hurricane fighters which were scrambled to engage the Italian escort of Macchi fighters, and one *barchina* was captured intact. All the crews were either killed or captured, while three of the Italian fighters were also shot down. The only British casualty was a Hurricane. But the pilot saved himself by baling out and then swimming to an abandoned E boat.

* * *

It was now time for everyone and everything to pause as if to make way for Winston Churchill. For he too, frustrated as he was with the failure of his baby operation in North Africa, was having his own idea of a crusade. His ultimate plan was to mount an operation which would vindicate his failed attempt to kick Rommel out. He had made his first step by removing Wavell from command and replacing him by Sir Claude Auchinleck. He had also changed both the force and the armoured division commanders and was now relying on different people. He brought over Lieutenant-General Cunningham, the Admiral's brother, from Italian Somaliland which he had conquered from the Italians. There was also Lieutenant-General A.R.Godwin-Austen for the infantry, and

Mediterranean Crusades

Lieutenant-General C.W.M. Norrie for the armoured corps. Then he set out to build up the army that was to be entrusted to them. This time Churchill had no illusions, and knew he had to have a powerful force. And this he could only have by recalling troops from the Far East, which raised the first difficulties. These came from the Chief of the Imperial General Staff, Sir John Dill who did not like the idea of weakening British forces in the Far East at this time when he felt that the situation there was becoming acute. The CIGS did not have any wild illusions about Churchill's bouts of pressure which sometimes followed his whims. He had in fact already privately warned General Auchinleck about any similar attitudes that may be forthcoming from Whitehall. And he had also indirectly exculpated Wavell of his defeat in agreeing that he had been pressed into attacking before being fully prepared to do it. Now to relieve Auchinleck of certain administrative and political responsibilities there was sent Oliver Lyttelton to Egypt. He was the President of the Board of Trade and could reduce interferance by the War Cabinet in what were strictly military affairs.

Japan had until now not joined in the conflict. But Dill was convinced that the latest British and American measures to curtail her resources might eventually prove to be the hair that would break the camel's back. There were also the first German successes on the Russian front to be considered, which could very well encourage the Japanese further. Were Japan to join the Axis in war, then British colonies like Singapore, Burma, Hong Kong and indeed even the Dominion of India would be found lacking after being depleted of their forces which the Prime Minister wanted to transfer to North Africa. But Churchill was adamant. It had now become for him like an obsession which indeed made his planned operation to be more than others like a crusade. He even code-named it Operation Crusader.

The build-up did not fail to create problems in Egypt. Reinforcements and masses of stores and equipment were soon flowing from England, the United States, Australia and the Far East. All of them having to go along the back door route up the Red Sea and converging on Suez and other ports of the Canal. It did not only create havoc with an administration never geared up for such an influx, but as was to be expected, it was soon attracting the enemy's attention who began escalating air attacks on Egypt, and mining the Suez Canal which had therefore to be closed for long periods. When the Cunard White Star liner *Georgic* was hit and set on fire there was place for more anxiety. Since there were expected to arrive next the big liners *Queen Mary, Queen Elizabeth, Aquitania* and *Ile de France*, all full of troops and equipment from the Far East.

This was a huge operation, but it was by no means monopolizing the British war effort in the Mediterranean region. Following what had happened in Crete there was now an effort made to reinforce Cyprus. So an army division was sent there with some units of the Royal Air Force as well as transport and stores. Entrusted with transporting them there was of course the Royal Navy now also concurrrently engaged in transporting troops to and from Tobruk and constantly being attacked by German aircraft. The Australian destroyers *Waterhen* and *Defender* were lost in these operations. The sloop *Flamingo* and the gunboat *Cricket* were also seriously damaged.

All this, however, seemed to lose importance, and was not even being noticed in the *maelstrom* being blown up by an excited Churchill. He was seeing his intended crusade taking shape. But then his balloon was pricked by General Auckinleck when no doubt remembering General Dill's warning, he told the Prime Minister that notwithstanding everything he would not be able to launch his offensive Crusader before November.

* * *

Three months were considered a long time. And anything could happen. Particularly from Rommel whose name had by now become like a fixation in every British mind. As it was, Rommel had his own problems too. It seemed that with the attention of the German High Command being concentrated on Russia, there was little or no interest in North Africa. Hitler had by no means given up his idea of an offensive against Suez. But he had decided it would have to wait until Russia was defeated. This affected Rommel in that he was refused additional reinforcements he asked for, while most of what was being sent to him was being intercepted and destroyed by offensive activity from Malta. This had become for him an ever increasing worry, the more so when he could see that notwithstanding the constant attacks on the island the situation had not changed. And during August 1941, 35% of his supplies were lost to Malta's aircraft and submarines.

To taunt further an already frustrated enemy there was the fast minelayer *Manxman*, just fresh from two runs to Malta carrying stores and troops, and now trying to pull a fast one on the Italians. She was detailed to lay a minefield off Leghorn. But to add to the element of surprise she was disguised as a French light cruiser of "LeTigre" class. In her fancy dress she penetrated right into the Gulf of Genoa undetected, then after dismantling her disguise and hoisting the White Ensign, laid her mines early on the morning of August 25th. At the break of dawn she got clear of the Gulf at full speed before the Italians could realize what was going on. They only knew of the minefield when some of the mines came to the surface and were sighted. The minefield was eventually swept before any damage could be done. But this still did not detract from the brilliancy of the feat.

Notwithstanding everything, Rommel made up his plans, and with or without encouragement from his Army Command he was determined to attack and capture Tobruk, which he believed (as indeed Wavell had often said) was the key for an advance into Egypt. But when he asked for permission to carry out his plan, even this was refused. Hitler and Generals Jodl and Keitel were most emphatic not to stir up North Africa while their hands were full in Russia. Then, information reached them of the intended British offensive, and this sealed their decision to bid Rommel keep quiet and husband his forces to meet the British attack.

While this was going on in the German camp, the British First Sea Lord, Sir Dudley Pound was complaining to Admiral Cunningham that too many ships were being allowed to reach Tripoli with supplies for Rommel. It was this then that made the Admiralty decide that apart from aircraft and submarines Malta should also be given a surface force. This could be considered as having obtained a promotion to the small battered island who had not only withstood all that the enemy was throwing against her, with the resulting destruction and loss of life, but had also arisen to hit back, first with aircraft and submarines, and now with ships. Even so, Cunningham did not lose sight of the fact that there had come the need for a further convoy to Malta. What had been sent with the last one in July was only expected to last three months and which would even dwindle down sooner with the added need of fuel and ammunition to be required by the ships being stationed there. The battleship *Barham* had now rejoined the fleet after being repaired, and was allocated to Vice-Admiral Pridham-Wippell, while Cunningham moved to the *Queen Elizabeth*. But he still could not afford the right escort for the convoy. So this had again to be formed in England and sent under the custody of Admiral Somerville and his Force H.

With the bulk of the Luftwaffe in Sicily having now been sent to Russia there was hope for the convoy to have a quiet crossing. But there were no chances being taken. Admiral Somerville, flying his flag in the battleship *Prince of Wales* was taking two other battleships with him, the *Nelson* and the *Rodney* as well as the aircraft-carrier *Ark Royal* with four escorting destroyers. He was taking with

Mediterranean Crusades

him as well Force X under Admiral Burrough with the cruisers *Kenya, Euryalus, Edinburgh, Sheffield* and *Hermione*, with an accompaniment of eight destroyers. It was a mighty array to cover the nine ships in the convoy i.e. *Clan Macdonald, Dunedin Star, Imperial Star, Breconshire, Rowallan Castle, City of Lincoln, Clan Ferguson, City of Calcutta* and *Ajax*. The operation was code-named Halberd. The convoy passed Gibraltar on the night of 24th/25th September. On the following day it was located by Italian reconaissance seaplanes which gave the alarm to Admiral Iachino who was defeated by Admiral Cunningham at Cape Matapan. Now he moved out with his more powerful squadron made up of the battle-ships *Vittorio Veneto* and *Littorio*, the cruisers *Trento, Trieste, Gorizia* and *Duca degli Abruzzi* together with fourteen destroyers, all intent to engage the British fleet. He was to be supported also by the airforce and 16 submarines he had sent to the intended area. This should have provided naval history with a stupendous battle. Instead, on sighting the British fleet the Italian admiral made an about turn and headed for Naples without firing a shot, because, as it transpired later, his orders were not to engage a superior enemy. But why did he dash out in the first place? It now fell to the *Regia Aeronautica* to attack the British fleet. The first attack was launched by squadrons of torpedo bombers heavily escorted by fighters. A fierce running battle ensued with the warships covering their precious wards with an umbrella of anti-aircraft gun fire. The *Ark Royal's* aircraft took care of the enemy fighters. In the heat of the action the *Imperial Star* was hit by a torpedo and seriously damaged, and rather than having it delay the convoy, Admiral Somerville had it sunk. The *Nelson* too was hit by a torpedo in the stern which reduced her speed. But that was all. Thirteen Italian aircraft were shot down, while another ten Macchi fighters which left their base and failed to find the British fleet ran short of petrol and were lost before they could return to base. The convoy of eight ships reached Malta.

Like never before, in October the British war machine in the Mediterranean began to function smoothly in final preparations for the November crusade. Air Chief Marshal Tedder had amassed some 700 aircraft which was the biggest concentration that theatre of operations had ever seen as yet. The Royal Navy continued with its runs to and from Tobruk, every time running the guantlet of newly placed German artillery. Submarines and aircraft from Malta increased their efforts and during this month had sunk 65% of Rommel's supplies. It was now too that the island had her promised surface force in the form of Force K composed of the light cruisers *Penelope* and *Aurora* with the destroyers *Lance* and *Lively*. But there was also a change in the naval command with Vice-Admiral E.L.S. King of the 15th Cruiser Squadron being replaced by Rear-Admiral Philip Vian.

In Egypt the last dispositions were being made, under the eyes of the Commander-in-Chief Sir Claude Auchinleck. The force commander Lieutenant-General Cunningham was given Captain Guy Grantham of the Royal Navy to act as liaison with his brother, the admiral. Lieutenant General A.R. Godwin-Austen commanding the 13th Corps was allocated the 4th Indian Division with a brigade of tanks. Lieutenant General W.M. Norrie was given for his 30th Corps the 7th Armoured Division, the 4th Armoured Brigade Group, the 22nd Guards (Motor) Brigade and the 1st South African Division. The 2nd South African Division was to be kept in reserve. What final plans there were to be made were then put into effect for the climax in November. This month promised to be a momentous one. And so it was.

It opened with feverish Italian air attacks on Malta, all being directed against the newly installed Force K. In the first days both the *Penelope* and *Aurora* were reported by the Italian radio to have been damaged and put out of action. But on the following day which was November 9th, they were out with *Lance* and *Lively* to intercept a convoy of seven ships escorted by two cruisers and ten destroyers. In the action lasting only seven minutes they had sunk the seven ships and one destroyer. The rest of the enemy squadron fled but with one further destroyer being hit and sunk.

It would not be surprising if this had something to do with Rommel flying to Rome to complain about the way his supplies were being sunk even when heavily protected, and this also gave him the opportunity to try again and obtain permission for his attack on Tobruk. It was a furious Rommel who from Rome telephoned Colonel General Jodl in Berlin to blow his top with him. Jodl told Rommel of the expected British offensive, and Rommel told him he could contain it with only his 21st Panzer Division under General Ravenstein who was there with him as well, while he could devote himself with the 15th Division to attack Tobruk. It was a very big task he was letting himself in for, but he was so emphatic in guaranteeing success, that Jodl gave in.

Rommel decided there and then he would attack Tobruk on 23rd November. In the meantime, however, he wanted to stay in Rome for his birthday on November 15th where he was also joined by his wife. His decision was a fortunate one, for that night, while at the invitation of the Italian High Command, he was seeing the film *On from Benghazi* depicting the advance of the previous April, a British Commando party under Lt. Colonel Geoffrey Keyes had landed in Libya and attacked the general's house near Beda Littoria in an attempt to kill or capture him. Four Germans in the house at that time were killed, and so was Keyes, for which he was awarded a posthumous Victoria Cross.

Rommel was back in Libya on 16th November in time for Keyes' burial. Then he lost himself seeing to the final touches for his attack on Tobruk. But he was not to complete them, however. For on 18th November, General Auchinleck launched his offensive which took the German General completely by surprise.

CHAPTER V

OPERATION CRUSADER

The 30th Corps under General Norrie was the first to cross the frontier with a 30 mile frontage. Its objective was Tobruk, 90 miles away, which was held by a British force. The much awaited Operation Crusader was on its way.

By nightfall the front elements had reached Trigh el Abd. The advance was then resumed in the following morning with the frontage now stretching to fifty miles, and in the process capturing the enemy airfield at Sidi Rezegh which was only 12 miles fron the perimeter of Tobruk. All seemed to be well. With no resistance being met. Neither from the Luftwaffe, probably grounded by the bad weather of the previous day, nor from Rommel's ground forces. Only, however, that the 22nd brigade, the 4th Armoured Brigade Group and the 1st South African Division, which had made the rear of the cavalcade now seemed to have lagged behind. In truth they hadn't. They had only run into the first troubles.

The 22nd Brigade had encountered Italian tanks and this was too good a temptation to follow a simple engagement with a chase which took the brigade out of its way. It might have been intentional when the Italians led the British force to the west towards Bir el Gubi, and right onto well placed anti-tank gun batteries which lost no time in mauling it down. The brigade lost 40 of its 160 tanks. The accompanying South African Division then was launched into an abortive attack on the enemy position. The 4th Armoured Brigade on the other hand was baited by a German Reconaissance unit, again tempting them for a chase. Then before they knew it there were two German tank units of the 21st Panzer Division coming from behind to maul their rear. And it would have been much worse had the brigade's front units not been pulled back to help driving the Germans away.

Although it might not have been realized at the time these enemy moves must have all been master-minded by Rommel, not as much to weaken the numerically superior British and Commonwealth forces of the 8th Army as to explore the situation of the offensive which had taken him by surprise. He had his misses too. Like sending his General Cruewell to Trigh Capuzzo expecting the British thrust to be strongest on that route, only to find nothing and no one there. And in the process Cruewell's forces exposing themselves to danger when they ran out of petrol. But still, there was the 15th Panzer division to make the day when it ran into the 4th Armoured Brigade looking somewhat lost and isolated, and giving it a sound beating.

Now, the elements of the German panzers were here, there, and everywhere, appearing like will-o-the wisps to hit hard and disappear. Then on 21st November, having gained a clear picture of the British lay-out Rommel ordered a counter-attack with his two divisions on the force at Sidi-Rezegh. This coincided with Norrie's decision to have his force drive towards Tobruk, and the garrison there to launch a breakout attack. These two contradictory orders by the two opposite commanders brought elements of their respective armies in confrontation earlier than expected and led to a series of separate tank battles, with positions constantly changing hands since the order in both camps had become to strike and destroy rather than holding fast. The 4th Armoured Brigade and the 8th Hussars were taken by surprise in a dusk attack and surrounded by the 15th Panzers. Most of their equipment was captured. The airfield at Sidi Rezegh was in the meantime overrun by a regiment of the 21st Panzer, while the British garrison at Tobruk having launched their breakout attack and made a way through the German lines surrounding their position, did not combine with the expected forces from Sidi Rezegh, since these had been engaged on the way.

Because of the fact that elements of the 8th Army were fighting on Libyan territory there was much over-optimistic belief of the Germans being beaten. However prudent, what reports by Auchinleck were reaching London were soon being interpreted as pointing at a massive British victory. To one such report, Churchill replied with a hint that he might be broadcasting the good news to the wide world. But the factual situation was far from being so clear-cut. The 30th Corps had certainly found itself in a confusing situation. Yet, it was only now on the 23rd November that Lieutenant-General Cunningham decided, rather late, to order the 13th Corps to start advancing. This second of the 8th Army's two corps consisted of infantry made up of the 4th Indian Division and the New Zealand Division, with two tank brigades. It was positioned on the right of the other corps, and its intended role was to contain and envelop the frontier defences. Its first move brought some initial compensation with the corps capturing Capuzzo and overrunning the German Afrika Corps Headquarters before setting on its way to join the forces of the 30th Corps at Sidi Rezegh. Nonetheless before the 13th reached this objective, Cruewell had struck at Sidi Rezegh and took the British and South African forces there by surprise. Fortunately he could not consolidate his attack because of the Italian element of his force (the Ariete Division) which had lagged behind. When it did reach him in the afternoon, however, he attacked again. But the brief respite had given Norrie a chance to strike a good defence. Still, the Germans broke through this to kill or capture 3,000 men.

Operation Crusader

The outcome of the 5 day dispersed battle could be best assessed by the loss of tanks, since it had been a predominantly tank battle. The Germans had lost seventy of their force of 160. But the British had lost 430. It was certainly not a result to inspire confidence, and the British commander Lieutenant-General Cunningham was now thinking in terms of a retreat back to the frontier from where he had started. But the Commander-in-Chief, General Auchinleck would hear none of this, and flying to the battlefield from Cairo he ordered Cunningham to keep fighting.

Had Cunningham been allowed to have his way a more serious situation might have followed since Rommel was now ripe for another of his tactical whims to make a deep thrust to and over the frontier into the rear of the 8th Army. And indeed, taking up the 21st Panzer division he led it himself on his stratagem. The 15th was to follow and meet him at a rendezvous. He covered the sixty mile run in five hours, went across the frontier into Egyptian territory, then turned back for his attack. It was here, however, that his plan was delayed when his car broke down. In a way it was fortunate for him that Cruewell was following in his command vehicle and picked him up but the ensuing delay made them reach the frontier when it had become dark, and they could not find a gap in the wire to get through. So there was nothing to be done but wait there until dawn, with British and Indian troops in the vicinity. It is ironic to realize how these forces never knew of the two German commanders in their midst, and how near they had been to be able to settle in one small stroke the war in North Africa. It was even more exasperating when at dawn, thanks to the fact that Cruewell was using a captured British command vehicle, they managed to slip away unchallenged.

This delay had already burdened Rommel's plan. There was an added obstacle when he reached the Headquarters of the 21st Panzer Division and found out that his other division, the 15th, had not yet reached its rendezvous. Therefore he could not proceed with his stratagem, which fizzled out. This provided much needed respite to General Auchinleck who had now to try and make some order from the very precarious situation he was in. But the first step undertaken was to have Lieutenant-General Cunningham replaced by General Neil Ritchie as commander of the 8th Army, with instructions to carry on with the battle, come what may. It was now the 26th November, and the 13th Corps was ordered to continue pushing forward in another endeavour to link up with the force at Tobruk. In the meantime there was a fresh delivery of tanks made to the 7th Armoured Division. This seems to indicate that Auchinleck might have been basing his intentions to recuperate and continue with the battle on the strength of his reserves. For although the 8th Army had lost almost four times as much as Rommel in tanks, it was assured of ample reserves which Rommel certainly did not have. So it might have appeared to Auchinleck that if he were to continue giving battle, the time would soon come when the Germans would not have enough tanks to continue the struggle. Provided of course that their line of supply from Italy would continue to be disrupted by the Malta based forces, and the rest of the Mediterranean fleet.

But what was in the meantime happening on that part of the front? For both Malta and the British fleet had their big part to play in Operation Crusader.

The island's aircraft, submarines, and Force K had intensified their efforts, and during November had destroyed 80% of the supplies intended for Rommel. And this at the most crucial time of his campaign. The German High Command was now giving Malta top priority, realizing that immediate action had to be taken. If Rommel were to be afforded a chance to hold to North Africa, Malta had to be destroyed. There had also to be the right man to do it, who had to be hard, decisive and already tried. These qualities were found in Field Marshal Kesselring, the same

Operation Crusader

man who had a year back been next to Goering in the Battle of Britain, and who was now in Russia. He was therefore appointed as Commander-in-Chief, and on 24th November briefed by Hitler himself on his new assignment. The order he was given was brief and specific. He was to forget about invading Malta. But the island was to be neutralized from the air, once and for all. The German squadrons in Russia were then swung back to Sicily as Kesselring arrived in Rome on 28th November. Two days later he was in Sicily to launch the one thousandth air attack against Malta which was to signal the beginning of a terrific air offensive the likes of which there had never been.

From Admiral Somerville's Force H, the aircraft carrier *Ark Royal* had made another of her trips on 12th November to fly more fighters for Malta. This time, however, on her return from the completed mission, she was torpedoed and sunk by the German submarine U.81. This gallant crusader was no more, and left an irreparable void. The more so now that the navy was being more heavily committed. Admiral Cunningham was indeed having his hands full in the Eastern Mediterranean guarding against enemy convoys that might escape the Malta forces. Two such convoys were reported to be making for Benghazi on 24th November, and Rear-Admiral Rawlings was out to intercept them with his cruiser squadron and destroyers. But Admiral Cunningham also left Alexandria with the *Queen Elizabeth*, *Barham* and *Valiant*. with eight destroyers to be within call should he be requested. On the afternoon of the following day, whilst the squadron was patrolling between Crete and Cyrenaica, the *Barham* was torpedoed and sunk by a German submarine.

This was another big loss. Both to Cunningham with his still depleted fleet and to British efforts in the Mediterranean. But it was time for sacrifices. Particularly now with Operation Crusader in its most critical stage, and Rommel badly in need of supplies which might very well bring his downfall. This sense of sacrifice could be seen two days later when notwithstanding the poor state of the Mediterranean fleet, the cruisers *Ajax* and *Neptune* with the destroyers *Kimberley* and *Kingston* were sent to Malta to reinforce Force K in its hard hitting operations against Rommel, who was now clearly showing the effects of this pressure.

In the Western Desert, the 13th Corps had now broken through the German investing troops, and linked up with the garrison at Tobruk. On 27th November then the two armoured brigades of the 7th Armoured Division now replenished with the new tanks, engaged the 15th Panzer and caused it much havoc, notwithstanding the usual tactics of bringing anti-tank guns into play. After fighting had stopped for the night, the Germans were not to be seen at dawn. They had pushed forward to join the rest of Rommel's forces.

It was now Auchinleck's turn to lay the ground for the next round which could be decisive in the battle. Rommel still had his two divisions, but between them they had barely 60 tanks. Auchinleck had much more which could decide the issue. Even so, he brought up further reinforcements from his reserve. And this time he flew again to 8th Army Headquarters to continue the battle. The main point in his plan now was to cut off Rommel's line of supply on land and his retreat. But somehow the German general came to know or anticipate this, and abandoned his investment of Tobruk which had always been his baby. He did reappear at Bir-el-Gubi to overrun the 11th Indian Brigade that was besieging the Italian forces defending that position. But this appeared to be his last spurt. On 7th December, he withdrew to Gazala.

This was a move that brought relief and satisfaction on the British side, which, however, turned into gloom when it was learned that Japanese aircraft had attacked Pearl Harbour which meant an escalation of the war. And there could not have been a more opportune time to bring the

Operation Crusader

North African campaign to a successful end. This appeared to be possible with Rommel now at Gazala licking his wounds, and with no more than 40 tanks to fight with.

There was now another cold douche from the Far East with the news of the sinking of the battleships *Repulse* and *Prince of Wales* by aerial attack on 10th December. It was another note of confirmation of the vulnerability of capital ships to aerial attack. The lesson given by the *Illustrious* and *Eagle* in November 1940 with the attack at Taranto seemed to have been learned, and would remain with modern warfare for posterity.

It was Lieutenant-General Godwin-Austen who went after Rommel with his 13th Corps, and he was soon engaging him at the Gazala line which apparently had been previously prepared and fortified as if the German general had indeed anticipated his present situation.Yet, notwithstanding his weakness he resisted the frontal attack by 13th Corps. Godwin-Austen was now on tenterhooks. He knew how much depended on a British victory now that his German opponent and much vaunted idol of military tacticians was caught in what could be described as a tight corner The British general was looking for a chance, and this came to him when the Italian Mobile Corps on Rommel's flank broke down under pressure. Godwin-Austen was quick to press the advantage and sent a brigade into the beach to run straight on to Sidi Breghiac 15 miles forward and in the Germans' rear. His idea was to have this force swerve and take Rommel from the back. But he had lost nothing of his cunningness and was suddenly launching a counter-attack which rectified the situation for him.

Godwin-Austen did not give up, and now he tried another stratagem. This time using the 4th Armoured Brigade and sending it to Halegh Eleba which was midway between Gazala and Mechili where it was intended to have it stay for the night. Then on the morrow it would draw Rommel's panzer reserves from the main Gazala line against which he would launch another frontal attack by the rest of 13th Corps. Unfortunately the brigade was delayed by bad going, and by the time the frontal attack was launched it was not yet in a position to carry out its part. And the attack failed again. There was a further ray of hope when an unobtrusive attack from the coast side managed to gain a foothold in Rommel's position, but it was soon beaten back again by a German counter-stroke.

The situation seemed to have resolved itself into a battle of wits between the two generals confronting each other. Rommel, the tricky customer that he was, now with only thirty tanks and his reputation, was trying to outwit Godwin-Austen with 200 tanks and a lot of determination to see this final phase of the battle through. The British general could afford to wait since he was hoping that the 4th Armoured brigade at Halegh Eleba would still carry out the assignment it had been given. Indeed it did, but apparently Rommel had also anticipated this and covered himself with the usual screen of anti-tank guns, which repelled the British force.

But this could not go on for ever. And Rommel knew it as much as anybody else, if not more. So on the night of 16th December, rather than risking a debacle he began to retreat. Derna had in the meantime fallen to the 4th Indian Division pressing forward on the coast and this must have pressed on Rommel the urgency of his action which was intended to take the British after him with calculated delays until he could get his hand on reinforcements which he knew were to be landed for him at Benghazi. When in fact Godwin-Austen caught up with him at Beda-Fomm, on 22nd December, Rommel stopped retreating and made a stand. He held up the British until the 26th, just enough to take possession of the two tank companies with 30 tanks which had arrived at Benghazi, then retreated a further 30 miles back to Agedabia. Hardly had he arrived there that he was attacked by the 22nd Armoured Brigade which he repulsed. But this was not all,

Operation Crusader

as the brigade fell back to recoup, Rommel went after it as far as El Hasciat and there destroyed 65 of its tanks.

It was a fantastic ending to Operation Crusader. And a very depressing one for the British. It is true that this operation had given them back most of Cyrenaica, with Bardia, Benghazi, and other isolated outposts eventually falling in the first days of the new year. As it was also true that the enemy had suffered some 33,000 casualties including 13,000 Germans, to a British total of 18,000. But the fact remained that Rommel was not evicted from North Africa. As had been the original objective. He was not even driven out of Cyrenaica. And no one was misled in believing that he would not strike again when he would have received reinforcements.

But during December there had developed an even more serious situation elsewhere. Under a determined Kesselring the Luftwaffe in Sicily had continued pounding Malta to smithereens. Dockyard, harbour and airfields were slowly but surely being knocked out. And so were the island's beautiful cities with their palatial buildings all being impressive monuments of European civilization and a western architecture of the sixteenth, seventeenth and eighteenth centuries. Royal Air Force fighters and anti-aircraft defences manned mostly by the Royal Malta Artillery were taking a heavy toll of the enemy raiders, but it seemed as if for every aircraft being shot down there would be a substitute in the next raid. This was bad enough in itself. But there was also the question of its effect on the island's offensive potential. Aircraft were being destroyed in the airfields, while warships and submarines were being sunk or damaged at their berths. Intervention with enemy convoys was already becoming forcibly less, and Kesselring knew it. That is why he continued with his offensive notwithstanding the astronomical losses in aircraft and crews he was sustaining.

But the month of December 1941 was blackest for the Mediterranean fleet. Not because of its further depletion with the departure of the Australian cruiser *Hobart* and minelayer *Abdiel* and other smaller craft. Now being recalled to the Pacific because of Britain's declaration of war on Japan within 24 hours of the attack on Pearl Harbour. This was certainly the least of Admiral Cunningham's troubles. Indeed there were even some bright flashes to mitigate it. Like the sinking of the Italian submarine *Caracciolo* by the destroyer *Farndale*, as it was evacuating Italian troops from Bardia, amongst them a general. Or like the engagement between the destroyers *Sikh, Legion, Maori* and the Dutch *Isaac Sweeers* with two Italian cruisers and one destroyer. But the mishaps started in mid-December, with an Italian convoy being attacked by the submarines *Upright, Utmost* and *Urge*, in the Straits of Messina. The *Urge* managed to hit the Italian battleship *Vittorio Veneto* with torpedoes, and this sent the convoy running back to harbour. Admiral Vian who was on his way to intercept this convoy with his cruiser squadron was then made to return to Alexandria where more urgent commitments awaited him. But on his way back the cruiser *Galatea* was torpedoed and sunk by a German U Boat. Hardly had he reached Alexandria that he had to leave again, this time to escort the sole *Breconshire*, a converted merchantman carrying 5,000 tons of badly needed oil fuel for Malta. Surviving all air attacks on his squadron, he handed over the *Breconshire* to the cruisers *Aurora* and *Penelope* with six destroyers from Malta, so that he could go back to intercept an Italian naval force that had materialised. Indeed nothing ensued more than a brief exchange of gunfire, but the presence of that force there, signified that the disrupted Italian convoy must have taken back to the sea, and indeed reconaissance reports confirmed it was quite close to Benghazi and Tripoli, where it was scheduled to arrive during the night of 18th December. So the cruisers *Neptune, Aurora* and *Penelope* with the destroyers *Kandahar, Lance, Lively* and *Havock* were despatched from Malta to intercept it. The *Neptune* exploded a mine in one of her paravanes, then realising he

Operation Crusader

had gone into a minefield, her captain reversed to get out, and in so doing hit another mine which brought the ship to a standstill. The *Aurora* and *Penelope* too hit mines, with the former having to be escorted back to Malta by the *Lance* and *Havock*, while the *Penelope*, although slightly damaged, stood by to take the *Neptune* in tow as soon as she would drift from the minefield. But rather than doing this the *Neptune* hit another mine and began listing over. The *Kandahar* dashed to rescue her crew and hit another mine herself which blew off its stern, and had eventually to be sunk. So rather than engaging the enemy convoy, the Malta squadron had lost a sunken cruiser and a destroyer as well as two other cruisers damaged. Then to add more troubles to Cunningham there was the Italian Decima Flotilla Mas launching an underwater attack on the battleships *Queen Elizabeth* and *Valiant* in Alexandria. The attack was carried out by three human torpedoes launched by the Italian submarine *Scire*. The two man crews waited outside the harbour until the boom had to be opened to let in some destroyers, and the three submarines went in beneath the British ships. Then the Italians fixed the explosive heads of their torpedoes to the battleships and to the tanker *Sagona* lying close by, which exploded at the set time. Both battleships were seriously damaged to be put out of action for months, while the *Sagona* was damaged beyond repair. Here the explosion also damaged the destroyer *Jervis* lying alongside. It did certainly not affect the issue that the Italian crews were captured, which in itself does not speak highly for security arrangements in Alexandria since some of them had even gone ashore in civilian clothes and left Alexandria to be captured at Rosetta later. But the most serious outcome of it all was that now Admiral Cunningham was without a battle squadron. He had not a single battleship in his fleet.

In the Far East too, Hong Kong had fallen on Christmas Day.

CHAPTER VI

TOWARDS A CLIMAX

Notwithstanding the failure of Operation Crusader, the Nile Delta towns began to live again. Streets, squares, bars and places where people normally gather were again teeming with troops. British soldiers, Australians, New Zealanders, Indians and South Africans. There were some French too. All mixing together under the ever present sun relentlessly burning the land. If green was the colour of England, then yellow had become that of Egypt, like the sands of the desert, the uniforms and Rommel's tanks and armoured vehicles. But the return of life could be seen more through the Egyptians in their white robes and sandalled feet. There were again the smells of cooking food and the muezzin who had started calling the people to prayer again from the top of the minaret. There were again the fascinating souks with their dark-eyed hawkers watching the jostling and noisy troops intently and without staring. It seemed as if they too were thinking what the next turn would bring, and wondering whether these men from across the seas would eventually succeed to push Rommel off their land. For they had heard of him too, this big man who seemed to have been receiving the favours of Allah on the battlefield to sweep anything and anyone that happened to be in his way. And even if they looked to be so uncaring and nonchalant amidst the mingling smells of dung and perfume one could detect an air of awareness in their attitude, and uncertainty in their side-glances. For

Towards a Climax

them as well Rommel had become a legend.

It was true that Bardia had fallen, but the least one would have expected was to have Winston Churchill suggesting at the Allied Conference in Washington during Christmas that there should be a British/American landing in North West Africa. Of course subject to the condition that the 8th Army would advance towards Tunis. It might have been too premature. But there had also been the disconcerting news of the Italian fleet now showing signs of activity, highlighted with the safe arrival of a large convoy to Tripoli without any of the usual interferance. One could only surmise what this might have taken to Rommel, last heard of as licking his wounds at Agheila. In the meantime Auchinleck had to wait until mid-February at least to recuperate enough to launch another offensive. That might have been considered to be too far away. But one could only hope for the best. This had become the standard slogan for everything and everyone. In the meantime Malta was still being pulverized by Kesselring's Luftwaffe forces, but now being temporarily brightened by the news of another convoy of three ships having reached the island. Thanks, no doubt, to the Royal Air Force which could keep surveillance of the combined operation from the forward airfields in Cyrenaica which were now again in British hands. But whatever was the occasion, everyone's thoughts were bound to fall back to the enigma in the Middle East that was Rommel.

Then the thunderbolt came on 21st January when against all expectations, Rommel launched an attack.

The intention behind this move was to reconnoitre. Now he had one hundred tanks. All he did was to tell his men of the Afrika Korps to take three days' rations and to follow him. The first British advanced force he met was the 1st Armoured Division. This was standing in for the 7th Armoured Division that had been withdrawn to rest and refit. But although adequately equipped with 150 tanks, was without any experience in desert warfare. The crafty general was soon back to his old trick of leap-frogging anti-tank guns from one point to another, always covered by his tanks, which soon had the British forces falling back in front of his push. His reconaissance soon developed into an offensive which brought chaos in the British camp.

Benghazi was the first objective, crammed as it was with supplies and the 4th Indian Division. But it did not take long for their leaders to decide to evacuate the town. In his by now characteristic way, General Auchinleck flew to the front to consult with General Ritchie, who was in Cairo when the attack began, but flew to be with his troops on the 23rd. Auchinleck impressed on the garrison at Benghazi to hold fast. Rommel played up by making a show as if he was only attacking Mechili which was in the vicinity, and this had the intended effect of drawing British reinforcement in that direction thus leaving Benghazi uprotected except by the 4th Indian Division. As General Francis Tuker, the divisional commander waited anxiously for the armour to join his division, he eventually learned this had been sent on a wild goose chase to Mechili where the Germans were feinting an attack. Benghazi could not be defended without armour and it had to be evacuated. So when Rommel suddenly swerved against Benghazi he found himself lord of all he surveyed. With the fall of the town and port the whole of the 8th Army withdrew to the Gazala Line.

The news shook Britain, already anxious for Singapore in the Far East. Churchill was trying to win a Vote of Confidence in the House of Commons. "I offer no apoligies," he said, "and I offer no excuses. As I will also make no promises ...". The British Command in North Africa now seemed to be burdened with many different conflicting orders, and General Godwin-Austen was soon at his wits' end unable to make neither head nor tail of what was going on. So he took the way of least resistance and resigned his command. In his place there was appointed

Towards a Climax

Lieutenant General 'Strafer' Gott to command the 13th Corps. Rommel seemed to pause for a while, but notwithstanding what respite this might have offered the British to recoup, the situation was far from being satisfactory. What plans had been initially made for a landing in French North Africa were to be shelved. And it was decided that rather than Africa, reinforcements would be sent to Singapore. Indeed there was not even time for this for the battle for this stronghold began a week later, and the Japanese captured it after a week's fighting. This started a new threat for Burma. It seemed there was to be no end of the setbacks for Britain. And Churchill had to bear them all. As General Alan Brooke wrote, "they would have crushed any other man."

In contrast, Rommel now had an additional harbour in Benghazi where to receive supplies and reinforcements, and with this being more advantageous since it was closer to his front. This automatically brought Malta back into the picture.

The island was now reeling under German savage air attacks. With her harbours full of wrecks and her airfields looking like a lunar landscape with bomb craters. These were being constantly filled or levelled by stand by troops, policemen and civilians after every raid, only to be hewn out again in the next attack, hardly leaving enough time for the fighters to scramble, and much less for bombers and torpedo aircraft to fly out and attack enemy shipping. Italian and German shipping losses had as a result gone down to only 20%, and in the beginning of February another big enemy convoy had reached Tripoli unmolested, no doubt carrying more reinforcements for Rommel. The little that was done must have been carried out by submarines since these managed to maintain their offensive and press their attacks, maybe now more than ever before. In January and February they had sunk 3 U Boats, one destroyer and eleven merchant ships. It might not have been enough. Moreover, it did not seem to be destined to go on for long, as it had now become only a question of time before the island's fighters would disappear. This drove in the point that the Hurricanes were proving to be easy prey to the latest type of Messerchmitt. It was obvious that this would raise the question of getting the faster and more powerful Spitfire fighters for Malta. If they couldn't save her, they would at least give her a chance of a fighting exit. The first batch was intended to be delivered in March. But Kesseelring was planning something else for Malta for that same time. What he had concocted was a terrific air assault by the pick of his airmen in an attempt to cripple the few remaining Hurricanes and anti-aircraft defences. Then he would follow up with heavy bombers to destroy once and for all the airfields and harbour installations. These attacks would also be consolidated by night nuisinance raids to hinder rescue and repairs. It was a diabolical plan entrusted to Air Marshal Deichman to carry it out, thus leaving Kesselring free to see to the final touches for an air and seaborne invasion of Malta which a hard pressed Hitler had finally conceded. It was by now already planned and code-named Operation Hercules.

It was now too that the ever present food situation in Malta had become even more precarious, with still less hope of relief now that the airfields in Cyrenaica were again in German hands. The little food that remained in Malta was now pooled to provide one cooked meal per person a day. The scheme was given the name of Victory Kitchen, but there was little if any hope of victory in it, because the thought behind it was that if the Maltese were to die of hunger then they would die together. Fortunately as much as the Maltese there were also the Chiefs of Staff in London and also Admiral Cunningham who were aware of this situation, and they became alive to the need of sending another convoy to the island notwithstanding the bigger risks involved. Only that they had fixed the date for this convoy to reach Malta for 22nd March. This, unknown to them happened to be also the date chosen by Kesselring for the launching of his air assault.

Towards a Climax

Malta welcomed the first 15 Spitfires on 7th March, 1942 after they were flown from the aircraft-carrier *Eagle* which had dashed into the Mediterranean with this purpose. Three days later while the Maltese people were rejoicing as they watched the Spitfires which had already become their darlings, go into action for the first time, their air of joy had to succumb to bad news. Rear-Admiral Vian had lost his flagship, the cruiser *Naiade*, which was torpedoed by a U Boat. Nonetheless, Admiral Cunningham carried on with his intended convoy. It was to coincide with an operation by Force N leaving Gibraltar with the battleship *Malaya*, a cruiser and eight destroyers, escorting only the aircraft carriers *Eagle*, and *Argus* packed with Spitfires for Malta. These were successfully launched on reaching the Balaeric Islands and merit no more detail. The dramatic and heart-rending drama was to be enacted by Cunningham's convoy which led to one of the most important naval battles in the Mediterranean.

The convoy left Alexandria on 20th March. It was composed of 4 ships escorted by Rear-Admiral Vian's cruiser squadron made up of *Cleopatra, Dido, Euryalus* and *Carlisle*, with the destroyers *Jervis, Kipling, Kelvin,* and *Kingston*. These were to be joined later by other destroyers which had gone beforehand on an anti-submarine sweep. The RAF was to provide fighter cover up to 300 miles from Alexandria, while bombers were to bomb airfields in Crete and Cyrenaica in an attempt to keep enemy aircraft grounded. As can be seen there had been a lot of planning, but there were still no illusions that this was going to be an easy operation. And indeed it wasn't. Yet, by the morning of 21st March there was no hostile action, and six of the seven destroyers that had gone beforehand had now joined the escort. These were the *Southwold, Beaufort, Dulverton, Hurworth, Avondale* and *Eridge*. The seventh had been the *Heythrop* which was sunk by a U-Boat during the sweep. Then it was in the evening that the convoy was located by enemy aircraft, and now Vian knew what he could expect. Truly enough he wasn't worried since he knew that he had enough warships to put up a good anti-aircraft defence. And on the following morning of 22nd March there were also added the cruiser *Penelope* and the destroyer *Lively* which had come from Malta to meet the convoy. What worried him was a message he received a little later about a squadron of the Italian fleet having been seen leaving Taranto in haste. Not that he did not welcome a skirmish, but he could bet that the Italians were certainly to have a 15" gun battleship and 8" gun cruisers in their outfit, which would outgun and outrange him.

The air-attacks by Italian bombers and torpedo bombers began some time later in the morning and did not cause any harm. The Germans that took over in the afternoon were a different problem. But still they didn't hit any ship. Some time after 2 p.m. then, the *Euryalus* reported smoke on the horizon, and Vian knew that the Italian Navy had arrived. Notwithstanding everything, he was now determined to fight the enemy to the last ship even if this was only to give chance to the convoy to reach Malta, now only about two hundred miles away.

Time began running fast, with a freshening rough sea and a moderate swell. Ten minutes later the smoke on the horizon seemed to be closer and Vian alerted his squadron for action. All knew that a battle was in the offing, and Vian sent the convoy ships forward with a close escort while he stayed behind with the rest to confront the enemy which was soon sighted and found to consist of two 8" gun cruisers, one 6" gun cruiser and four destroyers. This was much better than he had bagained for. The enemy opened fire at very long range, and now Vian rushed at them making smoke. When coming within range *Cleopatra* and *Euryalus* opened fire on one of the enemy heavy cruisers which immediately turned round and ran out of range. Another cruiser too had a few shots at the British squadron, but like the others ran out of range of British guns soon after. This was certainly not what the British admiral had expected, and although it was better that

Towards a Climax

things had turned out this way he could not help feeling disappointed. All he could do then was to turn to attend to the Italian and German aircraft that resumed attacks on the convoy. But he must have assumed things too soon, for it wasn't long that the Italian fleet appeared again. There was the group he had only just engaged, and another one. And this time there was the ship he had dreaded, the 15" gun battleship *Littorio* with an escort of four destroyers. Then before he could put his pre-arranged plan into action the Italian ships seemed to ignore him and his squadron, and steered hell for leather in the direction of the convoy ships ahead, obviously dead intent to sink them and prevent them from reaching Malta.

This was something different from what Vian had anticipated and required a change of plan. It appeared to the admiral that the enemy might have ignored his squadron to tempt him in making a run for it and abandon his wards to be cut to pieces by the heavy Italian ships, while he would make his escape. But this did not put him in any dilemma. He was the shepherd who would guard and even give his life for his flock in the best of British naval tradition.Without a further thought he gave his orders and steered on a straight course with all his squadron following him to get between the Italian waships and their prey, laying a pall of thick smoke which prevented the enemy ships from opening fire on the convoy's merchantmen. But this was not enough; the enemy had to be prevented from going round or through the smoke screen. And to do this Vian was the first with his flagship, the *Cleopatra* to dodge out of the smoke just enough to fire a salvo at the enemy ships and then dodge in again behind the smoke before they could reply. The other cruisers did the same in turn. Then followed the desroyers but in their case going closer to the enemy ships to fire their torpedoes. It didn't matter that none of the enemy was hit, but Vian's stratagem worked in keeping the Italians on the right side of the smoke screen, with none of them daring to cross and come within range of the British ships which they knew were waiting for them behind the smoke. So they too changed tactics and preferred to stay where they were, this time, however, alerted and in expectation of the British ships to dodge out of the smoke again, when they would be ready for them. Indeed, when the *Cleopatra* did dodge out to fire at the Italians she was hit by one of the cruisers, suffering both damage and casualties. So were the *Euryalus* and *Lively*. But it was the destroyer *Kingston* which got the worst, when she was hit by a 15" shell from the italian battleship on going very close to torpedo here. The Italian flagship was very closely missed and this might have made Admiral Iachino break up the action.

Since this action was fought off Sirte, it was recorded for posterity as the Battle of Sirte. It was one battle in which the British Navy suffered some damage without inflicing any on the enemy, but nonetheless achieved its objective in protecting the convoy it was escorting so that it could reach Malta.Indeed after being saved from this ordeal the four ships of the convoy had to face another one as they approached Malta which was now bearing the brunt of Kesselring's air assault. Having been set upon again by German and Italian aircraft the four ships decided to separate. So at dusk of the 22nd March the four of them were set on diverging courses, each with an accompanying destroyer or two. Thus dispersed they were to converge on Malta on the following day. From now on, each ship had its own dramatic story. The *Clan Campbell* was the first to be found by the Luftwaffe when it was still some 50 miles away from Malta. Escorted only by the destroyer *Eridge* she was no match for the low flying German bombers, one of which managed to hit her with a well placed bomb which sunk her. The *Breconshire*, an old-timer for Malta, was caught up with her escort the destroyer *Southwold* when only eight miles away from the island, and it was therefore possible for the island's Spitfires to fly out in defence. But then the *Southwold* hit a mine and was sunk, and the *Breconshire* was left alone to be hit by bombs. Although damaged, it did not sink, but

Towards a Climax

stopped, and this made her a sitting duck to the German Stukas. It was up to the Malta forces to come out to the rescue. And they did. The Spitfires to engage the attacking German aircraft in a terrible aerial combat, and two Maltese towing tugs to tow and beach her in the secondary harbour of Marsaxlokk.

The other two ships, the *Pampas* and the *Talabot* fell foul of the german blitz when they reached harbour. It was a too good an occasion for the Germans to be missed, and they subjected the two ships to several vicious attacks even while port workers began to unload them. Both ships were hit on 26th March with the *Pampas* beginning to sink slowly, while the *Talabot* was set on fire. Port workers were now being helped by soldiers to try and unload what they could before the ships were lost. Very often having to dive into the *Pampas's* flooded holds to release stores before it sunk. The *Talabot* had a further three hours' agony with fires raging and getting closer to the ammunition it was carrying. Then it had to be scuttled to prevent an explosion. Adding another to the many other wrecks in the once beautiful Grand Harbour, now a picture of doomsday with its docks, wharves and stores having become a foul area of cordite grey rubble.There had now also come the turn of submarines which began to spend most of their time submerged because of the attacks directed against them. Very often with some of them never coming to the surface again. Even the Governor, Sir William Dobbie was convinced this was the end of a climax, and he was already thinking in terms of a surrender.

The island was now very much in the enemy's mind with Kesselring all intent and ready to go ahead with the intended invasion. But Rommel being more than ever obsessed with attacking Tobruk for which he required the use of the Stukas in Sicily. Kesselring was adamant to send them and there soon developed an argument which had to revolve on which operation had to be undertaken first, the occupation of Tobruk or the invasion of Malta. It had to be Hitler to decide that Tobruk must take preference over Malta.

In contrast Winston Churchill and his Cabinet had realised by now that on Malta hinged the outcome in North Africa and in the Mediterranean. And that its destruction and demotion had enabled Rommel to rise again.As if to substantiate this, he had only just moved from his position to come closer to the Eighth Army still waiting at the Gazala Line as if intending to attack again. But Churchill was frantic now, and he wanted a British offensive. Even with the limited objective of occupying the airfields in West Cyrenaica from which British fighters would be able to defend Malta. Auchinleck was adamant however. He had still to build up his forces before he could launch another offensive. If he were to undertake one now, he told the Prime Minister, the chances were that he would not have enough strength to defend Egypt. Therefore, to defend Malta would be risking losing Egypt. So here too it had become a question of priorities. But Churchill and his Cabinet were decided on this point. They were ready to save Malta, even at the cost of losing Egypt. And Auchinleck had to compromise to launch an offensive by mid-June.

That was two months away, and something had in the meantime to be done to bolster the island's defences and the will of her people to resist. A further supply of Spitfires had to be made, and here the only difficulty was raised by the First Sea Lord, Sir Dudley Pound, who was adamant to spare any aircraft carrier to do it. Since all his carriers were needed for the battle against U Boats in the Atlantic, which he considered more important than the situation in the Mediterranean. So there was recourse to the United States which loaned the aircraft carrier *Wasp* for the mission. There was also the question of some sort of recoognition being made to Malta and her people for their heroic stand. Here it was King George VI who jumped into the breach and decided to award the island a George Cross.

Towards a Climax

There was also the question of her Governor to be considered since it was feared he could not take more. There was also a change of command for Admiral Cunningham who was sent to the United States to head the Admiralty delegation there. In his place as Commander-in-Chief Mediterranean, there was appointed Admiral Sir Henry Harwood.

April seemed to have become a month of reckoning for Malta. It was hard to believe that only since the previous month of March the Germans had flown 2,150 bombers against the island. They had indeed lost 350 of them to the defences, but this had not stopped them from dropping 6,556,231 kilograms of bombs, with 1,8659 tons of them being on Grand Harbour. Then the end came when there were only 7 serviceable Spitfires to face the German hordes on the end of April.

A furious Churchill was now ignoring everything and everyone. He was already snubbed by President Roosevelt having promised Molotov of Russia the opening of a Second Front in Europe during 1942. Britain was not ready for this. Besides, this meant the shelving of the N.W. African landing on which they had eventually agreed. Now he was sending on 7th May the aircraft carrier *Eagle* with 64 Spitfires for Malta and the fast minelayer *Welshman* to break the German blockade and carry foodstuffs and ammunition to the bealeagured island. At dusk on that same day that the *Welshman* reached Malta there was also Lord Gort VC arriving quietly by a flying boat to take over as Governor and Commander-in-Chief in place of Sir William Dobbie. He carried the George Cross with him and the letter by King George VI.

To honour her brave people I award the George Cross to the island fortress of Malta to bear witness to a heroism and devotion that will long be famous in history.

And so it was indeed, for as history was to prove, Malta had now become Britain's champion in the Mediterranean conflict as Rommel had become Germany's. The small island and the German General had become in the eyes of the world like two gladiators in a fight to the end, the winner of which would take all. Fluctuating circumstances saw both contestants taking turns in falling down only to rise again stronger than before. But all knew that there would come a day when one of them will drop out for keeps. And that would decide the war. Certainly in the Mediterranean; very likely elsewhere too. As true to Dill's warning, Malaya, Singapore, and Burma had all fallen to the Japanese in the Far East. If there were any reflection needed for this symbolic thought it came two days later when Kesselring stopped his air assault, as suddenly as he had launched it. The Luftwaffe had flown 11,500 sorties against Malta losing hundreds of planes and crews. But Kesselring informed Hitler that his mission had been accmplished and the air bases on the island had been eliminated. It was of course only wishful thinking. For Malta was only having her turn to fall down. Breathless and broken maybe, but convinced that she would rise again. Until then it would be Rommel's turn to have his fling. Which he did, on 26th May when against all expectations he launched an attack.

Unexpected as it was it did not, however, surprise Auchinleck, who had waited for this to develop against his lines at Gazala. Notwithstanding the fact that he had hoped it would not occur until he would launch his offensive in mid-June. Still, one cannot help realizing that Rommel must have been reading Auchinleck's mind when he started his attack by a feint with four motorized Italian divisions as if he was indeed attacking the Gazala Line as Auchinleck expected. But while the Italians were carrying out this make believe, Rommel was moving with his own three divisions and two Italian mobile corps, trying to go round the flank of the British defences under cover of night. Auchinleck must have impressed his commanders so much with his expectations, that although some of them spotted the German columns moving to the flank they persisted in thinking this was the feint move and not

Towards a Climax

the other. When they realized their mistake it was too late, for Rommel was in a very strong position and continued to advance. Nonetheless it wasn't made easy for him, and the new American Grant tanks the British had brought up made havoc in the panzer ranks. By the end of the first day's fighting the Germans had lost a third of their tanks. However, this part of the North African campaign became important when Rommel walked unaided into a trap which might have well finished him for ever.

This came about after Auchinleck had during the period of lull built up a system of defence based on a series of what could be called "defended cages". These were points, enclosed by heavy barbed wire entanglements, and minefields. The garrisons inside them were then supplied with enough artillery, stores and ammunition that would enable them to stand a siege. These cages had a double function. They could either guard the minefields and prevent the enemy cutting lanes through them. Or present him with a stronghold he must try to reduce. Otherwise the garrisons would sally out and take him from the rear.

When after failing to overrun the British lines at Gazala, Rommel decided to take a defensive position without knowing that he had chosen a spot between the fortified line he wanted to attack and a far-stretching belt of minefields laid as a corollary to the Gazala line. This meant that if he were to be attacked from the Gazala line he would have nowhere to withdraw except the minefield which was protected by such a "cage". The British realised this and acted immediately. The RAF was called in support and began a series of attacks on the German position. Then the 8th Army went into attack with everyone now confident that this was going to be the end of Rommel. He himself knew that he was in a fix, and one of his generals had occasion to confirm this after the war. "Never had Rommel been so close to a defeat and to capitulation," he said, and there appeared to be no possible way for him to extricate himself and his men." Yet, by luck or a miracle he did. He said it was neither. According to him there were two factors which helped him make his escape. Self-control in never losing his head to give up, and his powers of anticipation which made him believe that the British would not attack him with all their available forces and this would give him the chance to resist while clearing a way through the minefield. And things happened as he had anticipated, with the British attacking only with their mechanized brigades giving him time to clear his way through the minefield and get supplies.

Once free it was expected that he would put more zest in his efforts. Leading his forces personally he attacked another defence cage at Bir Hacheim which was held by the 1st Free French Brigade. Then on 13th June he went rampant amongst British troops before moving towards the coast road. Nothing and no one seemed capable of holding him. It became evident too that notwithstanding his devious advance he was edging his way towards Tobruk. And indeed on 14th June Winston Churchill was warning Auchinleck not to let go of this port. Its loss would weaken his stand with Roosevelt whom he was meeting in three days' time when he hoped the plan for an invasion of Europe would be dropped. Now that he was more inclined for the plan for N.W. Africa. But notwitstanding everything, when Rommel reached the coast road he made short work of capturing the Gambut airfields and that is where he had the Stukas he got from Sicily sent. Then rather than pursuing the forces he had dislodged he swung westwards towards Tobruk, taking General Klopper and his garrison by surprise. This was, however, an exploratory attack in the way of assessing the situation. The attack proper was delivered on 20th June, beginning with an aerial bombardment by the Stukas, which he then followed with an artillery barrage. Having thus softened the defences, he then launched an assault by the infantry. By the afternoon he had occupied Tobruk with 35,000 prisoners.

Towards a Climax

This was a lightning stroke which shook British prestige from its foundations. It put the British leaders into confusion, and General Ritchie began retreating fast with his remaining forces. This might have given Rommel a reason for a pause. After all he had a big victory to celebrate as well as his promotion to Field-Marshal which Hitler had given him as soon as Tobruk was captured. But Rommel would have no rest now and he went after Ritchie. He could afford to do so after having acquired what food, fuel and transport he needed from what was taken at Tobruk. He only lacked tanks, of which he had only forty-four. Yet, he continued to advance, and stopped only on reaching the Egyptian frontier on 23rd June.

An air of gloom had fallen on the Middle East. Silence reigned from desperation in Whitehall. The only good that was gleaned from this British disaster was the cancellation of the proposed invasion of Malta. Kesselring had flown to Rommel, and it wasn't just a social visit to congratulate him on his promotion. He wanted to have his aircraft back so that he could go ahead with his plans for Malta. But Rommel wouldn't hear of it. He had long suffered with being ignored and deprived of reinforcements, and he wasn't bending now when he could afford to lay it thick, with this being his moment of glory. He wanted to keep the aircraft for his last drive on Cairo and Alexandria. And both Hitler and Mussolini agreed with him. Hitler had never forgotten how the Italian fleet had let him down in the battle of Crete and was more than sure that it would do the same if Malta were to be invaded. So this gave him the chance he wanted and dropped this plan. Mussolini saw his one and only chance to appease his vanity and make a triumphant entry in Cairo. So Rommel was to carry on. Operation Hercules had thus fizzled out.

But what respite Malta had gained could not help her to escape strangling by the very effective blockade that was being imposed. It was one thing not receiving bombs and torpedoes with which to attack enemy shipping, but another not receiving any food. Her situation was now acute and generating even more desperate steps from Britain to mount two convoys from West and East as usual to converge on the island together. The first one, code-named Harpoon did in fact leave Clyde on 5th June with five merchantmen and an escort provided by Admiral Curtiss in the cruiser *Kenya*, accompanied by *Liverpool*, and the destroyers *Onslow*, *Middleton*, *Kuyawiak* (Polish), *Escapade*, *Bedouin*, *Icarus*, *Matchless*, *Blankney*, *Marne* and *Badsworth*. This was joined by Force T at Gibraltar consisting of the battleship *Malaya*, the aircraft-carriers *Eagle* and *Argus*, the anti-aircraft cruisers *Cairo* and *Charybdis* with the destroyers *Partridge*, *Antelope*, *Westcott*, *Vedette*, *Ithuriel*, *Wishart* and *Wrestler*, together with three minesweepers. But it was a different story for the other convoy from the East. Pressed as he was with lack of escort ships Admiral Harwood made available practically the whole of the fleet to escort the 10 ships he had earmarked for Malta, Rear-Admiral Vian in the cruiser *Cleopatra* had seven other cruisers with him, i.e. *Dido*, *Euryalus*, *Hermione*, *Arethusa*, *Newcastle*, *Birmingham* and *Coventry*, together with 26 destroyers, 4 corvettes and 2 minesweepers. No doubt an impressive escort, but the question was whether these could withstand what aerial attacks were bound to be launched on him, now that Cyrenaica was being nibbled back by Rommel. This looked like being the last confrontation with the enemy by the Mediterranean fleet, in the battle that had also reached its climax.

The convoy came under heavy attacks by the Luftwaffe flying from Crete, with the Germans then taking over from Cyrenaica and Tripoli. But the convoy was not yet half-way when the cruiser *Hermione*, three destroyers and two merchantmen were sunk, with another two damaged. it became obvious to Rear-Admiral Vian he could not continue, so the convoy and escort returned back to Alexandria. The convoy from the West was not doing any better. It came under heavy attack both from U Boats and aircraft sinking four merchantmen and two destroyers. The only two ships which reached Malta were of course useful but they weren't helping the island in her precarious position. It seemed as if after all Malta was losing her duel with Rommel.

The German Field-Marshal had in the meantime been given the go ahead to continue with his offensive and on the night of 24/25th June began pushing towards Sidi-Barrani. Auchinleck had now decided to make a stand at Mersa-Metruh with a 10th Corps made up of two infantry divisions under General Holmes, and further south in the desert with the 13th Corps supported by the New Zealand Division under Lieutenant-General Gott. Had one possessed full details of the enemy side there would have been no doubt that from a logistic point of view, the battle that was obviously being mounted up had all the dice loaded against Rommel. Because against Auchinleck's four divisions and 160 tanks, most of them powerful American Grants, he had only about 6,000 German troops and 60 tanks. And the obvious question was whether it was madness or audacity that was pushing him forward.

It was the 15th Panzer division or what remained of it that launched a frontal attack on the 10th Corps, and this was repulsed by General Holmes. In the meantime Rommel had edged the 90th Light Division behind Mersa Metruh to cut any eventual British retreat from that position and the 21st Panzer was sent in behind Gott and his 13th Corps, at Minqas Qain, hitting at his rearguard made up of the New Zealand Division. Commonsense would have dictated to anyone in Gott's position to turn back and fight the force at his back. But instead, on realizing what happened, Lieutenant-General Gott began to retreat leaving the New Zealand Division isolated to fight for dear life and escape from the Germans' surrounding movement. On the following day General Holmes with his 10th found out how he had been left to hold the baby with his way of retreat already cut off. His first thought must then have been to save his troops for another day, and rather than trying to fight his way out he waited for the night and began to get out his men from their position in groups. Most of them did get past the Germans, but 6,000 of them were captured with a vast quantity of supplies and equipment which went a long way to strengthen Rommel's position.

Certainly no one in his right senses could expect to withstand Rommel with this kind of tactics. The British retreat must have gone into history as a shameful disaster, with the German Field-Marshal now chasing their running forces. He only stopped on 30th June, no doubt to prepare for his coup-de-grace. For now he had reached his climax, and was only 60 miles away from Alexandria.

CHAPTER VII

THE TURNING POINT

The first effect of Rommel's arrival at El Alamein was immediately reflected in the Delta towns of Egypt. In a flash they had lost their cosmopolitan look. Crowds of people now began leaving their houses, and blocking railway stations to get away from an imminently looking German advance. And they couldn't be blamed since the British services themselves were making similar preparations. The military headquarters in Cairo had already began burning up files and records, and Admiral Harwood took out his fleet from Alexandria to withdraw through the Suez Canal into the Red Sea. The situation was not better in London. During a previous Cabinet meeting on June 29th, there had already been asked questions about arrangements to evacuate civilians from Egypt. President Roosevelt was himself warned by General Marshall that Rommel might reach the Suez Canal within a fortnight. Now on July 3rd, Ministers meeting at 10 Downing Street were being told what to expect when British forces were driven out of Egypt. In Cairo the rumour went round that the British had indeed decided to evacuate Egypt.

It was of course nothing of the sort. If there was a person who wouldn't even consider such a possibility, it was General Auchinleck. And here it must be handed to him that notwithstanding the obvious confusion around him, he never lost his head. And this was a good thing since Rommel had attacked again from El Alamein on 2nd July.

It seems that by now Auchinleck had learned of the weakness in the German panzers since he changed his tactics and began pushing forward heavy concentrations of tanks to halt the German attack. Rommel tried his hand again on 3rd July, but although managing to go forward about 9 miles he had no hope of overwhelming the massed British armour with the 26 tanks he only possessed by now. Neither could he hope for much from the Italian forces in support which continued to be no match to the British forces. On the following day, the 4th July, Rommel realized what he should have noticed long before, that his troops were exhausted and the time had come for them to be given a rest. He knew this would probably afford the chance to Auchinleck to bring up more reinforcements, but he could not avoid the issue. However instead of thinking about reinforcements, Auchinleck began attacking the Germans wherever they could be found. General Norrie's 30th Corps and Lieutenant-General Gott's 13th Corps both went into action, and the situation soon turned into one with Rommel's units having to fight in defence. This was something they had not done for a long time. And it seemed that the scale might have begun to tilt. London, Cairo and Alexandria however, still rippled with apprehension.

There is no doubt that this was a stage in the battle when General Auchinleck had gained the initiative, and had he decided on a general offensive it might have proved decisive. But even if he did not, he was at least now giving no rest to the enemy. His attacks served also another purpose when he came to realize that wherever they failed, this was invariably because his subordinate commanders were not always executing his orders to the letter. This must have been the cause of his failures which he could not have seen when fighting in defence. But now, when attacking, and with his being with the troops he could see it all, and would remedy.

On 8th July, Rommel received some reinforcements

Admiral Sir Andrew Cunningham on HMS Warspite at Malta. (Imperial War Museum).

British troops advance, protected by tanks, dust and smoke billowing across the North African desert. (Imperial War Museum).

HMS Penelope entering Grand Harbour in Malta. (Imperial War Museum)

Italian prisoners being taken into captivity from Bardia, after Australian troops captured the town. (Imperial War Museum).

Vice-Admiral Ford and Air-Vice Marshal Lloyd, the naval and air commanders at Malta. (Imperial War Museum).

German bombardments of Malta. (Top) A Stuka dive-bomber being loaded up at a Sicilian airfield. (Bottom) Pilots being briefed before flying to bomb Malta. (ECPA France).

Attack on an airfield at Malta. (National War Museum Association of Malta)

Attack by German bombers on Malta's dockyard. (National War Museum Association of Malta).

Hurricane pilot at Malta being briefed before flying into action. (Imperial War Museum).

British destroyers attacking and destroying German U Boat 138 in June 1941. (G.E. Fanthorpe).

Aircrew of an Italian torpedo bomber which sank the British destroyer Fearless in July, 1941. When the plane was shot down the italian crew were picked up by HMS Faulknor near Malta. (G.E. Fanthorpe)

A.

British aircraft carriers bore the brunt of enemy attacks while escorting convoys to Malta. In A the Illustrious is hit by a bomb from a Stuka. In B, the Ark Royal has two near misses. Then in C it is hit on the flying deck. D shows the Indomitable under another attack. (Imperial War Museum, J.J. Antier and G.E. Fanthorpe)

B.

C.

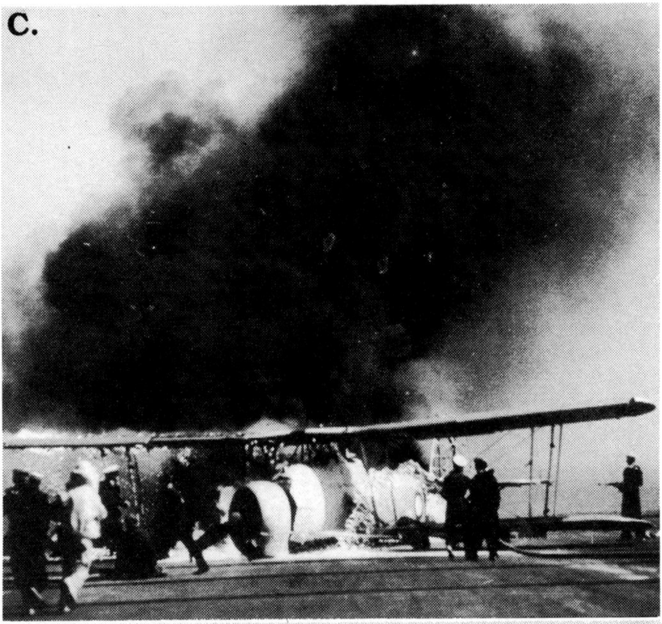

D.

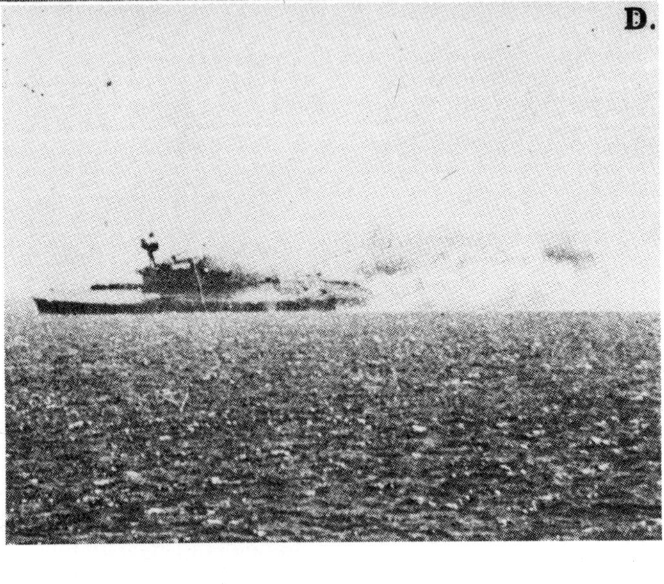

HMS Firedrake after being hit and damaged by italian aircraft. (G.E. Fanthorpe)

In North Africa, a member of a knocked out German tank crew surrenders as British soldiers rush forward. (Imperial War Museum).

British troops, mostly Maoris, after the evacuation of Crete. (Imperial War Museum).

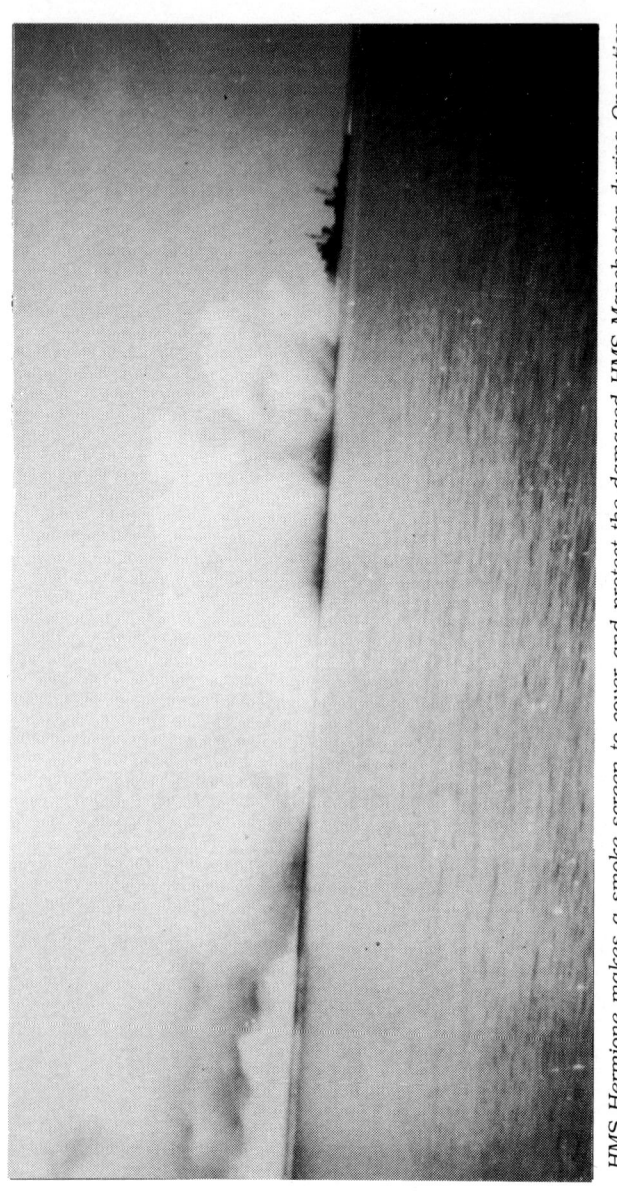

HMS Hermione makes a smoke screen to cover and protect the damaged HMS Manchester during Operation 'Substance' taking a convoy to Malta in June, 1941. (G.E. Fanthorpe)

The two German commanders, Field Marshal Kesselring and Field Marshal Rommel. (ECPA France)

British troops and tanks wait to enter the burning town of Tobruk. The armour displays the famous Desert Rats insignia. (Imperial War Museum)

Opening of Allied North African Headquarters in November, 1942. Left to right: Lieut. General Mark Clark (US); Admiral Cunningham (British); Lieut. General K.A.N. Anderson (British) and Admiral Darlan (French). (Imperial War Museum)

Prime Minister Winston Churchill and his Chiefs-of-Staff during the Casablanca Conference. Left to right: Air Chief Marshal Sir Charles Portal; Admiral Sir Dudley Pound; Mr. Churchchill in RAF uniform; General Sir Alan Brooke, and Lord Louis Mountbatten. (Imperial War Museum).

After the italian surrender on 8th September, 1943, elements of the intact Italian navy are anchored at Malta.
(National War Museum Association of Malta)

American troops entering Messina in Sicily on 17th August, 1943. (Personal collection)

The participants who signed the armistice terms are seen on one of the warships at Malta. Back to camera is General Eisenhower. On his left is Marshal Badoglio, then General MacFarlane, General Lord Gort, governor of Malta, and General Alexander. (Imperial War Museum).

mostly Italians. But there were also some tanks which raised his number to fifty, as well as some infantry. Auchinleck too had been given back the 9th Australian Division and two tank regiments which brought his strength to 200 tanks. The Australians were expected to give some more life to the 30th Corps where Auchinleck now replaced its commander Lieutenant General Norrie by Lieutenant-General W.H. Ramsden. But what must have improved the British effort was Auchinleck's new attitude in taking over command himself at El Alamein, thus avoiding the misunderstandings and shortcomings of before. Rommel himself had occasion to record this in his papers for posterity when he wrote that now General Auchinleck was handling his forces with considerable skill. The Desert Air Force had now also reached unprecedented heights in its effectiveness. There was no lack of airfields since these were being pitched where it was found convenient along the desert roads. Bombers and fighters would then land, refuel and fly westward. On July 3rd, the first day of the new set up, the RAF flew 900 sorties against the enemy.

Indeed there is a lot that could be said to his merit during July. When seen individually his attacks might have been considered as small localised operations. But put together they could be considered as a superbly fought battle which the noted military historian Sir Basil Liddell-Hart had called the First Battle of El Alamein. Again, looking at this battle statistically one might have got the wrong impression from the fact that it had cost the 8th Army over 13,000 casualties. The British had taken 7,000 prisoners, a thousand of which were Germans which Rommel could ill afford. Then, territorially too, this battle could not be said to have gained anything for the British since Rommel had retained his position at El Alamein. And the final outcome could be described as a stalemate. However there was one important achievement which one could not miss, as indeed it was not missed by Rommel when he wrote that in this battle General Auchinleck had halted the German advance.

With human nature being what it is, it was, however, expected that bad impressions would be left. But the worst one was that left on Winston Churchill who on 24th and 25th July had after all concluded plans with the Americans for the landings in French North Africa in the first week of November and which assumed a British advance in the Western Desert. This must have made the Prime Minster take the bull by the horns and go to Egypt on 4th August to see things for himself. He could appreciate all that Auchinleck had done but what mattered most to him was the fact, that notwithstanding all the reinforcements that had been sent, Rommel was still close to Alexandria. So he decided to change leadership again. His first thought was to replace Auchinleck by General Sir Alan Brooke, the Chief of the Imperial General Staff and who had accompanied him on his visit. Brooke however refused. Then Churchill turned for Sir Harold Alexander who was ready to take over. The surprise came when he chose Lieutenant-General Gott as 8th Army commander, since this General was not blameless in some of the blunders committed. It then happened that Gott was killed in an air crash on the following day and to take his place there was called General Bernard Montgomery. Two new commanders were also brought over from England. Lieutenant General Sir Oliver Leese for the 30th Corps and Lieutenant General Brian Horrocks for the 13th Corps.

The first disagreement with the new command was the usual one about how soon could be launched a fresh offensive. This time, however, Churchill was more pressing, with the French North African operation in mind. He wanted an immediate start, but both Alexander and Montgomery were firm about the time needed to complete training and to get what more reinforcements were required. Churchill could not but give way to their arguments. And he had to accept the risk of Rommel being able to get more reinforcements himself too, which could not but bring as well the question of Malta, that was the only obstacle between the German Field-Marshal and his supplies. It was, however, a smashed Malta which he had tried to revive again with the appointment of General Lord Gort as her Governor and Commander-in-Chief.

Lord Gort had indeed imbued Malta with a new kind of determination. More than on the dire need of a convoy he had concentrated on bringing back the offensive potential to the island. So while everyone did not know where his next meal was coming from, on Gort's insistence, there was another consignment of Spitfires delivered to the island by the American aircraft-carrier *Wasp*. There were also the first American Liberator aircraft landing at Luqa airfield to contribute to the air offensive potential. On 21st June, whilst Rommel was occupying Tobruk, Malta's torpedo bombers were attacking two 10,000 ships carrying German reinforcements, sinking one of them and damaging the other. There was the same fate for a tanker on the following day, and then again on the 23rd, two further ships were hit just as they had left Palermo harbour, and had to turn back. There was certainly a newly infused spirit in the RAF. And as if to reflect the change there was the Air Officer Commanding, Air Vice Marshal Hugh Lloyd who had endured the worst of the blitz being substituted by Air Vice Marshal Keith Rodney Park, one of the stalwarts of the Battle of Britain. It was now also time for the submarines to return to the island. The first to go back were the *Utmost* and *United*, to be followed by *Unbroken*. They were only the forerunners of the flotilla it was intended to send there, and notwithstanding everything, they had hardly arrived that they loaded up with torpedoes and left on operations. It had now come to that. There was not a single moment to be lost, because there was also a target date for the end of food and fuel supplies. In the last week of July there were only three weeks supply left. So the island was really living on borrowed time. But Gort's axiom was that Malta must be relieved, and it would. And his message shook the brass heads as it echoed in the corridors of Whitehall. Perhaps this was how he differed from his predecessor, Sir William Dobbie.

This was a dire situation which had to be faced by the British Cabinet if they were to make one more chance for Malta to go on living. And she must, if Rommel was to be defeated. The subject of risks was now taken off the agenda as they agreed to send a gigantic convoy to carry enough food, amunition and oil fuel to the island. There had to be the three of them, for if one failed to be delivered, Malta would still fall. It was obvious that the Italians and Germans would expect this last effort for Malta and indeed they got to know of it when the convoy began to be formed. They also knew its implications. Rommel had just conditioned the continuation of his advance into Egypt to the supply of 6,000 tons of petrol for his vehicles. And both General Caballero and Field Marshal Kesselring promised him he would have them as if they knew that soon their convoys would be able to go past Malta without impugnity after the destruction of the forthcoming British convoy.

Having taken over command of the 8th Army, General Montgomery was in a similar situation. He was alive to the likelihood of a German attack on his positions before he could launch his offensive. General Auchinleck had, before he left, also said that Rommel would strike before the end of August. So, rather than continuing with his preparations for the offensive Montgomery now felt it would pay him better to work on building defensive positions. If there were to be no attack he would have only wasted his time. But if there were indeed to be one, then he could not afford to be beaten since this would be decisive, and on which will depend his later offensive, and the future of North Africa, Egypt and the whole war. So after assessing the situation he concluded that if Rommel were to attack he would most likely aim at Alam-el-Halfa Ridge lying south east of El Alamein. And that was where he began to build his defences, as the days began to fly past towards the big climax that everyone could sense approaching.

The Turning Point

Vice-Admiral E.W. Syfret was placed in command of the decisive convoy code-named Operation Pedestal. He flew his flag in the battle-ship *Nelson* which was to be accompanied by her sister ship *Rodney*, as well as a squadron of four aircraft carriers under Rear-Admiral Lyster. Three cruisers and twelve destroyers then completed the group that was Force Z which was to see the convoy to the Sicilian Channel. From then onwards escort was to be provided by Force X under Rear-Admiral H. Burrough in the cruiser *Nigeria*, with two others and twelve destroyers. Force R was composed of two fleet tankers, a tow vessel and four corvettes. The important wards of this mighty armada were thirteen merchantmen and one tanker. Further back there was to follow the aircraft carrier *Furious* packed with Spitfires for Malta, and escorted by eight destroyers. From Malta's side there were to be provided only her eight submarines to be allotted billets on the more likely route to be taken by the Italian fleet which was expected to get involved.

But the Italians had no such intentions. Their plan was based on picked naval squadrons for lightning attacks where these were indicated, and for this they held in readiness two squadrons, one made up of three heavy cruisers and seven destroyers, the other composed of three light cruisers with four destroyers. In support there were to be two E Boat squadrons and eighteen submarines, with also two German U Boats and four motor torpedo boats. The main onslaught was to be made from the air.

The convoy and escorts left Britain on 10th August, went past Gibraltar and came in for the first attack in the morning of the 11th by Junkers 88. This was, however, beaten back by Fulmars and Hurricanes from the carriers. Two hours later the convoy had reached a position south of the Balaeric Isles and the *Furious* launched her Spitfires for Malta. There were 38 of them of which only one was lost. This completed the first stage of the operation, and Vice-Admiral Syfret might have complimented himself on a well done job as the *Furious* turned back to return to Britain. If he did, he must have spoken too soon for the aircraft carrier was attacked by an Italian submarine. Fortunately she was not hit and the submarine was also sunk by a destroyer. However, the carrier *Eagle* was not so lucky. She got the full four torpedoes from a German U Boat and sunk immediately. The merchantman *Deucalion* was also hit and had to leave the convoy.

The enemy increased his efforts on the following day with severe attacks by Stukas and S.79 torpedo bombers. Notwithstanding the interceptions by fleet air arm fighters, two aircraft carriers were hit, these being the *Indomitable* which was set on fire, and the *Victorious* which was lightly damaged. The destroyer *Foresight* was also hit and had to be sunk.

The most difficult part of the operation came at dusk, however, when Force Z turned back leaving the convoy and its escort without any air support. If the planners had thought that with night coming there would be no attacks they should have known the enemy would not sleep with such an important convoy passing close by. And it was now that there was a combined onslaught on both ships and escorts. Submarines hit the cruisers *Cairo, Nigeria* and *Kenya* with torpedores, as well as the tanker *Ohio.* Fortunately enough only the *Cairo* sank. But with three of the four cruisers now out of action, anti-aircraft defences were considerably weakened, and with their first swoop enemy torpedo bombers hit three merchantmen. Again, notwithstanding the damage incurred, the ships tried to go on, but two of them, the *Empire Hope* and *Glenorcky* were hit again by torpedoes from submarines, and sank. The *Brisbane Star* was hit by another torpedo and left the convoy to seek shelter towards the Tunisian coast. The next casualty was the *Clan Ferguson* which was sunk by an aerial torpedo.

By now night had fallen and there were hopes for a respite. If the convoy could make it till the morning then it would come within range of Malta's Spitfires. But the enemy had other plans for the night which he turned into a nightmare of terror. The two squadrons of E Boats pressed an attack home, firing torpedoes before escort vessels could bring their guns on the target. Not that the sleek boats could be seen in the darkness. They could be seen only for fleeting moments in the exploding flashes as their torpedoes hit home. The only remaining fit cruiser *Manchester* was sunk, and so were the merchantmen *Warrangi, Santa Eliza* and *Almeria Sykes*. Rear Admiral Burrough was now at a loss to know what had remained of his convoy.

When dawn came there were only three ships to be seen in their position. Then lagging behind there was the tanker *Ohio*, and still further back could be discerned *Port Chalmers* and *Dorset*. Only six ships out of fourteen. It appeared as if the enemy had won this second stage of the battle. If at least these six could be seen safety through, then the heavy losses suffered until now would not have been in vain.

By now all in Malta knew of the convoy. The sound and flashes of gunfire throughout the night had heralded its approach.

Lord Gort could only hope for the best, and the RAF fighters were getting ready to fly out in support as soon as the ships came within range. But the people of Malta, immune in their steadfast catholic faith, continued praying for the safety of the convoy, as indeed they had been doing for the last days. Now as the ships were known to be close, their prayers increased and their voices were rising in unison asking for the intercession of Santa Maria, whose fast would fall in two days' time on 15th August. But even while the people were thus congregated in churches, Junkers 88 were again attacking the remnants of the convoy hitting the *Dorset* and *Rochester Castle*. The tanker *Ohio* still making a heavy going after being hit by a torpedo now received the vengeance of a Stuka which crashed on its decks, and making it fall further back. The climax came later in the morning when Spitfires flew out and like shepherds rounded up what was left of the scattered sheep until they could reach their pen which was Grand Harbour.

But there were only three ships. The *Melbourne Star, Rochester Castle* and *Port Chalmers.* A look at the horizon showed nothing else in sight. Not even an eddy of smoke. Three ships were certainly welcome, but they were not enough. And no amount of food and ammunition that was carried in their holds would make up for the fuel required for aircraft and which had not arrived. All seemed to be lost, but the people continued to pray for what was now looking impossible. Then in the evening another ship appeared on the horizon. It was the *Brisbane Star* which had left the convoy in a damaged condition and sought shelter towards the Tunisian coast. It had carried out temporary repairs and made its way to Malta, unaided and unescorted. This was a welcome addition, but it still did not fill the void left by the tanker *Ohio* which carried 11,000 tons of fuel. It was now that hope was given up.

In truth the *Ohio* was still afloat. It was some two hundred miles away being cradled by two cables held fast by the two destroyers *Penn* and *Bramham* to keep it afloat. Smashed into smithereens, with decks awash and a still burning fire, the crippled tanker was still plodding forward as if in answer to an island's prayers. Then suddenly on the 14th the Italians got a hint about the stricken tanker which could still get them the victory they had been after. A squadron of four cruisers and eight destroyers left their hide-out in the Lipari Islands at full speed to the Straits of Messina from where they could pounce on the helpless tanker. Only that right in their way they found the submarine *Unbroken* which in truth should not have been there. But this fact did not make its skipper, Lieutenant Commander Alastair Mars, hesitate to fire his torpedoes at the rushing cruisers, hitting two of them. The remaining

The Turning Point

warships were then soon occupying themselves between picking up the cruisers' survivors and attacking the submarine. And their endeavours took just enough time to allow the *Ohio* to reach Malta on 15th August. This epic has gone down in Maltese history as the Santa Maria Convoy.

* * *

One decisive battle had been won. Now there was the other to follow. Until this convoy had reached Malta, there had been some respite for Rommel and he had received some reinforcements which included the German prachute brigade and an Italian Parachute Division which had been once intended for the invasion of Malta. They were now to be used as infantry. But from now onwards he could not hope for any more respite. Indeed the lack of balanced foodstuffs was now catching up with him. Dysentery and infectious jaundice became rampant amongst Italian and German troops, and Rommel was himself afflicted. He had now become so weak that he could not even get out of his truck. His medical officer was insisting that he should go back to Europe for treatment but the Field Marshal would not abandon or postpone the battle which he knew was going to be decisive. Maybe it was only his devotion and strength of purpose that made him feel a little better. So he attacked on 30th August.

The attack was launched quietly at night, and Rommel's intention was to proceed unseen through the southern sector of the front line and make to a point above the Qattara Depression. Then from there he would strike north to the sea hoping in the process to take the British positions by surprise just as he had turned the Gazala Line three months before. Since between the Qattara Depression and the sea there lay Alam-el-Halfa Ridge it was there that his ruse would have brought him in contact with the British troops had it succeeded. Which shows that Montgomery's anticipation had been correct. As things turned out Rommel seems to have miscalculated two important things. First there were the minefields the British had laid which delayed his going, and then there was the RAF which launched constant heavy attacks on his forces critically caught in the minefields. It took the Germans till the following morning to get clear, and all this time being harassed by the British planes which caused them heavy casualties, amongst them the Corps Commander General Nehring who was wounded.

Rommel was thinking of breaking off the attack. But on second thoughts he decided to carry on. Then rather than going deeper he made an immediate left wheel to take a short cut. This proved to be his undoing since it took him straight to the dominant part of Alam-el-Halfa Ridge where Montgomery was waiting for him. It looked as if he had played himself into the British General's hands.

Under continuous harassing by the RAF the German panzers covered the ten miles to the Ridge to come into confrontation with the 22nd Armoured Brigade which was holding that side with well sited tanks and supporting artillery. The Germans came under heavy fire and for long moments were pinned down without being able to move either way. They tried several of their old tricks to advance or move on the flanks. But all their moves were being checked, and they could not budge an inch until nightfall.

The following morning of 1st September, Rommel decided to make one last desperate move to occupy the Ridge, and he detailed his 15th Panzer Division to do it. He did not know that in the meantime, during the night Montgomery had brought down two further armoured brigades to help the 22nd which had proved to be so hard a nut to crack, when alone. With three the attempt became even harder and Rommel's attacks began to fizzle out one after the other. Seeing this, Montgomery began fresh preparations to counter attack. Rommel, however, gave him no chance and began to retreat.

This looked to be too good a chance to be lost by Montgomery. He could still have launched his forces to chase the Germans which might have even turned into a rout. But the British General remembered the many traps Rommel had engineered for his predecessors and he didn't want to be caught by any similar prank. So he let Rommel retreat, sending only a few patrols after him just to check his whereabouts. It was only when the Germans stopped at a point just six miles inside the frontier that Montgomery was satisfied. This was on September 6th. He could now let the Germans be. After all the battle of Alam-el-Halfa had been won, and he could use his time better in preparing for his big offensive. And fate favoured Montgomery for three weeks later Rommel was so ill from his jaundice that he was compelled to fly to Germany for treatment.

As if to make the best of a bad job he had an interview with Hitler before he went into hospital, telling him that if he was expected to occupy Egypt he must be assured of supplies and particularly petrol which Malta was preventing from reaching him. Hitler expressed himself to be positive of the outcome, and that petrol would certainly be sent. There were also new weapons mentioned that would help Germany occupy Egypt. But all the Fuhrer's talk was in the third person, and Rommel was no fool. Then Hitler came out with what he had in mind. He suggested that Rommel should not go back to North Africa. Instead he would be given an Army Group in Southern Ukraine after he would have left hospital. And it was with this premise that Rommel entered the hospital at Semmering. If he was not wanted again in North Africa then he wouldn't go.

On the following day Hitler appointed General Stumme to replace him.

What appeared to be a dallying attitude by Montgomery did not go down well in various quarters, the most important of which was no doubt the Cabinet where Churchill now continued to press the general to launch his promised offensive. He couldn't be blamed after the prolonged discussions he had had with the Americans about the intended British/American landing in North West French Africa, which had been finally concluded and agreed upon to be launched on 8th November.

But Montgomery wouldn't budge. And neither did Alexander. Their planned offensive code-named Operation Lightfoot was being worked out meticulously, taking everything into consideration to the minutest detail. Even to launching the attack when there would be a full moon to have the infantry in action also during the night. Churchill's own remonstrances continued about the importance of having a decisive result in time to soften French resistance in the forthcoming new operation. Also to discourage Spain from helping Germany.

"That's why I wouldn't be hurried," replied Montgomery, "so as to make sure of success."

"We only need to be allowed a fortnight before the attack on North West French Africa," added Alexander, "it will give us enough time to destroy the greater part of the Axis army facing us."

And that was that. Churchill submitted to their arguments, and the offensive was fixed for the night of October 23rd.

It was expected that by then the Germans and Italians would have something like 80,000 men between them, with about 260 German and 280 Italian tanks. Against this, Montgomery was building an army of 230,000 men with some 1,200 tanks, with a further 200 in reserve. As well as over, 1,000 guns. In the air too Air Chief Marshal Tedder was already enjoying superiority with 96 squadrons of 1,200 aircraft, all based in Egypt and Palestine. The Axis had only 350 between them. As September rolled into October there was the welcome news from Malta about her aircraft and submarines having picked up their activities again and destroyed a third of the enemy transports on their way to North Africa. Indeed the first two weeks of October were already indicating that there would even be a bigger toll during this month.

The Turning Point

The last few days to the target date were devoted to checking last details, and the meticulous Montgomery had everything ready and complete in time. Then on the night of 23rd October he launched his offensive with a barrage by more than one thousand guns intended to blast Rommel into smithereens.

But Rommel was still in hospital at Semmering in Austria. He had improved, but was not yet healed. He came to know of the offensive from Hitler himself when he phoned him up at noon on October 24th.

"Rommel, there is bad news from Africa," he told him. "The British have attacked and the situation looks very black. No one seems to know what happened to Stumme. Do you feel well enough to go back? And would you be willing to go?"

Rommel was certainly in no condition to return to the battle front and fight. And this could have been the right occasion to be exploited in a way to pay back Hitler for having distrusted him. But rather than in personal pique Rommel's heart was with the Afrika Korps. And it was this that made him accept. Nothing else.

"Yes, mein Fuhrer, I will go back. I shall be leaving tomorrow."

And he left by air early the following morning, stopped in Italy for a brief meeting to ensure supplies of petrol, and then flew to Crete. From there, then, he flew straight to his headquarters in North Africa where he arrived at 8 p.m.

"What's been happening?" were the first words he said to his generals when he arrived. Then they told him a story that was only 48 hours old.

General Stumme had followed exactly the plans that Rommel had left before going into hospital. But there was the unexpected barrage which had affected the outcome. Stumme had no doubt tried to counteract under the new situation, but barely twenty four hours after the attack had started he had driven to the front, ran into enemy fire and fell out of his car. Then he had died on the spot. The British had in the meantime driven a wedge into German defences, and the battle was as good as lost.

"Oh no, it isn't," told them Rommel. Then he retired to get some rest for the night that had set in. On the morrow he recalled his two favourite panzer divisions, the 15th and 21st, and led them himself into a counterattack.

* * *

Montgomery's bombardment had only lasted fifteen minutes. When it stopped he had moved his armour into attack. It was, however, unexpectedly delayed by heavy minefields, so while tanks and vehicles were left to make their slow and heavy going during the night, he took his infantry forward to catch up with them when they would emerge from the minefields. They did this in the morning and were pushed into the attack on the shaken enemy. Notwithstanding their suffering heavy casualties, they pressed on to drive a wedge in the enemy lines. When the attack was resumed on October 26th with the scope of widening and deepening the wedge, the British were checked by anti-tank guns which wrought havoc in their tank force. This was Rommel's doing after he had arrived on the scene. Rather than pressing on, Montgomery now decided to pull back his forces to regroup, then devised another attack which he launched on October 28th This time intending to move towards the coast from where he could swerve towards Daba and Fuka. This attack was again stopped by one of Rommel's characteristic counter-moves which, however, lost him many tanks. And now he had only 90 left, to Montgomery's 800.

Seeing this second move thus miscarried, Montgomery tried to revert back to his original thrust from the north, hoping the enemy would not be flexible to move enough forces to hold him. But if the Germans were slow in switching over, so were the British, and they lost what advantage there might have been created by the move.

There is no doubt that Montgomery had until now

The Turning Point

showed to be more intrepid in battle than the previous commanders. But it seemed that in confrontation with Rommel he as well could not obtain the desired results. More than worrying Churchill, this outcome worried Montgomery as well as he had to admit his anxiety. But the truth was that Rommel was on the verge of being beaten. he knew this, and was already playing with the idea of withdrawing to Fuka. But then he had delayed a little longer hoping Montgomery would break his attack, which in fact he did as if to oblige.

Montgomery's next attack came in the early hours of the morning of November 2nd, with his forces as before being bogged in minefields laid down by the Germans. With the light of dawn British armour was still at a standstill after finding a screen of anti-tank guns on emerging from the minefields. It was now that Rommel counter-attacked with what forces he still had, causing heavy British casualties. Sensing danger, Montgomery pushed forward more brigades to the front which got into the mettle and maintained the British lines until the night when fighting stopped. It was now time to regroup. Montgomery had lost 200 tanks that day, with Rommel having lost much less. But now the Germans panzers had only 30 tanks fit for action, and their 9,000 men had dwindled down to barely 2,000. Rommel knew he could not hope to resist Montgomery with these. That night he decided to withdraw.

Early the following morning of November 3rd, the first British aircraft on patrol spotted German forces withdrawing back. This was the tonic Montgomery needed. He sent forces to try and cut off the enemy's withdrawal, then with his main forces he decided to wait for the night to deliver a frontal attack. This he did, with the 51st Highland Brigade and the 4th Indian Division, both of which managed to cut through between the German and Italian forces. Now Montgomery pushed three amoured divisions into the gap with instructions to swerve to right and left in an attempt to cut Rommel's retreat. To consolidate the gap he brought up the motorized New Zealand Division and another armoured brigade.

Rommel realised what Montgomery was trying to do. What's more, he knew that this one move could destroy the Afrika Korps. So he decided to retreat, and gave the necessary orders to General Thoma. This general, however, was captured by the British before he could implement his superior's order, and it had to be Rommel himself to give the order to his troops on the following day of November 5th. With the resulting day's delay, however, now he told his troops to move fast if they were not to be caught by Montgomery's pincer movement.

Rommel was at last on the run. And the 8th Army was chasing him. Montgomery had finally done it.

The rest of that day was characterised by elements of the 8th Army trying to cut Rommel's retreat, with the Germans always managing to slip away before the British arrived. Fuka, Daba and Baqqush were all positions where the Germans could have been caught, but the British missed the bus in all the three occasions. It seemed that Rommel was as quick and sprighty in his retreat as in his advance. In the afternoon of November 6th, it started to rain heavily and pursuit had to stop. This gave Rommel all the time he wanted. He abandoned Mersa Metruh on the 7th and continued towards Sidi Barrani with the least that Montgomery could do being to have the RAF attack his transport columns.

Nonetheless Montgomery was not going to stop. However, his advance from now on needed only be in the form of a follow up rather than a pursuit. This would allow him to rest his troops and also allow supplies to catch up, as he was putting more distance between him and his base. He knew he had defeated Rommel, killing several thousands of his troops and capturing 10,000 Germans and over 20,000 Italians, together with some 450 tanks and over 1,000 guns. He had paid with 13,500 casualties of his own besides the hundreds of lost tanks. It might have been a fair price which, however, still left him with the one disappointment that Rommel had escaped.

But this might have been only a personal matter. And it could certainly not be considered against the significance of the outcome. To Winston Churchill this might have been a face saver for the operation that was to follow in North French Africa. But to the British nation locked in the Mediterranean struggle, this was without any doubt, the turning point.

CHAPTER VIII

OPERATION TORCH - THE FRENCH DILEMMA

The birth and planning of the Allied Landings in French North West Africa was not as easy and devoid of complications as one might have thought. This wasn't because it had to be the first major combined British American operation of the sort. And which was bound to bring forth the clashes it did between characteristic tendencies of the two nations. There were indeed many occasions wrought by pique and friction, but these were all eventually settled to bring the two allies even closer for the massive operation they were undertaking. The biggest difficulty, however, concerned the French. And who were the people to whom the torch of freedom was symbolically being carried by the British and American forces in this mission. Hence its code-name Operation Torch.

There were those of these people who were loyal to Marshal Petain as the head of the French Government, and others who one way or the other did not care, but who would still not be involved in any anti-Vichy commitment. Amongst the latter there were the military and naval commanders, still embittered against the British because of the attacks upon their fleet at Oran and Dakar, as well as for the other British intervention in Syria. On both occasions there had been shed French blood. And this was not to be easily forgotten. One had also to consider the French

Operation Torch – The French Dilemma

position with a part of France still unoccupied by the Germans according to the armistice terms, and this also included the harbour of Toulon with the main elements of the French fleet in there. Untouched and inactive, but still French. All this can be said to have been like a pistol being held to Petain's head. And if there were to be any change of loyalties in the North African colonies there were bound to be German reprisals in France. This had made it very likely from the very beginning that the French would resist the British American landings, and there were enough forces and defences in place to give the Allies a hectic time. Were the Allies therefore justified in fighting and destroying the people they were supposed to be going to liberate? And this was the big dilemma that had overshadowed the months of long preparations for Operation Torch.

There had been a series of moves carried out to try and come to some arrangements with the French through Robert Murphy, the chief American diplomatic representative in North Africa. And as far back as October he had discussed the matter with General Mast who commanded the French forces in the Algiers sector, and also with General Bethouart of the Casablanca sector. But all this was taking time which was not allowed to delay the preparations. The final plan was for three landings to be made at Casablanca from the Atlantic, at Oran and Algiers in the Mediterranean. The landing at Casablanca was to be under the command of Major-General George S. Patton who was allocated an army of 24,500 all American troops. The naval task force of 73 warships, escorting 29 transports carrying the troops and their equipment was to be under the command of American Rear-Admiral H. Kent-Hewitt. In the Mediterranean, the assault on Oran was to be carried out by 18,500 American troops under Major-General Lloyd R. Fredendall. But this time the naval task force of 70 warships escorting 36 transports was to be British and under the command of Commodore Thomas Troubridge. At Algiers then, the landing force was to be made up of 9,000 British and 9,000 American troops initially under the command of an American, Major-General Charles Ryder, but after the landing would be completed, command would pass to a Briton, Lieutenant General Kenneth Anderson who was also to take command of the British First Army that was to be created. The naval force for Algiers composed of 67 warships and 25 transports was to be under a British commander, Rear-Admiral Harold Burrough. There was also appointed an Allied Naval Commander of the Expeditionary Force, and this was none other than Admiral Andrew Cunningham who was thus to return to his old haunt, the Mediterranean. The air forces were under two commanders, Air Marshal William Welsh for the RAF and Lieutenant General James Doolittle for the USAAF. The supreme commander for the complete operation was to be an American, General Dwight Eisenhower.

With all this planning completed, it was expected that there would be more emphasis made on the diplomatic moves intended to ensure French collaboration rather than resistance. And some of these moves began to take the looks of cloak and dagger missions as usually found in fiction. General Mart who was being cajoled by Robert Murphy was ready to succumb to the American diplomat but he insisted that a senior American officer should discuss the whole matter with General Juin, the Commander-in-Chief in French North West Africa. Things seemed to be moving, and the Americans readily assigned this mission to General Mark Clark who was also to be Deputy Commander-in-Chief to General Eisenhower. His clandestine landing in North Africa was wrought with enough incidents to make it look like a thriller. Missing his first appointment, he had for the second time to be guided in landing at night by a lamp. Then when he reached his rendezvous which was a villa on the coast, he had to spend some heart throbbing moments as the place was raided by the police. When discussions began, then he had to find his own way out of an impasse when he realised

Operation Torch – The French Dilemma

that he could not tell the French that the British were having a good share of the operation. As otherwise they would have likely refused to negotiate, with their bad feelings for Britain. So he lied and told them that the operation was being carried out by Americans, with the British providing only air and naval support. The crux of the matter then came when it was suggested that there should be a French leader who would rally French forces to the Allied side. The obvious first thought was of General de Gaulle. But he was not wanted because of his unpopularity after having defied Petain. But anyway this was something Clark had to leave for someone else.

In fact there was a very good possible in Admiral Darlan who had once during a meeting with Murphy, expressed his possible willingness to throw his lot with the Allies. He wasn't popular with the general Frenchman, but all the senior French officers regarded him as their titular leader, no doubt because of his close relations with Hitler as much as his allegiance to Petain. And it was this long association of his with Hitler that weighed the choice against him. General Mart had also suggested General Giraud and he was accepted with all the difficulties this entailed. Still living in France under surveillance, Giraud had many a time expressed himself with friends that he would accept American aid to revolt against German domination. But then he had also explained that he would not want the Americans to free France, but rather have them help the French to do it themselves. And this could certainly not apply to Operation Torch. Then, when he was approached, his acceptance was given under the one condition of having him appointed Commander-in-Chief of Allied troops in French territory, which also did not fit in with the already laid down allied plans.

But what could Roosevelt do? It was now the 6th November and the landings were to take place in two days' time. He was all out to accommodate all as long as this would eliminate problems. So was Winston Churchill, by now having already made his historic sentence in dubbing himself "your lieutenant" to Roosevelt's directions, and was agreeing blindly to what the Americans were doing. He had even gone down to what bordered the ridiculous when he suggested that British commandos could wear American uniform during the assault. But this was refused by Roosevellt, who said that the Americans could go in the front ranks with the British to follow. So Giraud was picked from the South of France and taken to Gibraltar for talks. Even the British submarine *Seraph*, which picked him up was given an American captain for the occasion, and an American flag. Then when being transferred to a flying boat for the last lap of his trip Giraud was nearly drowned. Still, at Gibraltar on November 7th, the French General was met with two broadsides. First that the invasion of French North Africa was to take place on the morrow. The second was that he could not be appointed Commander-in-Chief of Allied troops since this appointment already belonged to General Eisenhower. Both statements shook him, and made him think of a trick having been played on him. But it wasn't. In fact he was offered the post of head of French forces and administration in North Africa, provided he would start by issuing an order over his signature to all French forces there to collaborate with the allies on the morrow. He didn't agree. But this did still not keep Murphy from going to General Juin in North Africa at midnight and tell him that in two hours' time the Allies would be landing, and that General Giraud was taking over command and that his first order was for all French forces not to resist. It was all sheer assumption on the part of Murphy. Or better still it was his way out of a desperate situation. Maybe he was thinking of risking all as long as there would be no resistance. Even if Giraud were not to accept, by the following morning all would be over, with the allied forces in control. And it might have worked had General Juin taken his word and the initiative. But he took neither of them. Instead, he said that Giraud's authority was not good enough for him, and that it should be referred to Admiral Darlan.

It was fortunate that Darlan was in North Africa that night. A quick telephone call brought him to Juin and Murphy, but his reply shook the American diplomat. He must contact Petain in France, he said. Then he would act according to his reply. More than that he could not do. And he did cable the French Marshal, and his message was also made out in a positive way asking to be given authority to decide himself what was to be done in the face of an Allied invasion. His idea was obviously to have himself covered in giving the order to French forces not to resist, which was what the Allies wanted. But when the message went out, Eisenhower had given the order for the assault to begin.

It must be said, however, that in the same way that Murphy had assumed responsibility of Giraud's eventual acceptance and informed Juin and Darlan accordingly, so had the French who were collaborating with the Allies. And they went into action in their respective sectors. At Casablanca the French divisional commander, General Bethouart, sent some of his officers to the beach where he thought the Americans would land and to welcome them. Then he took over the army headquarters at Rabat and also instructed General Nogues in Morocco and Admiral Michelier not to resist the Americans in the name of General Giraud. Therefore when General Patton arrived on the scene to land his forces at Fedala, Mehdia and Safi, the three landings were carried out without opposition. And for the next three or four hours until dawn the operation looked more like being an exercise rather than an invasion. At Oran too, the Americans landed at Arzeu, Les Andalouses and at Merse-Bou-Zedjar. And although it was known that the area was covered by thirteen coastal batteries, and there were about 10,000 French troops, there was no opposition to the landings until dawn. At Algiers too where General Mast had on his own initiative issued an order for French forces to collaborate with the allies, American troops landed without mishap at Cape Matifou and Cape Sidi Ferruch, while the British went ashore at Castiglione without any interferance. And all seemed to be working smoothly.

It was at dawn that trouble erupted. Darlan had not yet received any reply from Petain, while the promised Giraud had not made an appearance in North Africa, and much less delivered the broadcast that had been indicated. It seems that there were more French patriots than collaborators, and what truce had been self imposed was now broken, with patriotism weighing heavily against the attitude of wait and see that had been adopted. At Casablanca, Admiral Michelier ordered his naval forces to go into action against the Allies. A coastal battery at Cape el Hank and the French uncompleted battleship *Jean Bart* lying in harbour opened fire on the American ships. The French were, however, soon silenced by an American battleship and two cruisers which moved in and replied to the fire. This action, however, must have disguised the fact that there was a French naval squadron in harbour made up of one cruiser, seven destroyers and eight submarines. In the confusion these managed to slip out and launch an attack on the American transport ships. The American fleet reacted immediately and a battle ensued. When two French destroyers were sunk, the rest returned to harbour with most of them being hit. Then American aircraft from supporting aircraft carriers launched an attack sinking two further destroyers.

At Oran there was some sporadic but inaccurate fire from coastal batteries at dawn. The only serious resistance in the morning, however, came when two naval cutters with American troops went into the harbour to forestall any sabotage. These came under heavy fire and were both sunk. Armoured elements and infantry which had by now already occupied Tafaraoui airfield and were proceeding onwards began to meet the first resistance and were halt-

Operation Torch – The French Dilemma 143

ed. In Algiers, General Mast had been removed from command and arrested so there began to spring the first resistance. Troops advancing towards the town met a strong point which they had to subdue with force. A coastal battery at Cape Matipou too opened fire. Two British destroyers which had gone in harbour to land some troops were both hit. One had to withdraw, and the other continued to land her forces, which were taken prisoners, then left harbour again. The battery's firing was now getting too heavy for comfort and Vice-Admiral Neville Syfret's Force H which was supporting the invasion fleet by guarding against any Italian interferance was now called in to take care of the enemy battery. There were the two battleships *Duke of York* and *Rodney* in the squadron together with the battle-cruiser *Renown*, and their gunfire soon silenced the French guns. Then aircraft from the aircraft carrier squadron made up of *Victorious, Formidable* and *Furious* attacked the fort for good measure. This had brought the first day of Operation Torch to a close. But it was far from being the end to the diplomatic action that had been going on behind the scenes.

At 8 a.m. that morning in Gibraltar General Giraud had agreed to do the American bidding if he were made head of French forces and administration in North Africa. At the same time in Algiers, Admiral Darlan had sent a further cable to Petain saying the situation had become critical and suggesting between the lines that he should be given the authority to deal with the allies. And soon after there was Petain's reply agreeing to the request. Darlan ordered a French ceasefire in Algiers and instructed General Juin to do the same in other areas. But there seemed to be an element of procrastination in his action which made General Mark Clark who had just arrived from Gibraltar with Giraud, blow his top. The American general was soon insisting with the French admiral to issue a general cease-fire or get arrested. And the order was issued. He also wanted Darlan to send a message to the French fleet at Toulon, ordering it to leave harbour and join the Allies. The first order was issued, but as for the second, Darlan felt he could not do it. Instead he instructed the fleet to be ready to move out if the Germans entered unoccupied France, and that under no circumstances would it allow itself it be taken over by the Germans. But there had been enough to make Hitler aware of what Petain had been asked to do, and to get back to him through Laval asking him to withdraw the answer he had already sent Darlan, and to refuse any suggestion of an armistice in French North Africa. In the meantime he ordered Field Marshal Kesselring to intervene militarily. On receiving the counter order from Petain, Darlan was pounced upon by General Clark who insisted that the previous order should not be withdrawn or else he would carry on his threat of arresting him. And this is what the crafty Darlan wanted. "That seems to be the only way in which you can force me to do your bidding," he told Clark. So the American general had Darlan placed under house arrest, but he was allowed to send another cable to Petain telling him that while he had withdrawn his order for a cease fire (which he had not) he was placed under arrest. This brouoght the Marshal's reply removing Darlan from command and replacing him by General Nogues. Soon after there was another secret message from Petain telling him that he agreed with a cease fire but had asked him to withdraw it under German pressure.

These were two days of lost operations with the Allied forces and the French looking at each other as if in a dilemma without knowing what to do. It must, however, be handed to the French that they kept both their head and word, and when following Hitler's order the first German aircraft and troops arrived in an airfield near Tunis, French forces surrounded them and did not let them move out. By now all knew that Darlan's show of resistance to the Americans was only an act of subterfuge not to force Hitler's hand in taking some reprisal in France, and was only waiting for some move to break the dramatic exchanges that were going on. The break came soon on the

Operation Torch – The French Dilemma

10th when after Laval hedged to refuse a German request to make use of Tunisia for military operations, Hitler ordered troops to move into the unoccupied part of France thus breaking the terms of the 1940 armistice.

This gave enough reason to Darlan to cooperate. But when he sent a further message to the French fleet at Toulon, this time a little more pressing, Admiral de la Borde refused to leave harbour. So Darlan's authority was restricted to Algeria where it began to have the wanted effect. But there was still a nasty knot to be undone in defining what was being assigned to Darlan and Giraud. It was no easy matter because of the way the people were divided. And it had to be Eisenhower to have Darlan declared High Commissioner and Commander-in-Chief of French Naval Forces, while Giraud was to command the French Army and Air Force. Petain's appointment of General Nogues was cancelled, and Nogues was to remain Resident General of French Morocco and Commander of Western Sector, while General Juin was to be Commander of the Eastern Sector.

This collusion with Darlan after his well known pro-Nazi activities aroused a storm of protests in both Britain and America. But Eisenhower was not caring. His one thought was of the 120,000 French troops there were in North Africa who could forestall Allied efforts in this new theatre of operations. Neither Roosevelt nor Churchill had any love for the French Admiral. But in the circumstances both of them fully endorsed Eisenhower's step.

"Much as I hate Darlan," Churchill had said to Eisenhower, "I would cheerfully crawl on my hands and knees to him if by so doing I would get him to bring to us the French fleet."

Roosevelt too had sought to placate the tumult by saying that this arrangement was only a temporary expedient justified by the stress of battle. And indeed when Darlan came to know of this he did not like it, and protested. But by this time French troops had collaborated and Algeria was occupied. The pity of it all was that Darlan delayed in issuing similar instructions to the French in Tunisia. And this because of ramifications in the French military code. Without such instructions the Resident General and Admiral Esteva could not move as all his military and naval commanders were under Vichy orders. Then when Darlan could issue the order, it was too late, as the Germans had already entered Tunisia. The only consolation now was that in the attack on that country, the Allies were not only unhampered by the French, but they were also receiving their cooperation.

The Allied armies began moving into Tunisia by different means. Two divisions were transported by sea while paratroopers were dropped at Bone and at Souk el Arba, 80 miles away from Tunis. A column moved by road aiming to occupy the port of Tebourka where supplies could be landed before the fighting that could be foreseen would materialise. But even so, these could only be considered as advance units to pave the way for the main forces that would eventually constitute the main front. Until this could be established the various elements sent forward could not produce any coherent situation.

At this same time the Germans were more or less in the same position since the only fighting troops that had arrived did not exceed 3,000, and with only General Nehring whom we have already met as Commander-in-Chief of the Afrika Korps, as senior officer. In their case, however, the Germans were exploiting the situation better by making the Frenchmen believe that a much bigger German force had been taken to Tunisia. When there were the first clashes with Allied troops, these were found only in battalion strength and overwhelmed.

The outcome was that by November 21st Nehring was not only in control of Tunis and Bizerta, but he had also extended his sparse forces to control most of the northern half of Tunisia. By now he had received more reinforcements and it is estimated that he had some 9,000 men,

Operation Torch – The French Dilemma

with the addition of tanks and guns. On November 25th Anderson launched his first offensive.

It was the British General's intention to engage the main German forces in a pitched battle. And he was in fact using the 11th and 36th Infantry brigade Groups, with Blade Force, all supported by American armour and artillery units. But Nehring did not play up. Possibly because of his limited forces. Instead, he built his defence on a number of small counter-attacks which began harassing the Allied forces. One cannot help noting that this was similar to what Rommel used to do, and it seems that Nehring was copying his previous master. He had also the advantage of a strong Luftwaffe detachment which was continually attacking Allied troops with good effect, while a numerically superior RAF and USAAF were more intent on attacking airfields and harbours rather than defending their own men.

It seems that Nehring was then paid with his own coin when an American light tank battalion on advanced reconaissance came to Djedeida airfield which had only just been taken over by the Luftwaffe, and its happy go lucky commander went dashing in with his tanks destroying twenty parked aircraft. This shook Nehring up, making him believe that superior allied forces must have been near. And rather than risking facing them with the small force at his disposal, he decided to withdraw. Major-General Evelegh who was indeed not far with his 78th Division lost no time in pressing the advantage home and followed the Germans right to the important town of Tebourka, twenty miles away. Farther on, they were checked and Evelegh rightly decided he could not carry on until supplies and ammunition caught up with him. Moreover, attacks by German aircraft here became more persistent. So he decided to wait there until he received reinforcements.

There was now a flashback to Darlan's drama, after he had sent an emissary to Toulon with his orders to Admiral

La Borde to take the French fleet to North Africa. That emissary was captured by the Germans and never reached Toulon. In order not to precipitate things, when overrunning what remained of unoccupied France, the Germans had halted on the outskirts of the naval base. But now that they knew of Darlan's intentions they decided to act. Not hastily as one might have imagined circumstances warranted. But shrewdly, and in an attempt to get hold of the fleet for their use. First they laid a minefield in the approaches of the harbour, thus blocking the fleet's way of escape. Then their troops moved into Toulon on November 27th, to take over the ships intact.

They had misjudged Admiral La Borde, however, who faithful to his orders and assurance given to Darlan that the fleet will in no circumstances be allowed to fall into German hands, had prepared a plan. Now on realizing German intentions, he put his plan into operation, and the fleet was scuttled in harbour.

This was the last move which made all French forces in North West Africa throw their lot with the Allies. From then onwards they went into the fight, and were to stay there till the very end.

CHAPTER IX

THE FIGHT FOR TUNISIA

It was New Year's Day, 1943. Another German air raid on Bone was over. In the last few weeks the German forces in Tunisia had been considerably increased, and Colonel-General Jurgen von Arnim was appointed as Commander-in-Chief. Attacks on the harbour had been regular. But now they had intensified after this had become the main port of supply for the First Army in Tunisia. And with another imminent offensive in the offing. The statistics of destruction had increased, and even as the last of a hundred bombers that had taken part in a raid turned away, there were the palls of black smoke rising from two merchantmen in harbour. Two others that carried petrol had exploded and were instantly lost. The cruiser *Ajax*, just back from an extensive refit lay immobile, hit again and severely damaged. Nearby, the minesweeper *Alarm* lay helpless with her back broken by neat direct hits. Jetties were pockmarked by craters, and laced by twisted girders of ruined buildings. Adding obstacles to berthing facilities already made difficult by the many beached ships.

The first clearance operations were intended to start on the morrow. But on that day there were more supplies to arrive. As well as another air raid. Life had become like that all over the smaller part of Tunisia occupied by the Allies. And Eisenhower was feeling the pinch heavier, since his forces had been thrown back in November, and failed to launch the intended offensive in December. He would have wished to have engineered another offensive for January. But President Roosevelt and Winston Churchill were to be in Casablanca in that month and it would not be opportune to start anything. A general offensive could wait. But maybe he could manage a small thrust to Sfax. Even to block Rommel should he go in that direction when he would retreat from Tripolitania. Such a move might even help to trap the Afrika Korps, which would also hasten the coming of the 8th Army to attack von Arnim from the rear. But anyway he could always think about it. Rommel had still some battles to fight before he could be expected to appear in Tunisia.

Indeed Rommel seemed to have no intention to fight any more battles. Not in Libya anyway. During December, Montgomery had moved the 8th Army to Norfilia which brought him within 150 miles from Buerat where the Germans had dug themselves in. Had Eisenhower occupied Tunisia he might have co-operated with him to sandwich the Afrika Korps between them. But with this operation having failed, Montgomery now decided to launch another offensive himself. And judging from the rate at which he was now receiving supplies at Benghazi he was pretty sure he could mount it about mid-January.

Eisenhower did not give up his idea of a thrust to Sfax. But by the time he was ready and planned to allot it to his 2nd Corps there was the Casablanca Conference taking place which gave him the chance to talk it over with the Chiefs of Staff accompanying the Allied leaders. The reply he got could not have pleased him. It seems that there were those who remembered the mauling that American troops had received from the Germans in November. And the Chiefs of Staff were fearing there would be a repetition if the raw American 2nd Corps were to meet Rommel's battle-hardened veterans. So even this had to be off. It would have pleased Eisenhower even less had he known

The Fight for Tunisia

that his military abilities were also in dispute. And that General Sir Alan Brooke was only putting his hopes on General Alexander who was being appointed Deputy Supreme Commander and thus become responsible for day-to-day military decisions. Rather than the American Supreme Commander who was bound it have enough on his plate with political and inter-allied matters.

One thorny political problem which was temporarily solved for him at the Casablanca Conference concerned French leadership. After Admiral Darlan was assassinated in Algiers on 24th December 1942 there had to be someone else selected to take his place if civil disorder were to be prevented. The choice was between Giraud, proposed by the Americans, and de Gaulle who was now being pushed forward by Britain. Both men had for many reasons been found incompatible to work together. But on British insistence de Gaulle had now finally flown out to Casablanca to meet Giraud. No assignments were given to the two Frenchmen. But the first step had been made to get them to work together.

In a way, holding back the 2nd Corps from meeting the Germans might have been providential since von Arnim was now receiving heavy reinforcements. The 10th Panzer and the 334th Infantry Divisions had already reached him by the end of December. In January there had also arrived a Grenadier Division from Crete, and the 501st tank battalion, equipped with the latest Tiger tanks which Hitler had originally promised to Rommel. Besides the many Italian formations that were flowing in, and the Herman Goering Panzer Division that was still on its way. These were reinforcements that could give anyone a headache.

Montgomery, however, met his deadline for an offensive and launched it on January 15th. As before he had planned for a frontal assault by two divisions, detaching two others to go on a detour in an attempt to cut Rommel's way of retreat. This time without any aerial or artillery attacks, so as to gain the element of surprise. But when he reached Buerat, he found it empty. Rommel had slipped out of his reach again. The 8th Army followed the trail and hopes were raised when it caught up with some German elements. They stopped and fought for a while, but then withdrew again. It was realised that these must have been left behind to fight a rearguard action which meant that the Afrika Korps proper must have been well ahead. Nonetheless Montgomery kept his army on the go, moving relentlessly after Rommel, which after all was taking him towards Tripoli. He knew he was going in the right direction by the many skilfully placed mines his forces met on the way, the booby-traps and demolitions, which delayed him, as must have been intended by his crafty enemy. But on the night of January 22nd he reached Tripoli. And to defend it there was the 90th Light Regiment. It now fell to the 51st Highland Division to open the way. And they did it in cavalry style by assaulting the Germans with infantry riding on the back of tanks. The enemy was routed, and on the morning of January 23rd Tripoli was captured.

This was a much needed tonic for the Allies. Coming particularly as it did concurrently with the news of the retreat of the German forces from Stalingrad in Russia which was the first sign to the world that the German tide was ebbing.

It would have saved the Allies a lot of bother had the harbour of Tripoli not been put out of use by demolitions, for Montgomery would have continued in pursuit. But having need of the delivery of supplies he had to stop in Tripoli until the harbour could be brought back into use again. This had been another of Rommel's calculated plans. It now gave him enough time to cross the frontier into Tunisia where he found enough German reinforcements. In a question of days he had built up his divisions to a total of 30,000 Germans and 48,000 Italians. All he wanted now was to use them. A still weak Rommel from sickness and strain was suddenly living again.

Close to the frontier where he had stopped there was

The Fight for Tunisia

the abandoned Mareth Line. This was an old system of fortifications which the French had built to defend Tunisia against any Italian attack from Tripolitania. It had long been abandoned, and Rommel did not like it. But it was considered to be good enough as an obstacle for Montgomery's tanks should he eventually come. Even so, he knew this could not materialise before he would have cleared Tripoli harbour. And this was going to take him some weeks. In the meantime, what could he do? He knew there would be Allied forces too close for comfort in his rear when he would have to face Montgomery. So why couldn't he strike at them now and push them back while he could do it? His 21st Panzer Division had in the meantime been taken by von Arnim and was now under General Ziegler together with the 10th Panzer Division. On February 14th Ziegler was attacking the Allied lines at Faid, and was soon surrounding Combat Command A of the American 1st Armoured Division and making mincemeat out of them. On the following morning a second American Combat Command was sent forward to counter-attack but was similarly trapped by the Germans. Two fine American but inexperienced formations were thus wiped out because of someone's lack of foresight. Rommel was following all this and had it been for him, Ziegler would have gone forward and exploited the situation. But he preferred waiting for von Arnim's instructions.

Rommel, however, had nothing to hold him so on February 15th he launched his group at Gafsa and the Americans began falling like kingpins before him. He then continued with his advance on the semi-circular road leading to Ferranc and the airfields at Thelepte, 50 miles away. These he captured on February 17th, and put the British, American and French troops there into confusion. Allied fears were now for Tebessa, only 35 miles away, and which was a big supply depot. Preparations were therefore made to set it on fire should Rommel move towards there. But his mind was not there. Rommel wanted to exploit his breakthrough by going deeper. And he was convinced that within a few days he would force the Allied forces completely out of Tunisia. That he did not might have been due to von Arnim who was after all the official Commander in the field. Either because of his disbelief in the chances of a total success, or just to curb his exuberance, von Arnim failed to give any support to Rommel in his offensive against the Kasserine Pass. Now to make the lack of unity between them more obvious he held him back from carrying further exploits. So Rommel pulled a fast one on him and had recourse to Mussolini, with a message asking for his permission to continue with his advance. This was given on the night of February 18th, conditioned however, that he would advance towards Thala and Le Kef. Rommel was game, but to proceed to Thala he had to go through the Kasserine Pass, a naturally difficult outlet now made the more difficult by being held by American troops.

It so happened that the Americans there belonged to the 2nd Corps which was the same element which Eisenhower had been prevented from sending to Sfax for fear of meeting Rommel's forces. It seems that destiny had all the same brought them in his way, where they were to receive their baptism of fire. They might have made up heart when they repulsed what seemed to them to have been a German attempt to attack. But this had in reality been only a feeler by Rommel in the morning of February 19th to test their strength. The Americans were still taking no chances and reinforcements were sent to the Kasserine Pass as if in anticipation of the important battle that was to ensue. By the afternoon the Americans were numerically superior to Rommel who had only with him two small infantry battalions and one of tanks. Now that he had tested his enemy and noted positions he sent in the first units to infiltrate at some points in the enemy's lines in the evening. Then he made further infiltrations during the night while he asked for reinforcements. These arrived on the following morning in the form of three battalions. Then in the afternoon he personally led the

The Fight for Tunisia 155

assault by his whole force.

The Americans could not resist the hurricane like German attack. Those who tried to stand up to it were cut to pieces, and the rest withdrew, leaving the battlefield strewn with their blazing tanks and vehicles, as well as equipment which had never been used. This confusion was taking place with Eisenhower in command. When he rushed to the front he could not believe the situation was so alarming. His first thoughts were of reinforcements to be pushed in, and he hastened back to Headquarters to hurry them forward. But in the meantime Alexander was flown in a hurry from Cairo to take over as Deputy on February 19th and his first appreciation of the situation was that "in the confusion of the retreat, American, French and British troops had become inextricably mixed, and that there was no co-ordinated plan of defence and therefore uncertainty as to command.' His next urgent step to help him out of this situation was to appeal to his compatriot, General Montgomery, to do something and take Rommel off his back.

As Rommel stood at the Pass after the battle, lord of all he surveyed, he could see the two possibilities open to him..He could either attack Thala as was his original plan, or he could go to Tebessa with its supply dump. He could afford to take some time to think, because he was anticipating an Allied counter attack on the Kasserine Pass. But when this did not materialise he decided to proceed to Thala. As he set out he was soon confronted by a British brigade group under Brigadier Charles Dunphie who, however, seemed to be unwilling to make a stand for a pitched battle. The British force kept falling back after every skirmish. Their scope was realized when at dusk the British withdrew to Thala where a defence line had already been prepared. That was their chosen battlefield. But Rommel was not that fool to run into a headlong attack. He knew he would be outnumbered and at a disadvantage if he did that. So he had resort to one of his usual tricks.

Taking up a captured British Valentine tank he sent it in front after the retreating forces. But following behind it he sent a string of his own tanks. In the falling darkness the defenders at Thala could only identify the British tank which made them think the advancing column belonged to their own stragglers still falling in. When they realised it was a trick, Rommel's tanks were on them to overrun their infantry, shoot up vehicles and spreading confusion. A three hour battle followed in which the British lost 40 tanks to the German's twelve. At dawn then, Rommel withdrew, taking 700 prisoners with him.

After he had carried out this sortie, Rommel was tempted to go for Tebessa, and he did send a battalion towards the town. But this was met by heavy artillery fire from American forces which had in the meantime been sent there to reinforce the garrison. It immediately occurred to Rommel that if the forces at Tebessa were to counter attack while he was still there, with Thala behind him and the British force there which could any moment launch another attack, he might have his way of retreat cut. And he had already lost some of his force for he had not escaped unscathed. He found himself in a dilemma as to whether he should attack again or withdraw altogether from that area.

It was Kesselring who helped him decide when he flew to him on February 22nd to impress upon him that it was about time he should return to meet Montgomery and the 8th Army. And Rommel agreed and began withdrawing his forces.

His way had to be through the Kasserine Pass where General Patton had gone to wait for him. And his passage was not made easy. But he went through, although not without losses.

What happened in the days that followed can be described as the battle of fate. It began on February 23rd when Hitler and Mussolini, impressed by Rommel's victory at the Battle of the Kasserine Pass, placed all the axis

The Fight for Tunisia

forces in Tunisia under his command. Had this been done a day before, it would have given Rommel all the forces he required and the situation in Tunisia might well have developed differently. But it had come when he was withdrawing, to go and meet Montgomery. There was also von Arnim who had planned a new offensive which could not be spoiled in its last moments. In fact, it was launched on February 25th, and although the Germans managed to edge Allied troops from some positions and also take prisoners, they lost many tanks which they could not replace so easily. Still, they pinned down the British 5th Corps. This too affected Rommel adversely since it deprived him of the divisions he was hoping to have for his fast approaching encounter with the 8th Army which was going to be his last battle in North Africa.

In the meantime the situation was far from being rosy, and Alexander informed Churchill accordingly. "I am frankly shocked at the whole situation as I found it," he signalled him. "Hate to disappoint you, but final victory in North Africa is not just around the corner."

Ironically enough Montgomery too was momentarily in a difficult situation. His hastened run to the Tunisian front in answer to Alexander's appeal had made it possible for him to take only one division. Now that he knew that Rommel had cut off his offensive at Thala and was coming to meet him, he tried to redress feverishly. So the last few days of February and those at the beginning of March found both the German and British commanders doing their damnedest to build up their strength for the approaching decisive battle. Strange to say, that here too, Rommel must have been as usual guided by his sixth sense which had aided him so much throughout his campaigning. Now, with three depleted Panzer divisions (the 10th, 15th and 21st) which between them had only 160 tanks, 200 guns and 10,000 men, he was making haste to meet Montgomery, as if he knew of his plight. And he wanted to catch him off balance. But through fate, luck or more probably sheer hard work, Montgomery managed to bring up three further divisions with sme 400 tanks, 350 guns and what was more important many anti-tank guns. The weapon which Rommel had immortalized in desert warfare. Moreover, he had also brought up in support three RAF fighter wings, which the Germans certainly did not have. Then Montgomery stopped to wait for Rommel at Medenine, which faced the Mareth Line manned by Italian troops left there by Rommel. A couple of uneventful days passed, and Montgomery waited. Always finding ways and means how to improve his lines. Then on March 4th, Rommel was spotted by a British plane, and Montgomery was alerted. The Germans reached Medenine two days later, and Rommel lost no time in launching an attack on the British lines with his two faithful divisions, the 15th and 21st. There were now no minefields or wire to protect Montgimery's front, and a thick mist helped to shroud the first enemy movements at dawn. His tanks moved forward, and artillery opened up. But British artillery did not reply. Not even when the mist began to disperse showing the German battle array quite clearly. Their tanks continued moving until they were only about a mile and a half from the British lines. They stopped there as if awaiting an order, then after a while they moved to higher ground which made them easier targets. They had fallen into Montgomery's trap. It was now that the British opened a murderous concentrated fire from more than 400 anti-tank guns. At the same time well placed artillery began plastering the Germans. It immediately became obvious to Rommel that his forces would be decimated before they could get to grips with the British, and he stopped his attack.

There was another attempt made, and this time, Rommel, rather than leading the attack himself, found it more useful in mixing with his men trying to whip up their enthusiasm, and telling them tht this was a decisive battle for Africa. With his bandaged throat and his face covered with desert sores he must have presented a very sad sight, which might have made a strong impression on his men. But Montgomery's fire was even stronger. There were repeated attacks by the Germans, all of them different in style and strength. Attacking infantry that was all the time being dispersed by artillery fire before it could come to grips with the British. Mixed companies of khaki dressed Germans and dark green clad Italians tried advancing in close formations only to be broken down by Bren gun and rifle fire from the Argyles and Scots Guards at 400 yards range, together with mortar fire from the 28th Maori Battalion. Then tanks too failed to bring out a single successful strike, being badly mauled by the 73rd Anti-Tank Regiment. Many of them finished as mounds of burning hulks marking the line where German attacks had faltered against the British lines which were never reached.

By the evening, the Germans had lost 52 tanks with not a single one being lost by the British. Troop casualties were light, with only 645 Germans being lost, while the British had 130 in killed and wounded. But Rommel had used up all his tricks and strategies. And he knew he was beaten. So he gave up. Three days later he was in Rome. He had left Africa never to return again. But his legend remained.

* * *

In its time the Mareth Line had been a much vaunted French defence system, stretching for 22 miles from the coast to the Matmata Hills. But it had never been tried in action. Now in March 1943, manned by 80,000 Italian troops, with 150 tanks and 680 guns and three German panzer divisions of the Afrika Korps, it was going to have its baptism of fire. For Montgomery had to break through if he were to join the Allied armies in Tunisia. It seemed very likely that the spectacular battle that had not materialised at Medenine would now take place here. Indeed even the departed Rommel had his mind on the Mareth Line, for one of the first things he said to Hitler on meeting him was to have the Italians move out from the line and build a defensive position farther back at Wadi Akarit. Hitler had agreed but Kesselring had prevailed upon him to leave everything as it was.

Montgomery's first attack on the Mareth Line failed. It was delivered on March 20th by his 30th Corps under Lieutenant-General Oliver Leese. The 50th Infantry Division had managed to secure a bridgehead across anti-tank ditches in Wadi Zigzaou, just behind the Mareth Line, but before this could be consolidated for the tanks to come in, there was a German counter attack which made this impossible. Fighting continued for three days and when 42 British tanks managed to get into the breach during the night, most of them were destroyed in the morning. The rest had to withdraw. But the infantry held its place, notwithstanding savage attacks by the 15th Panzer Division which was now hitting at the part held by the Durham Light Infantry. An outflanking move by the New Zealand Corps under Lieutenant-General Bernard Freyberg had some initial success, but also finished by being checked. It now fell to Montgomery to act in his by now characteristic way by recasting his plan on the spot, rather than breaking off the attack. He switched his main strength on to the flank where the New Zealanders had had their slight initial success. He sent them the 10th Corps in support which reached the New Zealanders on March 26th. At the same time he had Air Vice Marshal Harry Broadhurst, commanding the Desert Air Force launch a continuous blitz by fighter bombers. The combined forces then launched an attack. By midnight they had broken the enemy defences and went through.

The Italian General Messe who was in command of the Mareth Line saw through Montgomery's intentions, and transferred troops to the side where an out flanking movement was being attempted. But then there was the dramatic intervention by General von Arnim who must have been following the fighting and realised that Montgomery

The Fight for Tunisia

was indeed outflanking the Mareth Line. So he ordered Messe to withdraw from there and move back to Wadi Akarit. This had been Rommel's suggestion from the beginning. It seems that even though he had left, his spirit was still hovering in the North African campaign. So Messe began to take his men out, and this could not but make Montgomery press with a second assault during which Major-General Raymond Briggs with his 1st Armoured Division advanced 5 miles right into the enemy lines. He continued to go forward during the night, and also turning right to the edge of the enemy defence line at El Hamma. Fighting continued for two days with the Axis forces. But theirs was only a rearguard action until the bulk of their forces had reached their new position at Wadi Akarit. So the Mareth Line was left empty and finished as a defensive line. Montgomery now had to attack the enemy in his new position at Wadi Akarit.

The 8th Army's task might have been eased when Patton with his 2nd Corps had taken Maknassy and proceeded along the Gafsa Gabes road thus threatening the Wadi Akarit position. But it seems that the American general was more concerned with his obsessions. He was now objecting to his being placed again under the First Army, after he had engineered to be detached from it. So now he was obligingly put on his own, while Alexander began planning a four pronged offensive which eventually failed. It was now Montgomery's turn to find that Wadi Akarit had been abandoned by the enemy, after General Messe had been deprived of two of the three German Panzer divisions he had. He had now withdrawn to Enfidaville, 150 miles away and that was where Montgomery was directed to proceed after first striking at Sousse. This meant that the 8th Army had now linked with the 1st Army. General Patton too was transferred with his 2nd Corps to the extreme north where he would have to fight on the left flank of the 1st Army and drive at Bizerta. As if to eliminate any more complications from his part, he was then relieved of his command to be given the time to plan the

American contribution in the invasion of Sicily, and his place was taken by General Omar Bradley.

Perhaps one should mention here the Royal Navy's activities which had been constantly directed towards intercepting supplies to the German armies in Tunisia which now numbered 250,000 men. Of 120,000 tons of supplies sent, only 29,000 tons had reached von Arnim during March. During April then, there were only 23,000 tons. Sacrifice was of course paid with a number of warships that were sunk. Like the destroyers *Lightning* and *Pakenham*, as well as the submarines *Tigris*, *Thunderbolt*, *Turbulent*, *Splendid* and *Sahib*. Admiral Harwood had now also relinquished his command in the Mediterranean, and was succeeded by Admiral John Cunningham.

But the climax was now being built in Tunisia where Alexander was having another offensive, and this time intended to be the last. Bradley moved against Bizerta. And Montgomery launched his first assault at Enfidaville where he met very heavy resistance. In fact this turned out to be one of the fiercest battles in North Africa. Strongly entrenched on mountain slopes, German and Italian troops seemed to be more than determined not to give way. The British troops and in particular men of the 4th Indian Division had to work themselves up the hills under heavy enemy fire and suffering heavy casualties. They had to go round rocky knolls, and run across wadis before they could come to grips with their enemy. Then during daylight men from both sides would kill each other with mortar and small arms fire, but in the darkness of night when every man would be only a waiting silhouette they grappled and slew each other at close quarters. In one day the British had only gained 3 miles, which more than being too little was exceedingly costly in men. The 50th Division which was moving on the coastal plain was having a different but also slow progress, and Montgomery halted his attack altogether, intending to give his men brief respite, before having another try.

The Fight for Tunisia

The 1st Army had in the meantime been launched into what was intended to be the final offensive. But this too was heavily resisted by the enemy, and it was soon to fizzle out. The 2nd US Corps under Bradley was also having a difficult going in its attempt to proceed towards Bizerta. It seemed then as if all Allied armies were destined to be blocked in their efforts. What the Allies did not know, however, was that von Arnim was reporting a worse situation for his armies to Berlin. His troops were all exhausted, and his petrol situation was critical. For him too the end was approaching, and he was looking at every battle as likely to be his last fling.

This question of the last battle had also become a point of contestation between the Allied commanders, although they did not show it. Both commanders of the 1st and 8th armies were on tenterhooks to get going again in a last attempt to get to Tunis. Montgomery planned his next assault at Enfidaville for April 25th, and although he had to leave for Cairo on that day, the 8th Army attacked in his absence. The outcome was a repetition of the previous ordeal, with troops again having to fight their way from one trench to another, crawling over rocks. The Indians again were making more use of their *kukri* knives than rifles. When Montgomery returned back after one day he was too sick with flu and tonsillitis to take personal command, and had to retire to bed in his caravan. But he could see that his troops had again failed to break enemy resistance. Then on the following day, the 27th, there was a bombshell from Churchill asking why he had found it necessary to go to Cairo when his forces were launching their attack. It was Alexander who covered for him by attributing the failure at Enfidaville to the fact that the men of the 8th Army were obviously exhausted and needed a rest. There were only two divisions, he told Churchill, that were still fit for combat and offensive action. He was referring to the 7th Armoured Division, by now known to all as The Desert Rats, and the 4th Indian Division. These had indeed been the best two divisions of the 8th Army, and had fought all the way in North Africa from the first Wavell offensive in 1940 and right through El Alamein. Alexander's reply served him another purpose. He could now order the 8th Army to rest. With the exception of these two divisions, which, together with the 201st Guards Brigade he transferred to the 1st Army to reinforce it in its imminent renewal of its offensive intended to capture Tunis. This time Alexander was going to do it or bust.

This offensive was launched on May 6th. Spearheading it there was the 9th Corps now placed under the command of General Horrocks, also taken from the 8th Army, who was made to move behind a massive rolling artillery bombardment in the early hours of the morning. When daylight came the airforces joined in with heavy bombing of enemy positions. A breach was made in the enemy lines for the armour to pass through. But both Germans and Italians were rallied again as the bombardments stopped, and they began to give fight. The British progress was slowed down and eventually halted by the evening, when they were only 15 miles away from Tunis. Bradley too had managed to advance with his 95,000 men of the 2nd US Corps towards Bizerta, but the plum of the fighting now went to Alexander. This final battle had become for him a tactical chess game. He now resumed the artillery barrage by 400 guns firing on picked targets, and began throwing in further units every time and wherever the enemy was being weakened. There was first the 4th Indian Division accompanied by the 4th British Infantry Division thrown in, then as dusk fell he pushed in the 6th and 7th Armoured Divisions with 400 tanks. A night battle ensued with no quarter being allowed, but results would only be known when it was dawn.

Indeed, at first light of the 7th, it could be seen that the enemy forces were reeling back under British pressure. Tanks and armoured cars of the armoured divisions were quick to exploit another breach in the enemy lines and dashed in. Within a short time the vehicles of the

Derbyshire Yeomanry and the 11th Hussars reached the outskirts of Tunis. With the enemy defences breaking down in several other points, the British breakthrough became an avalanche, and as enemy resistance continued to collapse, the above two regiments rushed forward to enter Tunis and reach the centre by the afternoon. At the same time the American 2nd Corps had entered Bizerta.

By May 8th all enemy resistance in Tunis and Bizerta had been completely subdued. The next few days were to see final mopping up operations, with the remaining Axis troops in the northern sector laying down arms to the Americans. The climax was reached on May 12th with von Arnim and Messe surrendering all the remaining Axis troops in Tunisia, which brought up the total of enemy killed or captured to over 600,000. British losses totalled 220,000.

On May 13th Alexander declared the official completion of the Tunisian campaign. It was done by a simple message to Winston Churchill. But behind it, there was the meaningful realisation that the whole of the North African coast was in Allied hands, making the Mediterranean safer, and for warships and merchantmen to ply across as they pleased. It was a wonderful and a historic achievement. But the struggle had not yet finished. And all eyes were now looking in a north easterly direction towards Sicily. That was going to be the next target.

CHAPTER X

LEAP TO SICILY AND ITALY

Hardly had the French North African issue been settled that the public in Britain and the United States, with no inkling of what had already been decided at the Casablanca Conference, began to clamour again for an immediate Second Front. This was being hinted wherever people met. It was reappearing in slogans on walls of buildings and factories. Notwithstanding what progress had been made on the Russian Front, Soviet troops were still locked in deadly battles, and President Roosevelt could not help shirk having to tell these allies again that notwithstanding his unwise promise to Molotov, there was still not going to be an invasion of France in 1943. Because now it was Sicily's turn.

None of this was surprising any of the leaders. Because after all, the American side of the Combined Chiefs of Staff, composed of Admiral Ernest King, General George C. Marshal and General H.H. Arnold had during the Casablanca Conference expressed themselves of being in favour of a Second Front in France rather than in Sicily After winding up the operation in French North Africa they had said, and which they had considered only as a diversion, they should go back to discuss a direct strike at Germany. It had only been the British side, made up of General Brooke, Admiral Dudley Pound and Air Chief Marshal Portal that had considered the time was not yet ripe for a cross channel assault. There had also been mentioned the possibility of an operation against Sardinia, but ultimate preference was for Sicily, which was also strongly subscribed to by Winston Churchill. So Sicily it was to be. The Chiefs of Staff had as far as that January conference agreed on the various commanders to conduct the operation, now also code-named Husky. General Eisenhower was again to be Supreme Commander with General Harold Alexander as his Deputy. The army commanders were then to be General Montgomery and General Patton, with the respective admirals to command the naval forces; Admiral Bertram Ramsay for the British and Vice-Admiral H. Kent Hewitt for the American side. Overall command of the naval side was invested in Admiral Andrew Cunningham, and the airforces were to appartain to Air Chief Marshal Tedder. From that day each and every comander began to see to his preparations which were to materialise by the target date which was fixed for July 10th.

None was deluded in thinking that Hitler would not expect another assault in the Mediterranean after the conclusion of the French North African campaign. The most that one could hope for was that he would not be able to know where this was bound to strike. Germany had the disadvantage of possessing a long stretch of conquests in the Mediterranean. From the south of France to the Aegean Sea. All of them with their strategic advantages. Hitler felt the Allies would fall on Sardinia with its being the most likely place for an easy springboard jump into France. But Kesselring and the Italians strongly favoured Sicily. It had therefore to be the Allies to push him into a decision, and to have him take the wrong one.

It fell to the British Intelligence Service to devise an ingenious deception which was to have a place reserved for it in the halls of military history. All they had to do was to procure a corpse of a British officer, complete with uniform and an identity, to be supported by documents purposely planted on him. As well as a letter supposedly to be carried by him from Lieutenant-General Nye, the Vice-Chief of the Imperial General Staff, to General Alexander. The contents of the letter were made out to concern the planning of forthcoming operations, but with a hint between the lines that while it was the Allied intention to land in Sardinia and Greece, they were to cover this by false indications to mislead the enemy in thinking that the real objective was Sicily. Whether Hitler and his cronies would fall for this was not known. Anyway, the 'fixed' corpse was secretly dropped off the coast of Spain at a time and place from where it would be carried ashore. And so it was. Hardly had the corpse been washed on a Spanish beach that the documents it carried with the obvious story they implied, reached the German Intelligence Service, to plant a dilemma in the enemy's ranks. Kesselring did not budge from his original belief, but he was not all, and the rest were convinced, including Hitler, that the Allies would be attacking Sardinia and Greece. An indication of the successful outcome of the ruse came with some of the deployments that were soon being made. The four Italian divisions in Sardinia were immediately reinforced by the 90th Panzergrenadier Division. And in support of an eventual assault on that island Hitler sent General Student with his 11th Air Corps consisting of two parachute divisions to the South of France to be ready to fly and drop in Sardinia when this was invaded. Greece too was being reinforced with the 1st Panzer Division from France. It certainly looked as if the stratagem had worked.

Planning for the Sicilian invasion could not be easy. The more so with the Allies having already been involved in French North Africa where they had learned many lessons. Indeed there was still much to say on the original plan which, however, had eventually to be modified. One important change that cried to be made and was in fact done was not to repeat the mistake of having the American force under Patton make a front of its own, as was done in

Leap to Sicily and Italy

Algeria with the negative results it had obtained. So Patton was now being made to land much closer to Montgomery as a precaution against the possibility of any Axis counter stroke, which would thus have a more likely chance of failure if it were to be contained by the two armies instead of one. Another point that was eventually raised concerned the two small islands of Pantalleria and Limosa which lay in a strategic position in the Sicilian channel. Notwithstanding the dismal forebodings that arose because of the possibility that these islands might be fortified and which could delay Operation Husky, it was decided to eliminate them. So both islands were bombarded and then assaulted on June 11th, with both garrisons surrendering after only a few hours.

On the following day there was a surprise at Algiers when King George VI arrived incognito to pay a visit to the Allied fighting men in North Africa. British and American servicemen as well as some discerning civilians knew he was there when they saw him. Then, while there he expressed a wish to pay a visit to Malta. This was quickly arranged, but similarly kept a secret. He left for the island on June 19th in the light cruiser *Aurora*, which for the occasion was escorted by the destroyers *Eskimo, Jervis, Nubian* and *Lookout*. The King must have been eager to see Malta as the Maltese were wishing to see him. But news of the impending visit was given only at 5 a.m. on June 20th. This was only three hours before he was due to arrive. But it was enough for the Maltese.

When the sun rose in its fiery splendour on that day, there was the ant-like community of the island already on the move. From an early hour, men, women and children left home, work and school to hurry to the cities round Grand Harbour to find a place of vantage on the bastions. It was now no longer an empty harbour, particularly with the already gathering fleet for the impending invasion of Sicily. By the time *Aurora* was due, there was not a single empty space on the bastions and jetties all packed with humanity. For moments they had all been silent. Then as *Aurora* swung slowly towards the harbour entrance with the white dressed figure of the King standing on the bridge, the thousands of people broke into a roar of welcome. Those who had taken Union Jacks began to wave them; others used handkerchiefs. Those who had neither waved their hands. These were the people to whom a year back the King had awarded the George Cross in recognition of their resistance and heroism under German and Italian attacks.

Coming as it did at such a crucial time, the King's visit was like an interlude of peace that all were craving for. But it had by now become obvious to everyone that peace could only be attained through war. And with the King's departure, the Mediterranean returned to its business in preparing the way for the Sicilian invasion scheduled to take place in less than three weeks time.

Force H which had been temporarily depleted after its new commander Vice-Admiral Willis had moved to Britain, had the battleships *Nelson* and *Rodney* recalled to the Mediterranean and deployed. The battleships *King George V* and *Howe* were sent to Mers-el-Kebir in Oran, while *Nelson* and *Rodney* to Algiers. The *Valiant* and *Warspite* proceeded to Alexandria from where they too had convoys to escort. Vice-Admiral Willis then took four other battleships, the aircraft carriers *Formidable* and *Indomitable* with a destroyer screen and went cruising in the Ionian Sea. The 15th Cruiser Squadron under Rear-Admiral Harcourt consisting of *Newfoundland, Uganda, Orion* and *Mauritius*, as well as the 11th cruiser squadron under Commodore Agnew with *Aurora, Penelope, Cleopatra, Euryalus, Sirius* and *Dido* were assigned the bombarding of shore targets.

As days ran on, and June turned into July, Malta which was to be at the front, was bustling with activity. Its 231st Infantry Brigade which had been the mainstay of the island's land forces throughout its siege and battle was

Leap to Sicily and Italy

now going to be in Montgomery's spearhead. Convoy ships began arriving, bringing trucks, tanks, landrovers, amphibian vehicles, field guns and troops. These were not only British and Americans, but Syrians, Mauritius, Basutos and Palestinians. Every creek in the island's harbours was being filled with warships and landing craft, while Spitfires from the airfields, now packed with all types of aircraft, were on constant patrol. Even the small sister island of Gozo, never militarily utilized, was being shaken out of its lethargy by the Americans. They bulldozed fields to make a landing strip which was soon taking aircraft. The majority of the forces to take part in the invasion, however, could not be accommodated in Malta. These comprised Admiral Ramsay's task force with 795 vessels and 715 landing craft which carried the 5th and 50th Divisions brought over from the Eastern Mediterranean. Two more convoys came from Britain carrying the 1st Canadian Division. The American taskforce then, under Vice-Admiral H. Kent Hewitt was bringing 580 ships and 1,124 landing craft in two convoys which carried the 1st Infantry and 2nd Armoured Divisions, as well as the 3rd Infantry Division.

On July 2nd, bombers from Malta began to hammer the airfields in Sicily in an attempt to put them out of action until the invasion date. Indeed their efforts were successful, not only in destroying 200 aircraft but in forcing the Italians and Germans to move the rest to other airfields on the mainland. Then when all seemed to be ready, Generals Eisenhower and Alexander, and Admirals Andrew Cunningham and Ramsay arrived in Malta for the final go, and control of the operation. It was then on July 9th that trouble loomed ahead when the weather began to deteriorate.

There was a heavy wind which made the sea choppy, and as the hours flew it began to get worse. There seemed to be no doubt that landing barges were not likely to be able to make the crossing to Sicily. Even with the danger of some of them foundering. On the other hand one could not very well turn these hundreds of ships back after their anxious two day vigil in the open sea East and West of Malta. It would raise the hell of a confusion. As time approached for the departure of the landing craft to reach their Sicilian billet in time on the morrow there was an all round flair of excitement. It had to be a big decision. But they were allowed to go. And once they had gone there was no more scope of worrying about the big ships. Operation Husky got under way.

* * *

As it was, the biggest effect of the stormy weather was on the paratroopers and their gliders. The US 82nd Airborne Division was to be dropped in the Gela-Licata area, whilst the 1st Air Landing Brigade of the British 1st Airborne Division was intended for Syracuse where it was to seize the Ponte Grande bridge leading into the city. Its 1,200 men entrained in 137 gliders towed by 102 C-47s, 28 Albemarles and 7 Halifaxes must have got the worst of the storm. They picked their escort night intruder Hurricanes of 73 Squadron from Malta. These were to strafe searchlights. In anticipation of their landing there were also 55 Wellingtons bombing the Syracuse area, with 19 more bombing Catania. A further 19 attacked other targets. Only a dozen gliders managed to reach their allotted destinations. The rest drifted away with 69 of them coming down into the sea. But the seaborne forces kept their appointment.

* * *

At first dawn on July 10th, the American 7th Army under General Patton landed at Licata, Gela and Scoglietti in the south of Sicily. Twenty miles away to the East landed the Canadians, while the British 8th Army went ashore at two points between Syracuse and Cape Passero. All these landing operations were covered by an umbrella of fighters and fighter bombers from the Desert Air Force, XII

Leap to Sicily and Italy

Air Support Command as well as from Air Headquarters in Malta.

There was little or no resistance on all beaches, and the three forces were able to begin landing their detachments and overrun beach defences. It seemed to the Allied commanders as if the Italians long on the alert might have chosen that night to rest, assuming there would be no assault because of the weather. But it is more likely that Italian troops had by then lost their belligerent enthusiasm and were more inclined to save their skin and get out of it all. This is indicated by the many surrenders there were on the first day. Spitfires and P.40s of the escorting air forces flew 1092 sorties during the first day. Fighter-bombers attacked airfields and defence positions, while fighters took care of any intruding enemy aircraft. Ten Italian Macchi 200 fighters were shot down, as well as three JU 88s. There were 16 Allied aircraft lost through various causes. The first worthwhile resistance came on the second day from one of the two German divisions that were in Sicily at the time. The reformed Herman Goering Division, which had escaped from Tunisia, now re-equipped with the 36 ton Tiger tanks delivered a counter-attack on the American 1st Infantry Division at Gela. Because of the still prevailing bad weather the Americans had not yet unloaded most of their tanks, so the Germans found it easy to overrun them. They would have pushed them into the sea had the British navy not come to the rescue. Informed of what was happening, the British warships moved forward and bombarded the German forces. Most prominent in the attack was the monitor *Abercrombie* whose 15" guns blasted the German tanks to smithereens. The inimitable General Patton had to admit to Admiral Cunningham later that it was the navy that had saved the day for him. When another German column made a similar attack on the American 4th Division with identical results, it had also to be the British navy to stop them in the same way.

The Allied Air Forces had a busier second day with having to deal with several formations of JUs 88 as well as Italian fighters and fighter bombers. Nineteen enemy aircraft were shot down.

Montgomery's forces had in the meantime made more progress. They had occupied Pachino and Syracuse on the first day and began moving steadily towards Augusta and Catania. Augusta was indeed captured on July 11th, but Catania, Montgomery intended to assault it on the 13th. There was an important bridge over the river Simeto that had to be secured before the city could be approached. Indeed paratroopers were used, and they captured the bridge intact. But in the meantime General Student had sent one of his parachute divisions from the South of France to be dropped in this area, which captured the bridge back from the British. It took Montgomery's men a pitched battle and three days of heavy fighting to re-take the bridge and open the way for a continued advance. But rather than continuing towards Catania, Montgomery decided to move further inland, and this paid dividends. He was soon occupying Leonforte and other hill towns, as well as Nicosia which caused the German 15th Panzer Division to begin retreating eastwards. Axis air operations had by now obviously decreased. But on July 19th the Luftwaffe made a final attempt in attacking Allies' shipping at Augusta with 15 dive-bombers. This was like an answer to prayers by the pilots of 162 Squadron frustrated by inactivity who lost no time in intercepting the enemy, shooting six aircraft down.

Following the occupation of Pachino, use was made of its airfield by 244 Wing. The Americans followed suit after having occupied the airfields at Licata and Ponte Olivio. As further airfields like Cassibile, Lentini and Comiso continued falling to the Allies, squadrons kept hopping from one airfield to the other. It was not long when with the exception of five resident squadrons, all the Spitfires at Malta were transferred to operate on Sicilian soil.

The American 7th Army had by now also broken enemy resistance. Patton might have profited by a decision by Kesselring to have German forces abandon the West of Sicily. Which might therefore have left only the Italians to stand in the American General's way. Indeed he was being handicapped more by blockages and demolished roads rather than enemy troops. Patton found the answer by using the navy to carry his forces by sea every time a heavy blockage was met, and to have them landed behind the enemy lines. And this hastened his advance towards Palermo. This was captured on the 22nd, while another column occupied Marsala.

Little did the British and Americans think that their old friend and enemy Field Marshal Rommel was in Italy at that time.

Yes, he was in command of Army Group B in Northern Italy, with headquarters near Lake Garda. This was a new command given to him by Hitler after he had come out completely recovered from the hospital at Semmering. Strictly speaking his new role was not an operational one, but he was acting as a military adviser. With the Allied advance in Sicily having taken a faster stride Hitler began thinking the worst of the Italians. One rumour which reached him, however, was that the Allies intended to start another front in Greece. So on July 24th he sent Rommel to Athens to advise what was to be done. But he had hardly been there twenty four hours when on July 25th there was the news of Mussolini's downfall. He had been overthrown by his own people. Hitler recalled Rommel immediately, and there might have occurred the slight possibility of asking him to take up arms again against his old enemies. But it is supposed that Kesselring would have resisted this for old time's sake. Besides, the situation in Sicily had already become critical and there were no visible means of how to stem the Allied advance.

Hitler sent a new division to Sicily now – the 29th Panzergrenadier. As well as General Hube to take over the island's defence. His instructions were not to try and defeat the enemy. But to delay his advance until the Axis forces could be evacuated to the mainland across the Straits. Sicily was given up as lost, and the Germans were now doing their best to save about 100,000 of German and Italian troops there to have them available to fight on the mainland another day.

The 8th Army occupied Catania on August 5th and continued in pursuit of the retreating Germans. By the 14th these held only Messina. Obviously as the last point of departure for their evacuation to the mainland. The two Allied armies were now rushing towards this port. And this gave scope for another of General Patton's high handed jokes when he rushed one of his patrols to Messina to be in place when Montgomery's men entered the city on August 17th.

What was left for Alexander now was to draw out statistics of what the Sicilian campaign had cost. There had been 5,500 Germans captured as prisoners. And considering that there had been about 40,000 others amongst those evacuated he could conclude that there could not have been more than a few thousands that were killed. The Allied casualties were 12,843 British in killed, missing and wounded, with 9,968 Americans. Allied commanders considered this to have been a fair price for the ultimate result obtained on August 17th, when there remained not a single Axis soldier in Sicily. After only a few weeks campaign, that battle was over and won.

* * *

If the Allies wanted to get the Italian campaign over because of the earmarked invasion of France, the Italians were now not less anxious to get out of it all. Following the formation of a new government after the downfall of Mussolini on July 25th, Italian intentions and efforts were directed towards reaching some form of a separate armistice with the Allies. But this was wrought with several difficulties. And they knew it.

Leap to Sicily and Italy

It wasn't a question of overcoming national reluctance to swallow the pill of "unconditional surrender" about which the Allies had already agreed at the Casablanca Conference. Because, notwithstanding the sense of humility there was attached to it, Marshal Badoglio knew that eventually it would have to be accepted.

But there had been the first difficulty experienced when as far as July there had been the initial Italian attempts to get in touch with the Allies. Two attempts through the British and American ambassadors at the Vatican had failed. More through the Allies seemingly being reluctant and more prone to avoid the issue than for anything else. Then there was the other difficulty through fear of the Germans, and this made the new Italian government titubate in trying different ways of approach.

Hitler had never trusted the Italians, and his fears were realized on July 25th when the Duce was deposed. Five days later German troops were already infiltrating through the North of Italy under the excuse of safeguarding supply routes from any surprise Allied attack. But the real intention was twofold – to put fear into the Italians lest they would go ahead with asking for a separate surrender, and to be in position should notwithstanding everything, this would materialise. Not less than eight German divisions flowed into Northern Italy. With Rommel being still there, Hitler now put his mind at ease that if it should come to the worst, he could always let him take command and move southwards. General Student too, was flown with his remaining parachute division from France. He was stationed in Ostia, the beach of Rome, to ward off any eventual Allied landing or parachute drop.

If the Allies did not give too much importance to these moves behind the scenes, it might have been because of what was going on in their own camp. The Americans had as far back as May expressed themselves as being against starting an Italian campaign after Sicily. No doubt after having learned at their own expense that these operations take time and sacrifices, and both of which they could not afford now that they were set on the operation in France, and escalation in the Pacific. It was only now when they learned of Italian feelings about surrender that they began to thaw. But they still insisted to have something more concrete in the way of an approach, which had as yet not been forthcoming.

The first tangible sign of an Italian move reached the Allies on August 17th, after Badoglio had sent General Castellano to Lisbon with a message for the British ambassador in Portugal asking him to negotiate for an armistice. This time General Eisenhower played up and sent his Chief-of-Staff Bedell Smith and Brigadier Kenneth Strong to talk with the Italians. There was no doubt left during the negotiations that followed that more than anything else, it was fear of the Germans that predominated over the Italian attitude. Castellano was allowed no quarter to negotiate and he had to submit to the Allied condition of unconditional surrender. But the Italians had also made a condition of their own from which they would not budge. If there was to be an armistice this would have to come into effect concurrently with an Allied landing in Italy. And since this coincided with the Allies' latest intentions there was no difficulty in accepting it. So the last preparations got under way.

As for the armistice it was agreed to have this signed secretly on September 3rd. On that day a British naval squadron under the command of Rear-Admiral McGregor, and composed of the battleships *Nelson, Rodney, Warspite* and *Valiant* carried out a heavy bombardment of coastal batteries at Reggio and Cape Pillaro. Then at first dawn, covered by a further bombardment by cruisers and monitors General Montgomery crossed the Straits of Messina and landed the 5th British and the 1st Canadian Divisions on the Italian mainland. The force was under the command of General Miles Dempsey. There was no resistance, and the few Italian troops found in the area offered to help the British troops to unload stores, rather than fighting them. They couldn't have known of the Italian surrender, because this was still a guarded secret. Not even Montgomery knew about it. The news reached him through Alexander two days later as his troops continued with their advance, still without meeting any opposition.

The fact that the Germans had abandoned that part of Italy makes it evident that they must have correctly anticipated Allied intentions of landing further up Italy's shin. Which would threaten to cut off any forces fighting in the south. And truly enough, on September 5th an Allied armada of about 700 ships had sailed from North Africa carrying a spearhead of 55,000 troops, and a further 115,000 for the planned landing code-named Operation Avalanche, under the command of General Mark Clark. Even with such a hefty operation the American commander was hoping to surprise the Germans. And he had insisted on having no preliminary bombardments. This might have been a silly notion of his. So much so that Kesselring had by then already moved six divisions under General Vietinghoff to Paola, which was quite close to Salerno where the Allied armada intended to land. This could have been neither guesswork nor a coincidence. Then on the afternoon of September 8th the armada was spotted, and the cat was let out of the bag.

The Luftwaffe began attacking the Allied convoys, and Allied air defence was soon forthcoming by aircraft from a carrier squadron made up of the aircraft carriers *Unicorn, Hunter, Stalker, Attacker* and *Battler*, under Rear-Admiral Vian who had his flag in the cruiser *Euryalus*. The squadron continued moving with the armada, providing cover until it reached the beaches. A couple of hours later then, there was the important announcement made, and the world knew of Italy's surrender. In the early hours of the following day, September 9th then, General Clark's Fifth Army landed between Salerno and Paestum. The fight for Italy had begun.

There were difficulties encountered by both the northern and southern flanks of the landing. In the northern flank where the British landed the 10th Corps composed of the 46th and 56th Divisions which had to go to different beaches, there was a mix up when both landed at the same place. This made them more vulnerable to attacks by the Germans who were immediately on the scene, causing them heavy casualties. Further north there were landed also some companies of American Rangers and British commandos who also found stiff resistance. In the Southern flank where the Americans had landed the 46th Division at four points close to Paestum the main difficulty seemed to have been caused by the American's persistance in having no covering bombardment, thus coming under heavy German fire without replying to it. By the end of the first day, with the help of a naval bombardment which they had taken the initiative to call for, the British forces had pushed two miles inland. The Americans had somehow pushed a column forward which penetrated up to 5 miles into the enemy lines. But that was all. And both allied forces had thus failed to achieve any of the intended objectives for that first day.

While this was going on there was a silent but more significant drama taking place with the surrender of the Italian fleet. It had been agreed by the Italians that as soon as their surrender was announced, their fleet was to leave its base at La Spezia and make for North Africa, from where it was to be escorted to Malta. Indeed with the declaration on September 8th, the battleships *Roma*, *Italia* and *Vittorio Veneto* left La Spezia in the afternoon. During the night there was a rendezvous made with 5 cruisers and seven destroyers which had left Genoa. However, whilst they were on their way there was a message supposedly from the Italian Admiralty ordering them to change venue and proceed to Sardinia. They should have never obeyed those instructions. But they did, and whilst on their way they were attacked by German aircraft which hit the *Italia*. Then the *Roma* was hit by a new type of a radio controlled bomb, and was sunk. The rest immediately changed course and proceeded to North Africa as originally detailed.

None could appreciate the significance of this event more than the people of Malta. Their country had been mostly involved with Italy since the thirties when the much vaunted Italian fleet, which had been the mainstay of the new Fascist government had started the race in armaments and pique which had eventually led to this struggle. And which was now nearing its conclusion. From the morning of September 9th crowds of people began flocking to vantage points trying to get a glimpse of the Italian fleet that according to spreading rumours would be going to the island. But there was nothing to be seen on that day. The expected spectacle materialized on September 10th, when in the afternoon the battleships *Vittorio Veneto, Andrea Doria* and *Caio Diulio*, with these last two having left from Taranto, as well as eight cruisers and eight destroyers appeared approaching Malta in a line. The crowds that had again gathered to watch the spectacle went into tumultous cheering. Not for the Italians, but for the British warships that were leading them – the old darlings *Warspite* and *Valiant*, with the accompanying destroyers on the flanks. This was only the beginning. In the days that followed there were still more Italian waships flowing in to surrender. The battleship *Giulio Cesare*, and the seaplane carrier *Miraglia*. A number of destroyers, submarines and torpedo boats. Until there were 65 ships in all. And Admiral Cunningham was at last to send his famous signal to the Admiralty saying that the Italian battle fleet was lying at anchor under the guns of the fortress of Malta.

In a way this could have been considered as the end of the battle of the Mediterranean. But on the other hand British and American forces were still locked in the struggle in Italy where things were not going so well for them. No element of the Allied fleets could as yet go about without the risk of meeting some German U Boat. Sardinia, Greece, Crete and Northern Italy still housed elements of the Luftwaffe ready to pounce on anything coming within their range. These risks had to be eliminated before one could say that the struggle for the Mediterranean would have come to an end. And this more than on anything else seemed to depend on the fierce battle going on in Italy.

In three days' fighting at the 5th Army's beachhead the situation had changed so many times. The British 56th Division had pushed forward and occupied Montecorrino airfield and Battiipaglia, only to be thrown out again by vigorous German counter attacks. The other British Division, the 46th had occupied Salerno but could not push on further. The American 45th Division too had made a substantial advance of 10 miles, only to be pushed back again. Thus all elements of the 5th Army found themselves confined to their original beachheads at the end of the third day. It had been programmed that they should have reached Naples by now, but they were still more than thirty miles away from the town. On September 12th after having for the second time occupied Battipaglia the British were pushed out again with heavy losses. This time the Germans were quick to exploit the situation and jumped into the breach opened between the two flanks of the 5th Army to hit harder at the Americans. These were driven back to within a half mile of the beach where they had landed. General Clark's answer to this critical situation was to ask to have his forces re-embarked and re-landed on the British beachhead.

Neither Eisenhower nor Alexander were impressed by this decision. And their reaction was immediate. Within hours there was dropped part of the American 82nd Parachute Division under General Matthew Ridgeway to bolster Clark's forces, while every available aircraft was sent forward to participate in a series of attacks on German troops and positions. Between 16 and 18 warships too started a systematic bombardment.

No force on earth could have withstood such attacks. The Germans had to stop for breath and the position was stabilized on the 15th. From all reports where their troops had been hit, the Allied burst of action had been successful. Now Kesselring had also to consider Montgomery and his 8th Army who had been rather slow and silent, but certainly very effective. When Taranto had been evacuated after Italy's surrender, the 1st Airborne Division of the 8th Army had occupied the town and harbour by what had been code-named Operation Slapstick. No resistance had been encountered and the British division had then pushed on to Brindisi which it occupied two days later. Now these same troops were aproaching Bari. But it wasn't this division that was worrying Kesselring. It was the rest of the 8th Army that had split into two columns. The 30th Corps moving up along the coast to join General Clark's troops, and the 13th Corps which was pushing up further inland and in the right position to outflank the German forces.

There was hope on the 16th when the first 8th Army patrols reached the 5th Army. It was a black day for the navy, however, when *Warspite* was hit by a German radio-controlled bomb and put out of action. On the 20th then, Canadian troops from the spearhead of Montgomery's inner column occupied Potenza. This brought the Allied forces in the level with the front running straight from Salerno on the western coast right to Bari, by now occupied, on the eastern coast. This showed the red light to Kesselring who ordered a tactical withdrawal to a line twenty miles north of Naples.

For the first time there seemed to be a more relaxed air in the Allied lines. Their forces from west to east began to advance slowly. Now Italian hopes were raised when the population in Naples and the surrounding countryside began to hear the muffled thunder of artillery getting near each day. There was much speculation although none knew what was happening. The 5th Army's slow advance had by September 23rd developed into an offensive with the 46th and 56th divisions now supported by the 7th Armoured Brigade taken from the 7th Army pushing forward steadily. Their going was made difficult by German battalions fighting a rearguard action in the many mountain passes. But only until September 26th, by which time the main German forces had made good their withdrawal. The rest was relatively easy. On September 28th, the Allies occupied Nocera. On October 1st then, they entered Naples.

The capture of Naples was an important achievement. Winston Churchill had described it as an important and pregnant victory. But the Germans were far from being finished. As was to be evidenced by their newly evident interest in the Aegean which was now ticking like a time bomb.

CHAPTER XI

FLARE-UP IN THE AEGEAN

Britain's interest in the Aegean can be traced to the early months of the struggle for the Mediterranean. As far back as November 1940, when an enthusiastic Churchillian whim to attack Pantalleria found no response, Admiral Cunningham had expressed his preference for an assault on the Dodecanese Islands. And notwithstanding the cold reception given to it, this suggestion was never put completely away. Indeed, what embers had remained were soon being rekindled enough to generate the first Mediterranean Combined operation by No. 50 Commando against the small island of Casteloriso on 25th February 1941.

This small island lying about 80 miles east of Rhodes and some 150 miles west of Cyprus boasted of a useful harbour which could be used by light elements of the fleet. More than this there was the likelihood of the island being used as a springboard for an assault on the rest of the archipelago. This plan, however, misfired. All because of the destroyer *Hereward* mistakingly withdrawing from the island where it had gone to deliver a message. Thus affording the chance to Italian reinforcements from Rhodes being landed in Casteloriso to neutralize the situation before the British main forces reached there. Three days later the island had to be abandoned, with another blunder being recorded in the annals of British military history.

More than the consternation this blunder caused in London and Cairo there were also the recriminations to follow. It is small wonder that the stigma left by this episode might have instigated American opposition to any further Allied involvement in the Aegean. The only mitigation came when Britain revived intentions of attacking the Dodecanese, but presenting their occupation as a way of creating a situation in which Turkey could be enticed to become an active ally. When the tide of war had then turned in Britain's favour in 1943 there was the additional influence of the need to forestall any Russian intentions for the Balkans as well as for what intentions there were on the Allied side to liberate Greece. Winston Churchill did not fail to keep on with his usual prodding, and plan after plan began to be made for the occupation of the Dodecanese without any of them ever materializing. Although ultimate objectives might have changed with the times and inherent developments, the lure of the islands seemed, however, to have remained.

The Aegean had in the meantime appealed to the Germans as well. They had occupied Crete and came to know it was a useful area from where to strike at British convoys. Also that it was a useful counter with which they too could influence Turkey away from the Allies. Only that they did not trust Italy who occupied the islands. So, in their own cunning way the Germans began to filter in. Following an agreement with the Italian Air Command in the Aegean, the first German troops arrived in Rhodes in January 1943, supposedly to train the Italians. But they never left, and notwithstanding Italian protests, they were soon controlling the more salient points of the island. Thinking no doubt of the eventuality of Italy getting out of the war. Whatever plans they had in this regard were kept secret. But after the downfall of Mussolini all caution was thrown to the wind, and the Germans began to strengthen their foothold in the island. It had now become not only a question of taking more troops and guns to Rhodes, but there was a string of high ranking officers visiting the island to inspect defences, like Admiral Fricke, the German Naval Commander Group South, and Field Marshall Kesselring.

None of this escaped the attention of the British High Command, and a decision on whether Rhodes should be attacked or not became imperative. But any Aegean operation had to be subordinate to what was going on in the Mediterranean, and plans kept changing before being put into operation. This did not in any way help to get the much needed support from the Americans. These were now convinced that such plans were only of a British periphereal strategy. And they might have been right, which, however, did not hold the British Commanders from going ahead with what was to become a purely British venture.

Following the successful landings in Sicily the time seemed opportune to finalize matters. And as barges and Tank Landing Ships now no longer required in the Mediterranean were being sent to the Far East, someone providentially kept five back. They would be enough for an operation against Rhodes. There was also the 8th Indian Division handy, which was soon put on intensive training. Sherman tanks which replaced the old Crusaders were soon being made waterproof. And General Wilson began seeing his last plan taking shape, to the extent that it was code-named Operation Accolade. Final instructions were issued to the elements taking part, now known as Force 292. Infantry landing barges were dispersed to Alexandria, Haifa and Beirut from where they were to embark the troops, and the date for the assault was fixed for October 20th.

Then on August 26th there was a thunderbolt by the Combined Chiefs of Staff. Acting on a decision taken at the Quebec Conference, they ordered every available tank landing ship together with a headquarters ship and cargo vessels in the Mediterranean to proceed immediately to the Far East for the Burma campaign. The 8th Indian Division too, on which depended the whole operation, was put under orders for the Central Mediterranean. Thus, overnight, General Wilson found himself without the men and means of transport required for his assignment. Operation Accolade was off. But rather than scrapping everything it was decided to substitute it by a smaller venture. One which was adaptedly code-named Operation Microbe. No longer intended for Rhodes, but directed towards the occupation of the three smaller islands of Cos, Leros and Samos, which could be undertaken by a small force needing more brain than brawn. It was for this reason that there was recourse again to the Long Range Desert Group. This unit which had first been formed up in 1940 had long established a reputation with its reconaissance and raiding activities behind enemy lines in North Africa. It had stopped functioning after the fall of Tunisia. Now it was re-activated for Operation Microbe. To work conjointly with it there was another unit called upon, originally being the Folboat Section of No. 8 Commando, now being recalled the Special Boat Section (SBS). It was in fact this unit which on September 9th spearheaded the operation by occupying again the small island of Casteloriso. There were only sixty men in the assault force, with a few anti-aircraft gunners and RAF signallers. But with Italy having surrendered on the previous day, the 300 strong Italian garrison on the island welcomed the British. Thus encouraged the two British units then moved to occupy the other three islands of Cos, Leros and Samos on September 12th.

The Americans relented from the stand they had taken and helped to divert the Germans' attention by a strike at Rhodes with 38 Liberators. As for the Italian garrisons on the three islands, all in a pitiful state, the arrival of the British was a godsend, and they cooperated. None, however, was deluded in thinking that things were indeed

Flare-Up in the Aegean

going to be so easy. On Cos there was the only airfield of Antimachia, and steps were immediately taken to make it ready to receive the first RAF aircraft. Two Beaufighters landed soon after, and before dusk there were the first six Spitfires. In the days that followed more troops and equipment were flown in, with Dakotas keeping a shuttle service from Egypt and Cyprus. The Navy joined in too, and the British destroyers *Faulknor* and *Eclipse*, with the Greek *Queen Olga* began to sweep the sea around the islands for any enemy activity. But there was nothing of this in evidence until the 16th. Indeed, the Germans had only learned of the British operation on the 15th. And this after seven Junkers 52 transport aircraft on a supply run to Rhodes flew close to Cos and were pounced upon by two Spitfires. One of the Germans was shot down, but the rest lived to tell the tale.

After the Italian surrender the Germans had taken absolute control of Rhodes. There had been some sporadic resistance by the Italian garrison, but the end came soon, with some 40,000 Italians laying down their arms. Anticipating an Allied move the Germans then turned their eyes on Cos which they considered to be next in importance after Rhodes. On September 16th they sent a sole Junkers Ju.88 to fly over the small island and report. But it did not return. So they followed up on the following day with five ME's 109 which swept in by surprise on Cos, strafing the airfield and destroying three Dakotas. A second strike soon after destroyed two Spitfires. The cat was out of the bag, and both Germans and British knew of the imminent flare-up in that part of the Aegean.

Much as the British had continued to strengthen their position in the three newly occupied islands, things didn't look so good. There was first of all the lack of the right kind of troops they could afford to send. Apart from a few seasoned battalions which General Wilson could spare from the 231st Infantry Brigade which he still controlled, he had nothing much. These battalions, like the Buffs, irish Fusiliers, the Durham Light Infantry, the West Kents, and others, had indeed been re-blooded in Sicily after their long garrison duties in Malta during her siege and could be used to repulse any attempted landing by the enemy. But they could not be expected to cover the airfield of Antimachia as well, which was already being attacked by the Germans, and was bound to continue-drawing the enemy's special attention. The alternative was to try and defend the airfield by units of the RAF Regiment. And these were soon being collected from all over the Mediterranean command, all of them being devoid of any battle experience, and what's more, being equipped with obsolete weapons, like Hispano anti-aircraft guns.

I can still remember those days myself when I was serving with the RAF in Malta. An urgent call was made for all those awaiting a commission who would be given a quick one in the RAF Regiment. The only condition laid down was that they would be given a week's training, then they would be posted on operations. I was almost caught myself. Those who answered the call found themselves in Cos within a fortnight, and were pressed in defending Antimachia airfield. Indeed this could not readily receive enough aircraft for the impending flare-up. But then there were supporting forces being earmarked to help from Cyprus and North Africa which between them comprised four Beaufighter squadrons, three Baltimore squadrons, one Hudson, and three Spitfire squadrons, as well as No. 38 of Wellington bombers (which I later joined). There were also a Photo Reconaissance Unit and two long range Hurricane squadrons.

Against this the Germans had built up a force of some 235 aircraft comprising Me 109's fighters, Junkers Ju 88 bombers, Junkers Ju 87 "Stuka' dive-bombers, and Heinkel He.111 bombers. Most of these had been flown to Rhodes from France and the Russian front, with the latter being still painted white. For good measure there were

Flare-Up in the Aegean

also some Arado float-planes for use in narrow sealanes between the islands, and a few Italian Macchi 202 fighters. This was a fairly powerful force, which was better placed than the RAF since it was backed by better facilities. Apart from the three airfields in Rhodes, the Germans had provided facilities in many of the islands they now occupied in the Aegean. These comprised Lemnos, Mytilene, Chios, the Sporades, the Cyclades (except for Icaria), Kasos, Kithira, and Antikithira. Besides, of course, Crete and Scarpanto which they already held. The British too had extended their tentacles, and after Cos, Leros and Samos, established themselves in Simi, Stampalia and Icaria. But besides the airfield of Antimachia they had only managed to improvise two landing strips at Lambia and Marmri, both in Cos.

The attacks by the Luftwaffe on Cos soon developed into a pattern of gradually increasing tempo. With its being constantly cratered the airfield was more often than not being made unserviceable, and troops had to be constantly on the alert to fill up craters and make it serviceable again. These were the same troops who might have been better used had they been allowed to dig themselves in and prepare to meet the now more imminent invasion. Two British and one Greek destroyers were now taken off their patrol duties to help in transporting more troops and stores to Cos. But on September 26th *Intrepid* and the Greek *Queen Olga* were sunk off Leros. On September 29th, the airfield of Antimachia was hopelessly put out of action. So all flying was transferred to the air-strips. A battalion of Greek paratroops brought over as reinforcements was diverted to Leros. Stores and supplies had similarly to be sent there. Confusion reigned everywhere, and it was in the midst of this confusion that an aircraft reported sighting the German invasion fleet on October 1st in the vicinity of Naxos. There was nothing to intercept the enemy, and the only Italian destroyer *Euro*, which was at Leros was sunk on that same day. A call for help went to Alexandria, and the British destroyer *Aldenham* and the

Greek *Themistocles* and *Miaoulis* sailed immediately from there. They were certainly far below what was required. What would have helped more to change the outcome were the battle-ships *King George V* and *Howe* which were then lying idle at Alexandria, but under orders to sail to the west. However, the Admiralty seems to have failed to appreciate the Aegean danger enough to change those orders. What's more, another four destroyers, the *Faulknor, Fury, Echo* and *Eclipse* were in harbour to proceed as escorts to the battleships. Then at sunrise on October 3rd, the German invasion fleet appeared off Cos.

Every available RAF aircraft from Cyprus was immediately launched into attack on the Germans which, however, put up a solid wall of anti-aircraft fire to smash the British planes. At the same time a heavy and continuous air bombardment by the Germans was delivered on the airfields and military positions. Cos became like hell, and the Germans proceeded with their landing.

Later in the day General Eisenhower, at last aroused from the unreasonable stand he had taken, signalled to the Combined and both British Chiefs of Staff saying that as the Middle East was having some trouble and needs help against increasing hostile air power he was throwing the entire Strategic Air Force against the enemy. And indeed heavy bombings of German bases were to start on the following day. The C-in-C Middle East too now asked for maximum Naval assistance. And from Malta there was despatched the 12th Cruiser Squadron made up of *Aurora, Penelope, Sirius* and *Dido*, together with a flotilla of 'Hunt' destroyers. The destroyers *Petard* and *Penn* left fromTaranto harbour. But none of these warships arrived at their destination before the night of 4th/5th. By then Cos was already captured by the Germans.

The Battle of the Aegean seemed to be as good as lost. No matter how much the Strategic Air Command attacked German installations in Athens, Eleusis, Salonika, Rhodes and Crete, nothing would dislodge General

Flare-Up in the Aegean

Mueller and his troops from Cos. But could this at least prevent them from getting to the other islands? At a meeting held on October 9th between General Eisenhower and the Commanders-in-Chief in the Mediterranean, including Admiral of the Fleet Andrew Cunningham it was decided to try and hold to Leros and Samos. They were, however, aware that this could hardly be undertaken without embarking on a major operation for which none was deluded in thinking that there could be the necessary forces available. However, the British High Command seemed to have been shocked by the ease with which Cos had fallen. And this made them adopt a more realistic policy about the Aegean. Some might have attributed this to the long finger of conscience pointing at the blunder so capriciously made. Others saw in it the repetition of other occasions when mistakes came to be rectified too late. And to support this opinion there was the abandoning of the island of Simi coming only three days after the decision was taken to hold to Leros and Samos.

As always happens in any theatre of operations there is always one position, very often an island, which is endowed with possessions that make it the key to control over a wide area. After the quick fall of Cos, this situation fitted Leros, more than any other place. Leros is a small island of about 30 square miles. Its coastline is deeply indented with bays, two of which, Alinda and Gurna almost cut the island in two. Under the Italians it was heavily defended, and was used as a submarine base. But because of its hilly nature there could never be an airfield. There were now new considerations influencing the holding of the island which was being seen as a bastion that could inflict much irritation on the Germans. More than this it could hold down their forces in the Aegean indefinitely. Also, if the fall of Cos had wrecked Operation Accolade, Leros could very well resuscitate it by affording the chance to have the operation mounted again in spring. It was this belief more than anything else that had influenced the British to fight as they did in Leros. More than a fight, theirs became an epic to go down into the annals of British military history, and to be thus recorded.

The fact could not be escaped that in reinforcing Leros and Samos for the now imminent second round of the battle in the Aegean the British had to contend with shortages and limitations, both in troops and equipment. Even if aircraft were available, the only airfield in the area had been that of Antimachia which was lost with Cos. To rectify this to some extent, there were allocated long-range Lightning fighter squadrons from North Africa. It therefore became quite obvious that the onus of defence now fell on the Royal Navy. Naval reinforcements that had arrived in the Aegean too late to save Cos were now to be left there. The meeting between the Commanders-in-Chief that had been held on October 9th was Admiral Cunningham's last direct involvement in this theatre of operations for he had already been designated as First Lord of the Admiralty to replace Sir Dudley Pound who was dying. His place as Commander-in-Chief Levant was taken by Vice-Admiral Willis who took up his appointment on October 15th when the navy was involved in some of its deadly engagements with the Luftwaffe. One day he was complimenting the submarine *Unruly* for sinking the ship *Bulgaria* carrying German reinforcements to Cos. And the "Nostril' Force made up of the cruisers *Penelope* and *Sirius* with the destroyers *Faulknor* and *Fury* for laying havoc with a German convoy of small transports, trawlers and lighters in the Straits of Scarpanto. On the next he had to commiserate with the *Penelope* after it was hit and put out of action by German Stukas. The whole force accompanied the stricken ship to Alexandria, while 'Credential' Force took over. This was composed of the anti-aircraft cruiser *Carlisle* with the desroyers *Petard Panther, Aldenham* and the Greek *Themistocles*. These too had their intermittent protection by Lightnings, but there were occasions when they had to be alone. It was in such circumstances that the Luftwaffe would pounce. And after such a nerve racking attack by Stukas, the *Panther* was sunk, while the

Carlisle was put permanently out of action. These were the kind of days that heralded Willis's command. Days full of the whine and howl of Stukas which many had thought to have been something safely in the past. Not that this worried him. He knew what to expect, and this can be seen from his first memorandum issued to the men of his command two days after his appointment.

> You are being called upon at the present time to undertake a task which involves a most strenuous routine. The garrisons of Samos and Leros, which include some 2,500 British troops, nearly all of whom are the old defenders of Malta, are dependent very largely on the Navy's efforts. The enemy is collecting a formidable invasion force for use against these islands but this force cannot achieve its object if we maintain in the area a naval force capable of destroying his assault craft and shipping. His own naval forces are insignificant.
>
> The scale of enemy air attack is considerable, but by operating at dark, lying up in neutral waters for most of the day, it is hoped that this threat is bearable. Gradually the bombing of enemy airfields is reducing his air potential. His crews are not so well trained or so determined as they used to be, and the experiences of last week have shown that our ships can continue to operate in the Aegean with very little air cover and from time to time damage may have to be accepted.
>
> There is evidence to show that while we are able to maintain naval forces on the present scale in the Aegean, the enemy hesitates to launch his invasion. Therefore in the defence

of our small garrisons it is essential that we should continue our present operations and endeavour to destroy the enemy's shipping and landing craft until his plans are defeated. The Royal Navy has never failed to do its utmost for the British Army in difficult situations and I know it will do it again.

This could be said to have given in a nutshell the plan of operations for the Navy in the running battle it was having with the Luftwaffe. Which, notwithstanding the losses in ships and men inflicted on the Navy, was indeed holding back the Germans from invading Leros. This assault was first intended for October 8th, but the sinking of a convoy then had made the Germans postpone the operation for the 11th. Then again, General Mueller, pressed by the heavy losses that continued to be incurred in his shipping, realized he was bound to have a serious supply situation on his hands, and had to postpone again. On October 17th then, while Vice-Admiral Willis was issuing his memorandum, the Germans were indeed seriously considering to drop the assault altogether. In the meantime occupying the islands of Calchi and Levitha which were not defended. On this same day too, following the hitting and damaging of the cruiser *Sirius* the Navy gave up sending cruisers right into the Aegean. They were ordered to keep away. And they could go into the Aegean only enough to give destroyers radar cover and direct British fighters during attacks. This placed a heavier burden on destroyers which was reflected in the *Hurworth* and the *Eclipse* being sunk on 22nd and 24th October respectively. The *Hursley* and the Greek *Adrias* were severely damaged on the 17th and 22nd. When the cruiser *Aurora* broke the rule and ventured in, on October 30th, she was hit and damaged.

However, even from the drama and carnage of sinking troopships, the destruction of British warships, and the hundreds of aerial dogfights in the always escalating bat

Flare-Up in the Aegean 197

tle, the Germans finally got enough reinforcements, mostly in ferries and lighters brought from France and the Netherlands, to enable them to mount the intended assault on Leros. Their troops were put on large scale landing exercises in Lavrion Gulf to the north of Athens. British intelligence received reports on this well in time, and recce flights over Greece were soon bringing confirmatory photographs. Then on November 5th there were no more landing craft to be seen in the bay. Instead, they were traced to a fleet, into which they must have amassed, which was moving eastward. There seemed to be no doubt this was the invasion fleet intended for Leros.

Both the Navy and the RAF were now ordered to attack it. But the enemy fleet moving slowly from island to island by night, and sheltering by day, soon proved to be very elusive. Destroyers and aircraft searched the many islands, and attacked what craft they found. But they never managed to get to any substantial part of the enemy force. The biggest concentration was sighted by Beaufighters at Naxos harbour on November 7th, protected by a strong umbrella of Me.109's and Arado 196's. However, the British attacks were sterile, and three Beaufighters were lost for their troubles. On that same day the Luftwaffe launched the first of a series of heavy bombardments on Leros, as if to confirm the imminent invasion. The British now went into a bustle which was not bereft of a certain amount of confusion. A further disposition of forces was made, now that a separate Aegean command was set up, with Major-General Brittorous relinquishing command and Major-General H.R. Hall being appointed General Officer Commanding Aegean. Then surprisingly enough he established his headquartaers in Samos, and Brigadier Tilney was appointed Fortress commander at Leros. The German bombardments continued, and despite everything the German invasion fleet reached Cos and Kalymnnos on November 10th. This was now zero hour for the Navy, and the destroyers *Petard* and *Rockwood*, with the Polish *Krakowick* sailed to intercept.

They went all over the coast of Kalymnos and also bombarded the port itself. The *Faulknor, Beaufort* and the Greek *Pindos* went to do the same with Cos. Both squadrons came under heavy aerial attacks, and the *Rockwood* was hit by a glider bomb. With *Petard* having to tow its stricken companion, and *Krakowick* standing by to ward off further attacks, the services of this squadron were lost. It therefore fell to the other squadron to cover operations on the 11th.

Captain Thomas of *Faulknor* was first told to stay nearer the Cos Channel to conserve fuel until reinforcements would arrive. But when in the first hours of the morning of November 12th enemy shipping was reported to be on the move into the Cos Roads, he was ordered to send his other two destroyers to investigate and ntercept if necessary. For some reason Captain Thomas did not carry out this order. And the enemy, for indeed the reported shipping belonged to the German invasion fleet, could proceed to Leros without any opposition. The only British craft that lay between the Germans and Leros was a motor-launch ML 456, which after duly reporting the enemy forces, dashed to attack all by itself, with its two Oerlikon guns which were like pea-shooters against the enemy's superior naval armoury.

The German invasion fleet was composed of two forces. Force West with the II/16 Infantry Battalion of about 800 men which had to land north of Alinda Bay, and Force East which had to go ashore at Palma Bay. The main objective of both landings was to get at the Italian Ciano coastal battery on Mount Clidi which dominated the coastal region where further reinforcements would be landing. It was also intended to drop a battalion of paratroops soon after in the centre of the island between Alinda and Gurna Bays. Fortunately enough some British aircraft managed to attack the Germans whilst on their way, causing them a delay. This meant that when they aproached the coast it was full daylight, and on being

Flare-Up in the Aegean

sighted they came under heavy and accurate fire from two Italian coastal batteries on Mount Cazzuni and Mount Scumbarda. Force West was thus held back and prevented from carrying out its scheduled landing. But Force East, being composed of smaller landing craft, and therefore a more difficult target, carried on.

"If only we had the Malta gunners here," remarked a Royal Irish Fusilier, "we would blow the whole lot of them in no time." He was referring to the exploit of Maltese coastal gunners of July 1941, when in a question of minutes they had blown out of the water the whole of an Italian assault force.

But at Leros it was a different story. When Mueller whistled his Stukas in support these flew in without being inconvenienced by anti-aircraft fire since 30 out of the 58 heavy anti-aircraft guns had been knocked out in the pre-invasion raids. And there was no fighter opposition. They would now weave their way about amongst the few exploding anti-aircraft shells, pinpoint their target, and dive. This, however, did not keep the 4th Buffs from launching a prompt counter-attack with some success. By this time, however, part of the force that landed had established a foothold at Grifo Bay, and because of a breakdown in communications a company of the Kings Own Royal Regiment was delayed in going in support. And the Germans had also captured Mount Clidi, with the Italian coastal battery that was located there. The landing in the south had in the meantime found no opposition and the enemy drove towards Castle Hill and Mount Appetia from where they could overlook both the town of Leros and Fortress HQ. The defence here was allotted to the Royal Irish Fusiliers, who although called late managed to push the Germans back with some stupendous fighting and also retake the battery which the enemy had initially captured.

This had made the first morning's, fighting. And although the Germans had two good footholds on the island, Brigadier Tilney, the Officer Commanding in Leros was satisfied that both of them seemed to be controlled. Then at 1630 there appeared fifteen Ju.52's flying low, and taking everyone by surprise. Before anyone could know what was happening, paratroops began jumping from the planes. It was a battalion of 500 men from the 2nd "Enheit Hase' Parachute Division. Because of the hilly terrain this hadn't been expected, therefore no defence against them had been envisaged. Hence the paratroops found no resistance. A company from the Royal East Kents and another from the Irish Fusiliers moved to intercept. Rather late maybe, but when they met, a bitter fight ensued. By dusk the Germans had achieved their main objective of controlling the neck of land between Gurma and Alinda Bays. This meant that they had cut the island's defences in two. And this had changed the situation.

The British had in the meantime taken control of the situation in the southern sector, but notwithstanding what gains were made, both sides had suffered heavy casualties and came to a standstill. When night fell both Mueller and Tilney realized they could not go on unless there were sent reinforcements, and both commanders were convinced that these would tip the scales in the battle that was being fought.

Tilney sent an urgent call to Samos, assuming no doubt that with this island being close and possessed of some fresh troops it could send, he might be with an advantage to turn the tables on the Germans. These too called for reinforcements, which they got in the form of the Western Force which had failed to land in the morning. It was still available quite close, and was landed on the north east coast in the morning of the 13th. Then the sea conditions deteriorated, and a full gale was soon blowing to make it impossible for any further landing craft to come close to the coast. It was now that Captain Thomas pushed forward with his flotilla, this time hoping to encounter any enemy shipping carrying reinforcements.

But obviously he didn't find any, and hadn't he been roped in to bombard German positions in Leros, his patrol would not have helped anyone. When it was time for his ships to refuel, the patrolling was taken over by another squadron made up of the destroyers *Echo, Dulverton* and *Belvoir* under Commander Sammy Buss. The flotilla was accompanied for part of the way by the cruiser *Phoebe*, then allowed to continue on its own to the north of Rhodes where it disturbed a hornets' nest. It was heavily attacked by the Luftwaffe, and the *Dulverton* was hit by a glider bomb and seriously damaged. Amongst the missing there was Commander Buss. The other destroyers rescued what they could of the *Dulverton's* crew, then they sank the stricken ship. Now they waited for dawn.

An attempt had in the meantime been made to send British reinforcements from Samos, but the first vessel MS.102 which tried to carry troops ran aground. The dawn of the 13th had also brought in the RAF in force. But nothing the Beaufighters did would take away the supremacy enjoyed by the Luftwaffe which continued to amaze everyone with is promptness when called in support by ground forces. This was something in which they had excelled in all their previous campaigns, which might have driven home a much needed lesson to the British. This had to wait however, for next on the programme there was another setback. Brought over by a flight of Ju.52's which again flew in low and calmly at seven in the morning to drop more paratroops this time on Rachi Ridge. The Bofors shot down three of them, and British defenders in the area gave the German troops a hot welcome, inflicting heavy casualties amongst them. But this still did not stop the Germans from occupying a good part of the ridge which had become so important. Brigadier Tilney agreed that Rachi Ridge had become the keypoint of the battle, and the Germans had to be driven away from there before he could think of anything else. This could only be carried out by a counter-attack which he decided to launch on the following morning.

What clarification of the situation might have been expected on the 14th never came. If anything, everything seemed to have become more confused. Before his counter-attack, Tilney had to send two of his battalions on a wild goose chase because of false messages, the originators of which are still not known to-day. So his attack had to be delivered with a depleted force which was no match for the German infantry now bolstered by paratroops. Then while he was burdened with news of the heavy going of his troops, there were the Buffs seizing the important point of Kidney which was only one mile from Rachi Ridge. The 15th was an even worse day, particularly for the R AF. Beaufighters could not make any headway with the Me.'s 109, while 12 Dakotas reported the successful drop of badly needed ammunition to the troops at Leros, only to be learned later that some of it was actually dropped on the island of Kalymnos, held by the Germans. Reinforcements were at last arriving from Samos. There were two companies of the Royal West Kents who on arriving were sent into battle piecemeal only to be wiped out. The destroyer *Rockwood* was crippled, and the other members of her squadron *Penn* and *Aldenham* had to retire to Turkish waters to embark wounded British troops taken there from Leros. Another destroyer *Blencathra* had to tow the *Rockwood* to Alexandria. These movements deprived the defence of the naval patrol, while land forces had to fight for dear life whether they were engaged in company or platoon strength.

It had become impossible to make head or tail of the situation. Then on the 16th the Germans began another series of bombings. It had suddenly become touch and go, with a successful action being reported at one point and reversals at two others. Brigadier Tilney was moving from one place to another trying to clarify matters and put things in order where they had gone wrong. He returned back to his threatened headquarters at 1545, none the wiser of what was going on. At 1730 he announced the surrender of Leros.

Flare-Up in the Aegean

There were those who had disagreed with Tilney's decision, because they knew this would be the end. And they were right on this, since in Samos Major-General Hall had only 220 British and 380 Greek troops, with which he could certainly not fight. They too would have to be evacuated.

But one could deduce whether Brigadier Tilney was right or wrong in his decision from the sight at Port Laki from where the troops that remained to him, after 3200 had been captured, were being evacuated after dusk on November 16th.

Illuminated by flares and tracers fired by the Luftwaffe still active to the end, the port presented a fantastic sight Crowds of soldiers were lying about, all too exhausted that they couldn't care less about the agressive enemy aircraft flying above them for the kill. Most of them were so exhausted that they were unable to reach the quayside. There were only 250 of them. All looking sorry and deflated. As the campaign they had brought to a close.

CHAPTER XII

THE BATTLE FOR ROME – FORERUNNER OF OVERLORD

The struggle for the Mediterranean had already taken the characteristics of a long campaign. But the Allied High Command was now determined not to allow anything to jeopardize the protracted invasion of Festung Europa. There had already been too many operations to take priority. French North Africa, Sicily, and Italy. But now the time had come to proceed with Operation Overlord, as it had been already code-named. If anything, the Italian campaign would help by keeping German forces tied up, and away from the new intended front in France.

This was more or less what Hitler was thinking. He was already convinced of Allied intentions to invade Europe from the West. And there had already been several false alarms with the Allied commando raid on Bruneval in February, which was followed by an equally successful raid on St. Nazaire. These must have indicated to him where the wind was blowing, and in March 1942 he had appointed Field Marshal von Runstedt in overall command of the West. After that there had been another commando raid on Dieppe, but now, with the approach of 1944 Hitler was feeling more than ever convinced that the time had come for this invasion. The study of moon and tides dictated to him that the most likely period for such an operation would be between July and September 1st. Until then he would have Europe's western coast fortified. But he would also drag and delay the Italian campaign so as to keep allied armies tied up there. It was in this regard that he instructed Kesselring about his withdrawals. The first one from Naples was to be of 20 miles as far as the river Volturno. And this position was to be held until mid-October. The next stand after that would be made 15 miles back on a front starting from the Garigliano River to the Rapido and the Lire, and this was to be called the Gustav or Winter line. Because that was where he intended to hold the ten divisions the Allies had in Italy throughout the coming winter

It had of course been a foregone conclusion that the launching of Operation Overlord would head the agenda at the meeting of the Big Three held at Teheran on November 28th. Stalin, accompanied by Molotov and Marshal Voroshilov would not have any more delays and was insisting that the operation should be proceeded with at the earliest time possible. On this there was general agreement. The first point of disagreement came when Churchill and the British side expressed themselves to be in favour of intensifying the Italian campaign. It was the American side headed by Roosevelt that disagreed with this, feeling no doubt that putting more troops in Italy was bound to weaken Operation Overlord. Instead, they proposed that there should be a simultaneous landing in the south of France, which seemed to reflect Hitler's feelings about another Mediterranean operation. The landing to be code-named Operation Anvil, was bound to draw many German divisions to the south, which would otherwise be utilized in the west resisting the main invasion. Operations in Italy could only be continued in earnest until Rome was occupied, and at the most with a further advance to a position running from Pisa to Rimini in the north. There was nothing further to be expected, and by which time Operation Overlord would be well on the way.

It might have appeared to Churchill that it was delay in capturing Rome that was drawing bias against the Italian campaign. He had himself said that he who holds Rome, holds the title deeds of Italy. And the time suited him in proposing something which he had already made up his mind upon. How about another landing behind the Gustav or Winter Line? Say, at Anzio. It could break the Germans' hold in the south of Rome. "Yes, why not?" said the Americans, "but Operation Anvil for the south of France would still be on". And that was that. The landing at Anzio, or Operation Shingle as it was code-named would take place in January 1944. Then there would be Operation Anvil concurrently with Operation Overlord which would have priority over everything.

In the same way as he had done in North Africa, when he launched an offensive at the time of the Casablanca Conference, Montgomery did the same in Italy. He launched an attack against the German lines on November 28th, while the Teheran meeting was in session. Who knows? He might have been trying to obtain some decisive results while the Big Three were at hand. And had he did, it would have saved a lot of bother. But he didn't. Under cover of a heavy air and artillery bombardment Montgomery broke through the German lines, but Kesselring was soon rushing up reinforcements to close the breach. On December 2nd General Mark Clark joined in by launching another offensive on his front. Like his English partner he had some initial successes but the Germans were soon pushing reinforcements. There was fierce fighting for positions to be wrenched from the enemy, but these were only small points and mountains. Monte Camino, Monte La Difensa and Monte Maggiora all fell in this way, taking the 5th Army a few miles forward but at an exorbitant cost in casualties. With an increasing German resistance and the bitter wintry weather having set in with cold, rain and mud, both offensives petered

The Battle for Rome – Forerunner of Overlord

out. Neither of the two armies had reached the German Gustav line.

The Big Three had gone away, leaving behind them the first arrangements they had made for Operation Overlord. General Eisenhower was to be Supreme Commander there, with Air Chief Marshal Tedder as his Deputy, no doubt indicating the importance now being given to air power. They were substituted by General Sir Maitland Wilson and Air Marshal John Slessor respectively. This latter being number two to the American General Ira Eaker placed in command of the Mediterranean Allied Air Forces. General Mark Clark too, now with more than 40,000 battle casualties in his army, and 50,000 ill soldiers, had to part with the British 7th Armoured and the American 82nd Airborne Divisions which were withdrawn to England for the invasion of France. General Montgomery too had to hand in his command of a stagnant army to Lieutenant General Oliver Leese, as he was transferred to take over command of the 21st Army Group earmarked for the cross-Channel invasion. Ironically enough also Kesselring had to part with Rommel, when the Field Marshal was transferred to assist Runstedt on the Western defences in Normandy.

Therefore in more ways than one the Italian campaign was being put aside. Subservient to Operation Overlord. In the meantime the year 1943 came to an end. With the result on all Italian fronts being a checkmate.

* * *

A new year dawned. And Field Marshal Kesselring was sitting pretty. What difficulties were caused in Italy by the flight of the royal family and the Government from Rome were quickly straightened out by the quick formation of a strong administration. This was being run by Italian bureaucracy under German control. Other difficulties for the Germans had begun to materialize when Italian and French forces in Sardinia and Corsica took control in their respective islands. Kesselring had now resigned himself to having all German forces evacuated from both islands. General Lungerhausen was skilful enough to get the complaisance of the Italian commanders in Sardinia and get out without much fighting. In Corsica it was a little different and there had to be some skirmishes. But finally General von Senger-Etterlin managed to get out. There were 40,000 men in all, complete with arms and equipment, that were evacuated in Elba, Leghorn and Piombino. No doubt serving the Allies in having had these two hornets' nests cleared. But similarly setting Kesselring's mind at ease with his being able to use these troops as reinforcements for his Italian campaign which now remained the only operation that counted in the Mediterranean.

In this regard his 10th Army holding the Gustav line had repulsed all Allied attacks thrown against it. And he had no fears that it would not keep doing so. He had his moments of reflection too. Thinking how he would have acted were he to change places with the enemy. He would have landed an army somewhere in the north of Rome, which would have produced a strategic threat to the German armies lying south of the capital. It smacked of the ideal military tactic. And he was so convinced that the Allies were bound to think of it that he had kept his 14th Army with eight divisions in the north to meet this threat when it would eventually materialize.

But it didn't. And the only innovation that irked Kesselring in the first days of the new year was the escalating rate of Allied air attacks on his airfields in the central sector. Ciampino, Centocle, Gardonia, Viterbo and Riete were all subjected to a heavy hammering by British and American aircraft. With the respective German commanders not being able to put up a single reconaissance flight. Thus being unable to get an inkling of what the Allies might have been concocting. Then on the night of 17/18th January Kesselring thought he had his reply when he was informed that the British 10th Corps under General McCreery had began an assault to cross the

The Battle for Rome – Forerunner of Overlord

Garigliano river on the western sector. He swiftly despatched his 29th and 90th Panzerdivisions which he reinforced with some battalions of the Herman Goering Division after General Fries, the GOC of the 29th complained about the depleted state of his forces. On January 20th then, the American 2nd Corps joined in, this time to cross the Rapido river. Kesselring knew by experience that this was uncrossable even without any opposition because of its current, and it was therefore less ameniable under the heavy fire from his troops on the northern side.

However, the Allies broke through in force at Castelforte, and the 10th Army was unable to seal off the breach with its weak reserves. Now there was a fresh trend of thought to occupy Kesselring. He had already had occasion to think that the Allies' reckless expenditure of troops in capturing San Vittore, Monte Trocchio and Monte Santa Croce between the 6th and 15thJanuary must have concealed some ulterior motive. With the new impetus evident in this new offensive this feeling was revived. He had no doubts that the fresh assault begun on January 20th on the positions north of Monte Cassino by the American 2nd Corps and French troops was co-ordinated with that of the Garigliano. But it became obvious to him that rather than being complementary to each other, they must have constituted one move, in aid of something else. Admittedly it was just a hunch. But he could not afford to take any chances. So he ordered an emergency alert throughout the whole of Italy. Notwithstanding the many emphatic warnings he had been having against tiring his troops by such continuous alerting.

He was conceded a moment of grace when he learned that the first two regiments of the American 2nd Corps that had tried to cross the Rapido river had been wiped out. There was also the relief from the fact that the bombings had stopped. One of his air commanders had also managed to put up four FW 190's in the air which were sent to reconoitre towards the western coast as if to see if anything was brewing up. But the only hostile element they found was a squadron of Spitfires which chased them away, shooting one of them down in the process. The next incursion in Allied air space was made on January 22nd by a single BF109 which managed to approach the coast. And its pilot was stupefied with what he saw. He quickly turned back to report to Kesselring, that an Allied armada was lying off the beach at Anzio, and that an army seemed to have already landed.

Indeed this had been the Allied plan. Operation Shingle as it was code-named was to have a first stage of heavy bombings to ground all German reconaissance aircraft. Then there was to follow the second stage with an offensive being mounted up by the 5th army against the Gustav line, drawing all enemy troops and attention there. And finally there was the landing on the beaches of Anzio and Nettuno which lay south of Rome, but north and behind the Gustav line.

It is unbelievable how the Allies managed to take the armada of 243 vessels carrying 50,000 British and American troops under the command of Major-General John P. Lucas to their points of landing under complete secrecy. And the first report of the landing by the sole aircraft to spot it had reached Kesselring two hours later. Which was already six hours after the troops had begun to land. Initially the 6th Corps had landed the 1st British Infantry Division on the northern beach and the 3rd US Infantry Division on the southern, both accompanied by their respective Commando and Ranger units, a parachute regiment, and two tank battalions. Then there followed up the American 1st Armoured Division and the 45th Infantry Division.

Since the predominant factor behind this operation had been the element of surprise, and which was achieved, it was never understood why Major General Lucas's first efforts were all concentrated on consolidating the bridgehead rather than moving inland. There was lit-

The Battle for Rome – Forerunner of Overlord 211

tle or no resistance to the landings since the nearest German forces consisted of a battalion on leave to rest. And even when the first German fighter bombers began arriving to attack the Allied forces, now well covered by their own fighter screen, which anyway showed that the cat was out of the bag, there seems to have been no attempt at moving forward before the Germans arrived on the scene.

In contrast with this Allied procrastination, on learning of the assault, Kesselring moved General von Pohl to surround the beachhead with a ring of guns while General Schlemmer was ordered to send every available battalion he would be receiving straight on to halt the enemy advance. The 11th Parachute corps, the 76th Panzer Corps from the Adriatic and the 14th Army Corps under General Eberhard von Mackensen from North Italy were quickly moved to stem the expected Allied push. This, however, was rather slow in coming. Sir Basil Liddell-Hart says in his History of the Second World War that the first real attempt to push inland did not start before January 30th which was a week after the landing. Kesselring, however, says in his memoirs that the first violent attack was delivered by the American 6th Corps against Cisterna which is about 20 kilometers inland, on January 25th. This was then followed up by two further attacks again on Cisterna and Campoleone on January 31st. But even if Kesselring is right one cannot fail to point out that by January 25th he had already built and consolidated his defences where three days before there had been none. By the end of the month something like eight German divisions were taken to the bridgehead and the harsh battles that were to follow.

Kesselring could now give his attention to the 5th Army which, however, slow, was pushing forward. Its French corps had been steadily moving towards Colle Belvedere and Terello, which it eventually occupied on January 31st. This time he had to pick the right kind of seasoned troops to halt the Allies, under two similarly proven commanders. Generals Heidrich and Baade. On February 6th the French troops were beaten back after a fierce battle which Alexander declared to have been a German success. Having found this unsurmountable obstacle General Clark decided to try again to overcome the Gustav Line from the north through Cassino. This had been tried on January 24th, and the American 34th division supported by French troops had managed to make a bridgehead. But the Germans had slowly recovered and closed the breach until lthe Americans had to withdraw mauled and depleted on February 11th. Now this second attempt was to be made by the New Zealand Corps, made up of the 2nd New Zealand and 4th Indian Divisions, under the command of Lieutenant General Bernard Freyberg whom we had already met in Crete and North Africa. Only that now it was decided that the attack should be made through the mountains which necessitated that the assaulting force should first tackle Monte Cassino, on the top of which there lay the historic monastery which was to influence war history for posterity.

This was a Benedictine monastery renowned for its art treasures and historic library which on the onset of war had all been removed to the custody of the Vatican. The monks had, however, remained and continued with their ecclesiastical rites for the benefit of the inhabitans of the town of Cassino. Because of its strategic position the hill of Cassino was taken over by the Germans, but the monastery was not touched. Indeed it was closed against unauthorized entry, and for this purpose was guarded by German military police. Still as the Allied troops tried to fight their way up the hill they could not help being effected by the look of the dominating edifice which looked even more sinister every time their progress became more difficult. The belief was rife that the Germans might have been using the monastery as a redoubt. This wasn't so, but there was nothing and no way to persuade the Allies. So someone suggested to have the monastery destroyed. It

The Battle for Rome – Forerunner of Overlord 213

was a very big and delicate decision. But it gained support as well as the approval of both Freyberg and Alexander. So leaflets were dropped by aircraft over the monastery asking the monks to leave the place as it was being bombarded. Allowing them enough time to evacuate it, the monastery was then subjected first to a heavy artillery bombardment, then to a similarly destructive aerial bombing. This obtained opposite results, for now that the monastery was desroyed, the Germans felt justified in entrenching in its rubble which strengthened their positions in resisting the Allied attacks. The rubble also helped in blocking the way for Allied tanks. All further attacks by both Allied divisions were now being beaten back. And in one counter attack the 2nd New Zealand Division was not only pushed out of Cassino but also driven out of is bridgehead over the Rapido river

The Germans were now like hounds hot on the scent and there was a determined effort to deal the same kind of treatment to Lucas's force in the Anzio bridgehead. But it is in such moments that men are liable to make their own traps, and the Germans made one for themselves. They crammed so many troops and tanks in their counter attack that they made an easy target for both Allied naval artillery and aircraft, which brought them heavy casualties. Notwithstanding this, they maintained their attack and it was only some brilliant do or die fighting by two British and an American division that won the day. Lucas was replaced by General Lucian K. Truscott and as the Germans seemed to go into a brief lull as if to remuster, it was the turn of the Allied Air Forces to attack the enemy concentrations with deadly precision. On March 4th, the Germans were compelled to stop their offensive. What little of Cassino had been left standing was demolished on March 15th after a fresh and heavier bombardment by the Allies. This time this was aimed to destroy the German troops in the area. But even now, when they seemed to have at last broken enemy resistance, and the Indian Division had already reached Hangman's Hill, which was just below the monastery, the Allies met an unexpected new enemy. Torrential rain, against which no countermeasures could be taken. So by March 24th the attack had to be discontinued.

It looked like another checkmate. The fighting had all been in vain. But Kesselring called the result a draw. To Hitler it was more than that. After the fall of Sicily, he had gloomily concluded that there was little or no chance of saving the German forces fighting south of Rome. But after Kesselring had many a time shown his ability of extricating his forces from tight corners, and also how he managed to halt the Allied advance from Salerno, Hitler changed his mind. His only pessimism changed to new optimism, and Kesselring was given instructions to stay and fight south of Rome. The Italian capital was now invested with a new significance for Hitler which in a way was also reflected on the Allied side.

* * *

There was now the dawn of Spring. Calling for changes and a clean up. More than anything else tiredness and exhaustion had become the order of the day in both camps. What remained of the New Zealand Division was disbanded. The men were to be given a rest and then put in other units. Alexander took away all but one corps from the Adriatic side of the front, to put them in the Liri valley sector. Those at the Anzio bridgehead were now to be considered as forming part of the 5th Army, notwithstanding the fact that the two elements were still separated by the Gustav Line.

This too had to undergo some changes. Not as much in troops as in fortifications. But by having a reserve position which the Germans had begun working on as far back as December. This was to be like another line of defence, about 8 miles behind the Gustav Line and beginning from Piedimonte, running across the northern half of the Liri Valley to Pontecorvo. All of it being bolstered by concrete emplacements, anti-tank ditches, mines and wire. It was

The Battle for Rome – Forerunner of Overlord

to be called the Hitler Line. Kesselring was also thinking of laying another line farther back, just before Rome and which was to be called the Ceasar Line. It was his intention to fall back there should the Gustav and Hitler fortifications be eventually pierced. He was well aware that building another line needed time, but he was similarly convinced that the Allies would not attack so soon. And he was right. As notwithstanding the fact that Alexander was soon planning a Spring offensive there again arose the old divergence with the Americans about Operation Anvil. They had not only not given it up, but were now more insistent about it. General Maitland Wilson, the Supreme Commander, tried to find a compromise and asked Alexander about the likely time for his intended spring offensive.

"Not before May," had replied Alexander.

And this immediately meant to him that allowing for preparations and regrouping, "Anvil' would not be able to be put into operation before July. And with "Overlord' drawing near, this was not considered practicable. A long wrangle ensued between the Allies which reached right up to the top, involving Roosevelt and Churchill. There had to be a compromise, and the British gave in, with the Americans agreeing it would have to be in July.

This spurred Alexander to bigger efforts in forcing the issue of Rome before then. And he set himself on a very ambitious plan which he was convinced would finally help him to break through the enemy defences on the road to the Holy City. From this he must have drawn the codename of "Diadem' for the operation. But until he would launch it, the Allied Air Forces were let loose against the enemy 's lines of communication.

Air Vice Marshal Broadhurst had now left the Desert Air Force and gone to the United Kingdom to take a command in 'Overlord'. With him went nine squadrons. His place was taken by Air-Vice Marshal Dickson who lost no time in launching a series of attacks on the Italian railway system in conjunction with the United States Army Air Force. As this air offensive got under way, the Strategic Air Force joined up with heavy bombing raids being extended as far as Hungary and Rumania.

Now there had also developed a new operational front for the Air Forces in Yugoslavia where Tito's partisans had risen against the German army of occupation. Theirs was no longer the type of guerilla warfare that had began as far back as 1943. Aiming at the destruction of plants and communications or ambushing enemy units. The Yugoslavs had come out into the open like an organised army to fight pitched battles with their enemy. It had become a situation which required much assistance in arms, food, equipment, and also air strikes in support. And these the Allied Air Forces began providing from Italy. One particular unit was No. 7 Wing of the South African Air Force, made up of not less than four squadrons of Spitfires which alternated between operating as fighters and fighter-bombers, generally in this last capacity carrying a pair of 250 lb bombs. Very often they did both by first dropping their bombs then go back to strafe. There were now different types of aircraft operating with the Allied Air Forces. Baltimores, Bostons, Mustangs and Kittyhawks; with as many different nationalities in crews. French, Polish, Greeks, Australians, New Zealanders and South Africans were all there. Besides of course the British and Americans. And the airfields at Biferno, Marcianisi and Foggia, in Italy were all bustling with their activities. There had been such an escalation in operations that a detachment known as Balkan Air Terminal Service was sent to Yugoslavia to find landing strips where supplies could be flown to. Also from where it would be possible to evacuate Yugoslav casualties for treatment in Italy. The landing strip at Kupresko Polje was thus established. But it was also found expedient to form what came to be called the Balkan Air Force under Air-Vice Marshal W. Elliot with headquarters at Bari in Southern Italy. At least on one occasion Marshal Tito himself with British and Russian

The Battle for Rome – Forerunner of Overlord 217

missions were lifted and taken to Italy for a conference at Bari on closer air support for the partisans. Guerilla warfare also erupted in Greece, and air support was extended to that front as well, adding a difficult, but nonetheless welcome task. What difficulties had to be surmounted were now being balanced by the general feeling that the rest of the Mediterranean had joined in the struggle, determined to oust the Germans from that theatre of operations once and for all.

But the last decisive move had perforce to be made by the 5th and 8th Armies which in the first week of May were ready for Alexander's spring offensive 'Operation Diadem'. General Clark was waiting with seven divisions at his Salerno Beachhead, and another six constituting the 10th Corps at Anzio under General Truscott. General Reese had assembled ten divisions for the 8th Army made up of British, Indians, New Zealanders, Canadian, Polish and South African troops. The operation had long been planned and rehearsed, and time had seemed so endless for the 100,000 men to be involved. Finally D Day had come, and on May 10th every Allied soldier in Italy had Alexander's special order-of-the-day read to him. Operation Diadem was being launched with the ultimate objective of capturing Rome.

Most of the day of the 11th was spent in seeing to final touches. And it could be deduced how much had everyone waited for this day from the almost mechanical way in which everything was being done. When dusk came there was a change of scene. Work stopped, but a new kind of activity had taken over all along the front. Thousands of men now began leaving their bunkers to reach forming up positions, others uncovered assault boats to be used for river crossings. Tanks, armoured cars and other vehicles were reviving up to move into position, while artillery men were already checking and caressing their guns. As the night became older all movement stopped, and silence returned to the front as all began to wait for the expected signal. This was given at 11 p.m., and the combined artillery of the 5th and 8th Armies, made up of sme 2000 guns opened fire with an intensity not yet evidenced since El Alamein.

Within minutes, General Clark launched his 2nd Corps forward under General Geoffrey Keyes, as well as the French Expeditionary Force under the command of General Juin. And the shells were still raining down on the German positions as the American and French troops approached to make contact, with the flashes lighting their way and the black shapes of hills where the enemy was waiting. The 13th Corps on the right under General Sidney Kirkman allowed some time for the barrage to get hotter in order to have its noise cover the rattle of boats and rafts which his troops would be using to cross the Rapido river. The Polish 2nd Corps under General Wladyslaw Anders had to wait too as it needed moonlight to find its way over the rough hillsides which covered its objective that was Colle Sant'Angelo, before moving to attack Monte Cassino. But an hour later all four corps were going. Operation Diadem was in full swing.

The Germans had of course not been idle, and they had taken the necessary precautions to contain the Allied offensive. To confront the 5th Army Field Marshal Kesselring had assigned the 14th Army under General Mackensen. He had surrounded the Anzio beachhead with the 1st Parachute Corps under General Alfred Schlemm and the LXXVI Panzer Corps under General Traugott Herr. For the rest of the front he had General Heinrich Trettner's 4 Parachute Division, General Hellmuth Pfeiffer's 65 Infantry Division, and General Fritz-Hubert Graser's 3 Panzer-Grenadier Division. The eastern side of the 5th Army beachhead was then strengthened by the addition of two other infantry divisions: the 362 under General Heinz Greiner, and the 715 under General Hans-Georg Hildebrand. The Gustav Line was being held by General Vitinghoff's 10th Army comprising General von Senger's

The Battle for Rome – Forerunner of Overlord

XIV Panzer Corps of 3 divisions, and the LI Mountain Corps under General Feurstein, retaining the Gruppe "Hauck' of 3 divisions on the Adriatic side. It was a line-up which promised to produce the biggest battle in the struggle for the Mediterranean.

The first sketchy reports of the fighting that reached Alexander were not very encouraging, and would have spelled disaster to any less seasoned campaigner. But he knew what to expect at such an initial stage of a major offensive. In fact he had already told his commanders not to expect any decisive results before two to three weeks of fighting.

If there was any confusion in the first days' fighting this was certainly not restricted to the Allies. Conjointly with the ground assault the Allied Air Forces had launched a series of heavy air attacks on the various headquarters of the German chain of command. Moreover, something like 3000 sorties were flown against the enemy communications system. This had the intended effect, and as Kesselring confirmed later, many of his formations were out of contact with each other and also with headquarters during the first three days of fighting.

"It is intolerable," he had written for posterity, "that troops could be fighting the enemy for two days without knowing whom they are fighting ... the Army Group was not in possession of data on which to make a far reaching decision on the 14th and 15th May."

Nonetheless German formations fought fiercely, sometimes on their own, and results for the first two days' fighting showed that Allied troops were having a rough time and not making headway on any part of the front.

There was only one exception, and this came from where it was least expected. The French Expeditionary Force under the command of General Juin, consisting of a Pursuit Corps under General Larminat and a Mountain Corps under General Guillaume, was generally considered as not being up to scratch for modern warfare. This might have been because its two mountain divisions were relying more on pack-mules for transport rather than on vehicles. However, the French were lucky in being confronted by the not so tough 71st Infantry Division on their first day of fighting, while the two forces on the sides, i.e. the 2nd US Corps on the left, and the British 13th Corps on the right, met murderous resistance. They could thus move forward while the others were halted. The French penetrated to the Ausente valley beyond Gariglione on the 14th, and on the strength of this move the German 94th Division which was confronting the 2nd US Corps was ordered to fall back and contain the French advance. In doing this, however, it took a different road from that leading to the hard-pressed 71st. So rather than contributing to have a common front, the two German divisions found themselves isolated and with a mountain range between them which they could not penetrate. This suited General Guillaume better who set his troops on the range and proceeded to capture Monte Faito and Castelforte.

Kesselring had explained this situation by saying that the 94th Division had its instructions to assemble its reserves on the mountain range, and this would have placed it in the right position to halt the French advance. But his instructions had been disobeyed, and the reserves were placed on the coast road leaving the wide open gap on the mountain which the French exploited. But he failed to mention anything about his own delay in moving reserves to the Liri valley where the French were obviously heading to reach before the Germans, and thus opening the much wanted breach in the Gustav Line, which in fact they did.

General Reese's main objective had been to break German defences in the Liri Valley to open a way to Route 6 which was the road to facilitate an advance towards Rome. This would also have helped him to reach and attack the Hitler Line before the Germans would have time to man it properly. But all this was very much dependant

The Battle for Rome – Forerunner of Overlord

on the occupation of Monte Cassino in the north and Monte Majo in the south. For from these two dominating positions the Germans could bring accurate artillery fire to bear on anything in the Liri Valley. Reese had decided that the two attempts to cross the river Rapido and put more forces in the valley, and to occupy Monte Cassino, should be undertaken concurrently. The first assignment was given to the 13th Corps, which succeeded to put a couple of bridges across, which however were not enough. The task of attacking Monte Cassino, which had already defied American, British, New Zealand and Indian troops, was now given to the Polish Corps under General Anders. These too, however, were met with fanatical German resistance and halted.

This must have been frustrating to Leese, particularly when on the morrow the French who had continued with their advance had captured the other controversial height, Monte Majo. General Sidney Kirkman must have been similarly frustrated with his 13th Corps having made a balls up in crossing the Rapido. The only two bridges that were put across could not take more than small vehicles across, and one of them required immediate repairs. He realised he must have more bridges, and quick if he were not to put a spanner in the wheels of the whole operation. He gave a quick order for another Bailey bridge to be built at once. He took precautions to have the area smoke screened from the enemy, and this included an intensified bombardment of Monte Cassino with smoke shells to blind German observers on Monastery Hill. It was a slow and murderous work for his sappers who worked like dogs, still exposed to sniper and machine gun fire, as well as hand grenades that were often being rolled down the slopes to burst amongst the sappers. Eighty three of the 200 employed on the job were killed. But in ten hours a bridge that came to be known as Amazon Bridge was completed. The reserve brigade of the 4th British Division, and the 17/21 Lancers of the 6th Armoured Division were soon rolling across to be committed in the Liri Valley.

With the 13th Corps thus also past the Gustav Line it became more pressing on General Leese to settle the issue at Monte Cassino. General Anders himself wanted to renew the attack, but Leese went to him personally to make him do it. He wanted it at all costs now, and it had to be successful. Anders only asked for artillery support which Leese gave him from the 13th Corps. The 78th Division had now been committed to the Liri Valley as well to join in the attack towards Route 6, which began on May 15, when incidentaly the French having surmounted all the mountains in their way swooped down to occupy Ausonia. The Canadian Corps under General Burns now joined the army in the Liri Valley. And on the following day, May 17th, the Polish Corps launched its second attack on Monte Cassino.

There was the expected stiff rsistance from the 1st Parachute Division still holding the mountain, and first indications were that again the Poles were not going to make it. Canadian troops were pulled back from the Liri and pushed in support, artillery and armour were boosted up, but the German paratroopers still held their lines.

One would have expected Kesselring to be more than satisfied with the performance of his troops. And he was. But his mind was now more on the Liri Valley where the British 13th Corps had cut across Route 6. The French too had maintained their advance and occupied Esperia, while their mountain artillery was shelling the Pico-Itri road. The 2nd US Corps had also come round the corner and occupied Formia. This meant to Kesselring that his Gustav Line had collapsed. And if there were any lurking doubts about this they were quickly swept away when the 8th Indian Division penetrated his lines between Pignatoro and Cassino Now he acted quickly and sanctioned the withdrawal of his forces to the Hitler Line from the Fuhrer himself. In the meantime he despatched the 26th Panzer Division to block the French advance which was nearing Pico. His next order was to the 1st Parachute Division at

The Battle for Rome – Forerunner of Overlord

Cassino to withdraw. This, they refused to do according to their code of conduct as paratroopers of fighting till the end. But this counted only for normal situations. The battle there with the Polish and Canadian troops pressing like mad, supported by armour, artillery and aircraft was no longer a normal one. So on May 18th, the Germans withdrew and Cassino fell. The Polish Corps walked amongst the ruins for which they had paid with 4000 lives.

It had been a bitter fight, and very costly. But it had brought the collapse of the Gustav Line in five days. Alexander now tried to forestall something similar happening in the Hitler Line, and the 13th Corps and the Canadian Corps were rushed to attack this new line of fortifications. Hoping the Germans would not have had enough time to settle down. The Poles were diverted to drive towards Piedimonte so as to turn the line from the north. The French were in the meantime to continue towards Pico, trying to overpower the 26th Panzer Division awaiting them, which would bring them behind the Germans facing the 8th Army in the Hitler Line. The only snag that arose here was that the 13th Corps realised on reaching its destination that it wasn't that easy to breach the German defences. Such operations require time with a thorough examination of defences,ways of approach, and other details which they hadn't prepared. It was a situation which required Alexander's way of doing things. Real and methodic; very often as near perfect as success can be. And this was something which sometimes drew criticism from both Clark and Juin. Probably because it took longer to obtain results. Now General Leese was already thinking in terms of postponing the operation. It was again the French who saved the day when they reached Pontecorvo which was a salient position in the Hitler Line. Farther south the 2nd US Corps had captured Fondi on its way to join the American forces from Anzio. It was therefore decided to have another try at penetrating the Hitler Line. This time, however, to be undertaken by the Canadian Corps. Their attempt was code-named Operation Chesterfield.

How did the Germans react to this situation which prevailed on May 20th? Kesselring was determined to resist any attack on his defence line on the spot. So he had all German troops south of the Liri pulled back to the part of his line now being called the Senger Line after the general who was in command. He was well aware of the intention behind the move by the American forces which had occupied Fondi. So in order to prevent them from joining any force from Anzio he despatched the 29th Panzer Grenadier Division to Terracina which lay in the Americans' way. As for the French obvious new move to Pico, another salient point in his line, he ordered the 305 and 334 Divisions from the Adriatic to move there to intercept them. There was nothing of this that Alexander had not expected, for here too it becomes obvious how Kesselring was being made to dance to the Supreme Commander's tune. Even so, Alexander was taking no risks. Before he took his next step he wanted to be sure he would be playing his cards right. He waited for the following day before he acted. Until he knew that the French had overwhelmed German resistance and captured Pico, and that the 2nd US Corps had reached Terracina notwithstanding German attempts at intervention. Now he could act and agreed to let go the Canadians with their attack on the Hitler Line. At the same time he also ordered Truscott and his force to break out of Anzio, and move in the direction of Valmonte where he anticipated they would be in time to cut off the retreat of the German armies from the line.

This brought another move from Kesselring, and in an attempt to halt the American breakout from Anzio he detailed the Hermann Goering Division. But this still did not affect the main issue. And on May 23rd the Canadians penetrated the Hitler Line. On that first day it was just a narrow breach which involved attackers and defenders in some bitter fighting. But on the following day it became wider. Enough for armour to pass through, and also the stand-by elements of the 13th Corps. Before Kesselring could realise what had happened there was the news of

The Battle for Rome – Forerunner of Overlord

the defeat of his forces at Terracina by the 2nd US Corps which captured the town and proceeded forward until its leading units met those of the 6th US Corps which had broken out from Anzio, at Borgo Grappa. With this unsurmountable reversal to his forces, Kesselring ordered his troops to abandon the Hitler Line and withdraw to the Ceasar Line to fight the final battle for Rome.

It can also be seen here how Alexander's timing had been almost perfect. With the Canadians and the 13th Corps rushing forward to reach and cross the River Melfa, about 4 miles beyond the Hitler Line, it was obvious that the German 10th Army would have to pass through Valmonte in its withdrawal, where, Alexander knew it would find Truscott with his 6th US Corps waiting. This move had been code-named Operation Buffalo, when it had first been planned as far back as May 1st. But on that day General Clark had also told his subordinate Truscott to keep Operation Turtle also in mind, which was the code-name for a break-out towards Rome. And this was to start one of the biggest altercations of the Italian campaigns.

On moving out of Anzio on May 23rd, General Truscott had pushed his 6th Corps northwards towards Cisterna according to the plans of Operation Buffalo. He had to fight hard and suffer many casualties. Probably these being more than he had inflicted on the Germans. The second day was a repetition, with both sides letting no quarter. Nonetheless Truscott persisted and on May 25th he captured both Cisterna and Gori which formed a triangle with Valmonte where the plan required him to go. To fit with these plans, any moving object in the area between these three towns was on that day being heavily attacked by Allied Air Forces, and one element to be thus caught and badly mauled was the Hermann Goering Division still on its way to meet the 6th US Corps. Operation Buffalo was working nicely, and Truscott was soon all set to continue moving on his last lap, more than ever confident of meeting the German 10th Army in retreat towards Valmonte. But suddenly he received fresh orders from General Clark. Dominated more by emotion and political fervour rather than by military logic, Clark ignored Alexander's orders and ordered Truscott to change direction and proceed north west towards the Alban Hills, and Rome, which was operation Turtle that he had mentioned to Truscott only a few days before.

A lot had been said and written about this spectacular move by the American General. It cannot be said that it was just a change of mind. For had it been so, he would have consulted Alexander before implementing it. So much so that three days before, he was heard reiterating at a press-conference that it will be the 5th Army that will take Rome – and no one else. But what does it matter what anybody might have thought? The fact remains that while Churchill and Alexander fumed with irritation, the 6th US Corps was already thrusting forward on its new route for Lanuvio which formed part of the Ceasar Line. And on reaching it they launched several attacks, all of which, however, failed. On May 30th it seemed that after all Clark's switch of plan had only served the Germans by giving them more time to close the Valmonte Gap, and thus make things more difficult for the Allies.

Clark had foreseen this possibility too, and he had recorded in his diary that if he would not crack the Ceasar Line at his first try he would wait for the 8th Army to help him do it. And this is what seemed that he will have to do. But the 8th Army was heavily engaged elsewhere. What with fighting reaguard actions by retreating Germans, and trying to deepen beachheads over the Melfa it had been delayed. Now it was approaching Frosinone which, however, was still about 20 miles from Valmonte. The French too were still ploughing forward across the Lepini Mountains. So by the looks of it there appeared to be a long wait for Clark. And most of the people involved must have been thinking that this would have served him right.

The Battle for Rome – Forerunner of Overlord

But luck favoured Clark. And this was on May 31st when the news reached him that the 8th Army had just captured Frosinone and was rushing towards Ferentino on its way to Valmonte. The lucky strike came to him in the form of a silent challenge by a 3000 foot high mountain which stood in his way. Mount Antemisio, which overlooked the back of the German lines from Velletri to Lanuvio had not been showing any signs of activity. Clark's sappers were sent up to investigate on the night of 30th/31st, and finding no resistance they were followed by two infantry regiments. They also reached the top unchallenged. By dawn the 5th Army was in complete control, and resisted what German attacks were belatedly launched against the mountain. On June 1st, Clark had built his forces there so much that he decided he would not wait longer for the 8th Army's help. So he ordered a drive to the east and west of the Alban Hills.

The 8th Army was now hurrying forward, not as much to help Clark as to be at the final kill. Anagni was reached. The French too had met the Canadians and the 2nd US Corps at Collefano. They too seemed in a hurry now to join in the race for Rome. But Clark had a distinct advantage, and on June 3rd they found only German rearguards to resist them when they reached Lanuvio and Velletri. The capture of these two towns meant the end of the Ceasar Line. On the following day, the Germans evacuated Rome, and the 8th Army had reached a position east of the city. Only a few miles away. But General Clark's leading troops had reached the Tiber bridges. Then the main part of his troops entered Rome in the evening to the rejoicing of the population.

In the morning of June 5th, General Clark drove triumphantly into Rome. "This is a great day for the Fifth Army," he said in his official speech, "and for the French, British and American troops of the Fifth Army who made this victory possible." There were no further credits given. It seemed as if the Italian campaign had been fought only by the 5th Army. Still, what mattered to General Clark then, was that he had achieved his ambition and drew the publicity he had always been after.

But this only lasted for a few hours. For the victory of Rome went out of the limelight that same afternoon. When the news flashed all over the world of the launching of Operation Overlord. The Allied Armies had landed at Normandy.

CHAPTER XIII

THE WINDING UP

The Allies had every reason to be elated with the way the invasion of Normandy was going on. The first six seaborne and three airborne divisions were catapulated to create a good bridgehead, with the enemy not being able to deliver one dangerous counter-stroke, until the Allied position was consolidated. Yet, this headline making feat, so eagerly followed by the free world was now presenting the Supreme Commander in the Mediterranean with a series of complex decisions that had to be taken.

There was first of all Operation Anvil, which was the intended Allies' landing in Southern France and on which he had compromised with the Americans to carry out in July. It was no secret that General Maitland Wilson might have still been hoping to be able to postpone it. But with the Allies' forces now going rampant in Western France he knew he would have to give in. There was also Operation Diadem in Italy, which, notwithstanding that it had attained its object with the occupation of Rome, Alexander was now enthusiastically clamouring to extend his plans further to include an advance right up into Austria. Going by past experience in that theatre of operations this could be considered to be a very optimistic plan. Nevertheless it appealed to both Churchill and the British Chiefs of Staff.

It would however be useless to argue this point without having a look at what was going on in the enemy's camp. Kesselring was not deluded in thinking he had not been beaten in the acquisition of Rome. This he admitted himself. But he had also admitted that had the Allies seized their chances and continued with their advance and aerial attacks after the capture of Rome, they would have probably wrought havoc amongst his troops which were still running into the rear in disorder. The Allies' pause that followed was therefore considered to be a godsend which gave him enough time to rally his forces and complete another defence layout in the Appenine region. Now Kesselring was not resting on his commanders, some of whom he even changed. He was now convinced that every new defence point to be constructed had to have his own personal attention. And this conviction forced on him a lot of bother in having to run about from one spot to another in building his new line of defence to be called the Trasimere Line, which centred on Lake Trasimere. Even this, was to be only a temporaray arrangement however, intended to hold the Allied advance until he would have completed a more formidable system of defence in the North Appenines which he was calling the Gothic Line.

In the meantime the Allies too were consolidating their lines, and this had made it imperative to clear the island of Elba on the western side of Italy, which by virtue of its position still constituted a threat to the rear of their new front. This new task was code-named Operation Brassard, and was allotted to French troops from Corsica. Spitfires and P.47's of the USAAF from the French island began softening the German defences on Elba. Then the French troops landed on the island on June 17th. It took them two days of hard fighting to overcome the German garrison there. Killing 500 in the process, and capturing 2300.

There was now a bonus being given to the Allies in the form of the Italian partisans. According to Kesselring, cells of partisan resistance had first appeared in Italy between July and September 1943. Being inspired by Colonel Count Montezemolo who was Badoglio's aide. But after the country's surrender the network spread, first to

The Winding Up

release Allied prisoners of war, then to take to the mountains from where they could deliver occasional raids. In April 1944 then, they had become more active after receiving arms and food supplies. They began to jeopardize German lines of communication. When Rome fell, the partisans then became more aggressive. So even as Alexander was now moving against the enemy in the Trasimere Line he was being helped to some extent by the thousands of partisans who were acting independently behind the enemy lines. This might have had something to do with the swift advance of the 5th Army, which, supported by the reactivated Allied airforces cleared the Trasimere area by the end of June, and was soon moving towards Florence. On July 11th, the 8th Army occupied Arezzo, while the IV Corps of the 5th Army captured the town of Arno on the following day which was just south of Pisa. On July 18th the Polish divisions of the 8th Army entered Ancona while it was the 5th Army's turn to occupy Leghorn. Considering the German determination to resist, this was certainly some quick work by the similarly determined Allied forces to wind up their campaign. Indeed there seemed to have been born this new determination to hasten things up in the Allied Command which was now seemingly being involved into a race to reach the German Gothic Line. But against what?

The Allies could not have known of Kesselring's own determination to halt them on reaching his Gothic defences. The German Field Marshal had his own preoccupations, there, too. Particularly with a furious Hitler now insisting that the Allies should be stopped at all costs. He was now demanding again, and for the first time Kesselring lost his patience and blew his top. He flew to Germany and said what he had to say to Hitler himself.

"The point is not whether my armies are fighting or running away," he told him., "I can assure you they will fight and die if I ask it of them. But now we are talking about something entirely different and more vital. Whether after Stalingrad and Tunisia you can afford the loss of yet two more armies." Then he continued to say to the exasperated Fuhrer, "I beg to doubt it. The more so that if I were to change my plans and do what you say, sooner or later the way into Germany will be opened to the Allies. On the other hand I guarantee that, unless my hands are tied, to delay the Allied advance and even halt it at the latest in the Appenines, thereby creating the right conditions for the prosecution of the war in 1945 which can be dovetailed into your general strategic scheme."

For once Hitler was silenced. But rather than ignoring and forgetting Kesselring's previous occasions of failing to substantiate by facts the guarantees he gave in words, it is very likely that he was realizing the end that was approaching. Even so, notwithstanding what sound plans the Field Marshal might have had this time, he was not allowed to put them into operation. And this because of the other contestants in the race who were the Americans now dead intent on their invasion of Southern France.

Backed to the hilt by Eisenhower, the code-name of Anvil was scrapped, and changed to Operation Dragoon. As was to be expected there were several of General Clark's divisions taken for this new front. Particularly his four French divisions to be used fittingly in liberating their motherland. On the other hand this was weakening Clark's chances for a further advance by depriving him of his only mountain troops which were expected to be used in his approaching battle in the Appenines. This effect was felt immediately, for notwithstanding the fact that Florence was captured on August 5th, the rest of the 5th Army slowed down on reaching the hilly terrain. And it was left to the 8th Army to try and pierce the Gothic line which they were approaching.

By now it was August 10th. There began a systematic bombing of the Marseilles/Toulon area in Southern France, while the railway system from Valence to Modane was devastated. Four days of heaving bombings followed.

The Winding Up

Then on the night of 14/15th August, 400 American C-47's dropped thousands of paratroops on the southern coastal belt of France. At dawn, beach defences were subjected to a heavy bombardment, then by the time the last bombs had exploded, American and French troops began landing at Cannes and St Tropez. The third wave consisting of 9000 troops carried in gilders, together with guns and large quantities of supplies, then made the German airborne invasion of Crete of two years before look like child's play. The damage caused to roads and railways during the bombings of the previous days delayed frustrated reinforcements enough to allow Allied troops to go ashore with little or no resistance. What few aircraft of the Luftwaffe scrambled to attack the Allied forces were taken care of by British and American carrier-borne fighters. Then when the airfield of Ramatrielle was captured four days later, 225 Squadron was flown in there from Corsica to be soon followed by other fighter wings. Gop and Chatillon were occupied after a week. In the next, the Allies captured Grenoble, while Lyons fell in the third week.

It was now the turn of the French partisans the Maqui to come out fighting. They had done a considerable service to the Allies in the past in helping escaped prisoners of war, reporting troop movements and also disrupting communications. Now, simulating the Italians and Yugoslavs they resorted to open warfare. With their help it became easier to capture Marseilles, Montelima, Bordeaux and Toulon. But the optimum of the operation was reached on September 12th when the US 7th Army from Operation Dragoon made contact with General Patton's 3rd Army advancing from Normandy. Now the armies in Southern France ceased to be on their own, and they were brought under the command of General Eisenhower.

* * *

In contrast there weren't any bright prospects on the Italian front. With the 8th Army now lying in the centre and closer to the 5th Army no hopes were being entertained for the forthcoming attack on the Gothic Line. General Leese felt they would stand a better chance if they were to launch their attack from their original position on the Adriatic side.

"Why?" asked him Alexander.

"Because we would cetainly draw most of the German forces there. And that would weaken them in the centre and make them ripe to an attack by the 5th Army. Besides, I'd rather have two armies attacking on two fronts, than both of them attacking on one."

The point was made and Alexander agreed. It only required a short delay until the 8th Army could move back to its old billet on the Adriatic. And it was from there that the attack was launched on the Gothic Line on August 25th. There were involved the 5th Corps, the 1st Canadian Corps and the Polish Corps. Nine divisions in all. The Germans became aware of the offensive four days after it had started and the Allies had reached Foglia, just a couple of miles from the eastern end of the Gothic line.

According to Kesselring this attack found him on the wrong foot whilst he himself was switching over his forces. And he tried to play safe by ordering all his troops to withdraw behind the line of defence. The 8th Army continued pressing the advantage and on September 2nd reached Conca which was part and parcel of the defence line. Here it was halted after meeting heavy enemy resistance. But this served in rattling Kesselring who was now insisting on what units were still outside his lines to hurry back in. One such unit on the western side had to withdraw across the river Arno, where the 5th Army was still standing by waiting for such a possibility. Indeed, as the Germans withdrew across the river there was little or no attention being given to any rearguard action, which was what General Clark wanted. He struck immediately at the breach made by the withdrawing enemy who however stopped to fight. It took a week of fierce fighting to force

The Winding Up

the issue, but eventually General Clark's forces wre through, and were soon driving towards Bologna.

The Gothic Line was thus pierced. This however did not worry Kesselring. He began pushing his strongest divisions to the breach hoping to stem the Allied advance until he could recoup. His only help came from the weather which produced some heavy rains on that side of the front, bogging all Allied armour. There was a warning note when it was learned that the Canadian Corps of the 8th Army had crawled forward and occupied Rimini on the Adriatic. As things were he needn't have worried for the 8th Army could not go any further. But Kesselring did not know. Now he began to insist again on giving his personal attention to all sides of the front as if more than ever obsessed not to let the Allies move another inch. On October 23rd he had been on his inspections since four in the morning, and was returning to his quarters at seven in the evening, doubtlessly very tired. But so must have been his driver who drove straight into a long-barrelled gun coming out of a side road. Kesselring received a concussion and had to be taken to hospital where he was to be detained for the rest of the year. General Vitinghoff took his place.

It is sometimes argued that had the Allies exploited this situation and took the initiative during Kesselring's absence they might have brought the Italian campaign to an early end. Indeed their attacks had by now petered out, and no one seemed to be worried by the situation. It must be said in fairness that Alexander was already thinking in terms of another offensive in the spring of 1945, but none was expressing any opinion for or against it. What had happened?

To get to the answer we must digress in time to the aftermath of the invasion of Southern France, when a fresh offensive was being launched on the Russian Front. The Army of the 3rd Ukranian Front under General Tolbukhin had on August 20th struck together on their respective fronts. Their scope was to clear up what

German pockets had remained in Bessarabia. But in their way lay also Rumania who was quick to join the war on the Allies' side against Germany. All the same the Russians swept in the country, occupied the Ploesti oilfields and entered the capital Bucharest on August 27th. Six days later they had already covered 200 miles and reached the Yugoslav frontier. Just in time as the German forces were posed to launch an offensive against Tito's partisans who had occupied the country's capital Belgrade. This German intention now misfired since they were constrained to defend their rear from the Russians. But it did not take them long to realise that even so they could not hope to hold them off. It became obvious too that within a few days the Russians would not only be controlling the Greek frontier but also that of Yugoslavia, and this would trap all the German forces in the two countries. One had only to remember how a few days before the Red Army had surrounded and captured a German army of 100,000 men in Bessarabia. It had suddenly become touch and go for the German High Command. So rather than trying to halt the Russians, the German troops were ordered to fight only a delaying action until all their forces in Greece and Yugoslavia could be evacuated. They had also to face the problem of the only roads still open which were those so often used for ambushes by partisans, and this was partly solved by trying to extricate some of their forces by air. So in the next few days 150 transport aircraft arrived to carry out this task. As well as flying boats. Anything that could fly was put into service. An enemy exodus from the Balkans had begun.

The Allies did not miss this opportunity. And their air forces went into action immediately trying to get some of the ecapees who had taken to the road. The British acted quickly on their own too and landed a small force on the Greek island of Kythena after it had just been vacated by the Germans. Six days later they moved further up and used both paratroops and seaborne forces to seize the airfield of Araxos on the Greek mainland, which had also been abandoned by the Germans. Immediately this was secured, aircraft were flown over from Italy, and these were soon harassing even further the retreating enemy troops, and hastening their escape. From Araxos it was the easiest of operations to take the other airfield of Megara. And this was only 20 miles away from Athens. From there British troops proceeded towards the Greek capital which they occupied on October 14th. It then only took them four more days to occupy other islands in the Aegean which the Germans had abandoned. Syros, Lemnos, Scarpanto, Santori and Thira fell down like kingpins. Germans were found to be still in Naxos, and there was some resistance to the British forces. But this was soon overwhelmed. The only islands which did not surrender were Crete, Rhodes, Leros, Kos and Melos. Between them they housed some 19,000 German and 5000 Italian troops. And rather than provoking a long battle it was decided to neutralise them by aerial bombing and a blockade. It is no wonder then that the Italian campaign had moved out of the limelight. And indeed Alexander was now burdened with a further task of trying to pick up again the lost morale of his troops who were justly feeling that they had been edged out of what looked like the beginning of the end of the war in Europe.

The situation there was however not so clear cut. Notwithstanding the advance of the Allied forces, a power struggle was on between Britain and America about the division of Germany. On both sides of the Atlantic, diplomats and military advisers of the two nations were trying everything to bring some sort of agreement which appeared to take long in coming. It was Russia that forced them into it. By hinting that if this dispute was not settled, she would not participate any further in discussions on the subject and would consider herself free to act on her own. This showed the red light to the Americans. And Roosevelt, by now failing rapidly in health, hence tired and frustrated, gave in. The Americans acquiesced to British demands. Only as a safety measure, since it was expected they would raise these matters again at the Yalta Conference for the big three, scheduled to be held in February 1945. It had suddenly seemed that as 1944 was drawing to an end, all the war leaders had their own brief for the final reckoning. Alexander might have been the only one to be left frustrated by the fact that the Italian campaign did not in any way feature in all that was going on. And notwithstanding the fact that the Canadians in the 8th Army had managed to occupy Ravenna on December 5th, he realised that trying to attract interest in his theatre of operations might as well have been like flogging a dead horse. Hopes for an early winding up disappeared. Then as if to dampen his hopes still further, the Chiefs of Staff took away his two Canadian divisions together with three others, to be sent to the Western front.

There were two more thunderbolts to hit the Allies before the end of the year. The first was the unexpected German counter-offensive in the Ardennes launched on December 15th, which looked like halting their advance. Then, while British and American military leaders were going all out to contain this threat there was a new trouble erupting in Greece. It was nothing less than a civil war between the ELAS Communist forces which had made most of the underground elements in the country, and the Royalist government. This might have been considered a minor matter had it not found the British forces in the country between the two elements. On the night of 18/19th December, the British Air Headquarters in Greece was overrun by ELAS attackers and RAF personnel were captured. So while the situation in the Ardennes was being controlled, the British found themselves engaged on a new front. It was a desperate situation requiring similarly desperate measures if there were to be the so much wanted winding up in the Mediterranean struggle. Now wave after wave of RAF planes began attacking ELAS positions, motor transport and ammunition dumps, and there was no rest until the ELAS men were forced to take to the hills.

With the dawn of the new year there was some respite. The Ardennes situation was rectified and that in Greece quietened down bringing a cease-fire on January 12th. But neither of these two developments resolved the impasse in the Mediterranean with one leg still bogged in the mud of the silent batlefield of Northern Italy, and the other lost amongst the islands still in German hands. The struggle for the Mediterranean was still on.

February brought an improvement in the weather. Maybe not enough for the offensive which had been brewing in Alexander's mind and in the head of every Allied soldier in Italy. But it added more scope for air assaults, which were taken up again in earnest. This wasn't an ordinary air offensive. As front line squadrons began hammering the enemy wherever he was to be found, air forces from the rear were being pushed forward to occupied enemy airfields, thus bringing them closer to their targets. A South African Air Force Wing was moved to Pontedera, while the RAF took over the airfields at Rosignano and Falconara in the north. Even Ravenna which was the latest acquisition was soon hosting 324 Wing of the RAF. Squadrons were also changing to the latest aircraft, and Liberators 6s, Halifax and Mosquitoes 19s began to take over. And as the offensive kept mounting up there was the contrast of interceptions by the Luftwaffe getting less until they could be counted on the fingers of one's hand. It seemed as if the Luftwaffe had been swept away from Italian skies.

Never in the history of air warfare had so many aircraft flown into action so fast. The speed of the offensive was contagious, and taking on the proportions of a contest. There was no doubt it was having the intended effect on the enemy. But it must have driven the point in also with the Allied Command for there was soon a change of heart becoming evident regarding the Italian campaign. Some of the new equipment that had appeared on other fronts was soon being diverted to Italy. At first it was a trickle, but soon Alexander was receiving the new Sherman and

Churchill tanks, tank dozers, and amphibian tanks in quantity. There were also the new flame throwers, and to back them all followed huge quantities of ammunition. Morale of Allied troops rose skyhigh again, and all became more eager for the offensive which everyone could now see looming ahead.

The Germans must have known of this too. But the only indication that reached the Allies was in the way of a rumour that they had had enough. Indeed, the paralysing effect of the Allied air offensive had caused a shortage of weapons, fuel and ammunition to the Germans, besides the loss of men and equipment. And Hitler's confused orders to transfer forces from one side of the front to the other now began falling on deaf ears. A similar confusion reigned in the enemy's camp on the western front where Hitler, deluded by the belief that the Ardennes offensive had crippled the Allies, began having troops transferred to the East to stem a similarly fast Russian advance. And this helped in no small way the British and American armies to push ahead across the Rhine. But in Italy, there was General Karl Wolff who commanded the SS to reach the conclusion that the terrific Allied air offensive was spelling the beginning of the end on that front. And he realised that to wait and hope to resist Alexander's forthcoming offensive which must follow, would be courting a bigger disaster for his side, and unnecessary loss of life. So taking matters in his own hands he started the ball rolling to meet Allen W. Dulles of the United States, in order to ask for terms of surrender. So the rumour was well founded. But things were not that easy to move fast, and by the time Wolff managed to arrange a meeting with the American diplomat in Switzerland, March had set in with a further improvement in the weather, and an Alexander now giving the final touches to his planned offensive.

The race was on. Days were flying past. And with each one of them bringing fresh news of Allies successes else-

The Winding Up

where, now making the Allies Supreme Commander more impetuous to get going. General Wolff sighed with relief when he concluded his efforts to bring about a surrender on the Italian front, and it began to appear to him that he might have after all won the race. To bring a cease-fire before the offensive. But he was then stuck on the last stumbling block – Himmler, who would not hear of it.

March was nearing its end and German hopes were being revived with the return of Field Marshal Kesselring from hospital and convalescence after his October accident. But on March 23rd he was taken away from Italy to replace Field Marshal Runstedt in command of the German armies on the Western Front. He left General Vitinghoff to hold the baby again. With 23 German and 4 Italian divisions on paper, spread out on the northern edge of the Appenines, supposedly ready to resist Alexander's now imminent offensive. But Vitinghoff knew better than Kesselring what he could reasonably expect from his depleted divisions. He had been with them throughout the Allies air offensive and knew what was left. He had also known of General Wolff's attempt to surrender which had misfired, and with which he had agreed. Now there was March coming to an end. But not the air offensive, in which by then the Desert Air Force had flown 27,000 sorties, and destroyed 1064 vehicles, 5007 railway trucks, 531 locomotives, 485 barges and 26 ships. Besides the thousands of troops killed in the offing, leaving only shattered remnants of the two powerful german armies. General Vitinghoff was now faced with the biggest decision he was to take in his life. And he took it. Taking up where Wolff had left he ignored everything and everyone, and on his own initiative decided to offer to surrender. And he set about to make contact with the Allies.

But he could not reach them before April 9th. And on that day Alexander launched his offensive.

In the afternoon some 1800 Allied bombers and fighter bombers flew to attack enemy troop concentrations. To supplement them there was a bombardment by 1500 guns, which stunned the enemy forces. Then as night fell the infantry of the 8th Army began moving towards the enemy lines. Because of the bad weather on its side, the 5th Army could not start. The first German troops to be encountered were all in deep dugouts, sheltering from the bombardment, and as the Allied troops arrived they began to get the Germans out by using flame throwers. On April 10th, the 8th Army occupied Lugo.

The Germans now began recovering from their shock, and as they left their dugouts opposition became stiffer. But this did not keep the 5th Corps from crossing the Santerno river and press ahead on April 12th.

On that day there was the sad news of President Roosevelt's death, which Hitler was soon interpreting as being the miracle he had been waiting for. He had hoped this was going to drive a wedge between the Allies. But what it did was to bring them closer, as they were sweeping forward to reach the Elbe in Germany, from where they were to push towards Berlin.

In Italy, too, the American President's death seemed to bring the good weather to the 5th Army waiting impatiently to join in what they knew to be the final battle of the campaign. And on April 14th it went ahead. The American troops here had the disadvantage of having to overcome stiff resistance by alerted German forces of Vitinghoff's 14th Army, and it took them three days to do it. They were also hindered by having to cross a mountain ridge before reaching the plains leading to Bologna. This took them another four days, which gave enough time to the 8th Army to reach there as well. The two Allied armies could thus enter Bologna together.

But the significance of this move did not lay in the occupation of the city. The 5th Army had by its advance cut the German 14th Army in two, with one part being trapped against the western coast, and the other being caught between the Americans and the part of the 8th

The Winding Up

Army on the Adriatic side, which had also trapped the German 10th Army on that part of the front. Thus both German armies were cut in three. Vitinghoff's men were now running in disorder, leaving transport and equipment behind, and the German general lost control of his forces which brought their collapse.

The Allies could now move swifter. Modena was taken on April 23rd, with Ferrara and Mantua falling on the following day. La Spezia and Parma were occupied on the 25th. It was now the turn of the partisans to emerge out in the open, and some 60,000 of them began waging open warfare on the fast retreating Germans. Piacenza and Genoa fell to the Allies on the 27th, by which time the partisans had blocked all the Alpine passes out of Italy to trap German troops now all wanting to escape. But the morrow, April 28th, pushed a different kind of escapee in the partisans' trap. Benito Mussolini and his mistress Clara Petacci were caught whilst trying to escape. Their end came quick by a firing squad. It was all finished for the Germans, and rather than running away they now began surrendering on meeting Allied troops. On April 29th Padua was captured by the 5th Army, while the 8th Army reached Venice.

A desolated General Vitinghoff now knew that all was lost. Of the 27 divisions he had three weeks before, he was left with only 4. More than a defeat it was a disaster for the German armies. He now got in touch with General Wolff, and disregarding all attempts from Berlin and Kesselring to hold them back they asked Alexander for terms of surrender. In the meantime the Allies occupied Turin on April 30th. On that day German envoys were at Alexander's headquarters in Caserta to sign an unconditional surrender in Italy which was to come into effect on May 2nd. By that time too, Trieste, Cremona, Milan and Udine were taken over which closed the tally. The whole of Italy was occupied, and all fighting stopped.

A sudden hush had taken over from the thunder of

guns on the battlefields. The war was not yet over. But hearts were no longer throbbing with fear or trepidation. There was hope and excitement in waiting for the end. Hitler was dead and Germany was beaten. The total German surrender came on May 6th. Eyes now turned on the islands of Crete, Rhodes, Melos and Leros in the Aegean. But for them too the end had come. On May 8th Major General Wagener, the German commander in the Dodecanese, as well as the commander in Crete surrendered to the Allies.

Now the silence was broken, and rejoicing took over. Finally it could be said that the struggle for the Mediterranean was over. There remained only the situation in the Far East to be resolved. But that is another story.

Bibliography

Alexander, Field Marshal Earl, *The Alexander Memoirs.* Edited by John North (Casells, London)

Attard Joseph, *The Battle of Malta* (William Kimber & Co., London)

Bekker Cajus, *The Luftwaffe Diaries* (Macdonald, London)

Churchill Winston S., *The Second World War.* Vols. II & III (Cassells, London)

Cunningham, Admiral Lord, *A Sailor's Odyssey* (Hutchinson, London)

Hughes Quentin, *Britain in the Mediterranean and the defence of her naval stations* (Penpaled Books, Liverpool)

Jackson W.G.F. *The Battle for Rome* (B.T. Batsford, London)

Kesserling, *Memoirs of Field Marshal Kesselring* (WIlliam Kimber & Co., London)

Liddell-Hart, Sir Basil, *History of the Second World War* (Cassells, London)

Macmillan Allister, *Malta and Gibraltar* (W.H.&G. Collenbridge, London)

Mars Alastair, *British Submarines at War 1939/45* (William Kimber & Co., London)

Parkinson Roger, *The War in the Desert* (Hart-Davis & McGibbon, London)

Playfair, Maj. General I.S.O. *Official War History, Campaigns in* Mediterranean & Middle East)

Roskill S.W., *The War at Sea Parts II & III* (HMSO London) and *The Navy at War* (HMSO London)

Shores Christopher F., *Mediterranean Air War* (William Kimber & Co., London)

Simpson Tony, *Operation Mercury* (Hodder & Stoughton, London)

Smith Peter & Walker Edwin, *War in the Aegean* (WIlliam Kimber & Co., London)

Young Desmond, *Rommel* (Wm. Collins, London)

INDEX

Abdiel, HMAS, 96
Abercrombie, HMS, 173
Abyssinia, 9
Acropolis, 50
Aden, 7
Admiral Graf Spee, 15
Adrias (Greek destroyer), 196
Aegean, 1, 30, 185, 192, 244
Afrika Korps, 44, 131, 150
Agedabia, 94
Agheila, El, 43, 49
Agnew, Commodore (later Captain) W.G., 170
Air assault, 102
Airborne forces, 55
Air Headquarters, Malta, 173
Air offensive (on Malta), 90
Air raid precautions, 16
Air Support Command III, 172
Ajax, HMS, 40, 62, 68, 72, 92, 149
Ajax, M/V, 83
Akrotiri, 59
Alam-el-Halfa, 122, 127
Alamein, El, 117, 122
Alarm, HMS, 149
Albania, 11, 30, 35
Alban Hills, 227
Aldenham, HMS, 191, 194, 202
Alexander, General (later Field-Marshal) Sir Harold, 120, 151, 157, 162, 165, 167, 171, 179, 182, 211, 215, 241
Alexandria, 7, 12, 23, 26, 69, 75, 96, 126, 187
Alfieri, (italian destroyer), 49
Algiers, 1, 137, 143, 169
Alinda, 193, 198
Allied Air Forces, 174
Almeria Sykes M/V, 125
Amazon Bridge, 221
Anders, (Polish) General Wladyslaw, 218

Anderson, Lieut. General Kenneth, 138, 147
Andrea Doria (italian battleship), 181
Andrew, Colonel Les, 61
Antelope, HMS, 114
Anti-aircraft guns, 12, 16
Antikithira, 191
Antimachia, airfield, 189
Anti-tank 73rd Regiment, 159
Anzio, 206, 210, 217/8, 224
Aphis, HMS, 20
Appenines, 232
Aquitania, SS, 80
Arado (German) float-planes, 191, 197
Araxos, airfield, 236
Arethusa, HMS, 12, 114
Argus, HMS, 15, 103, 114
Argyles & Scots Guards, 159
Ariete Division, 88
Ark Royal, HMS, 23, 40, 76, 82/3, 91
Armistice, 178
Armoured, 4th Brigade, 42, 71, 84, 87
Armoured, 7th Brigade, 184
Armoured, 22nd Brigade, 94, 128
Armoured, 1st. (British) Division, 99, 161
Armoured, 1st. (US) Division, 153
Armoured, 2nd (British) Division, 44
Armoured, 2nd (US) Division, 171
Armoured, 6th Division, 164
Armoured, 7th Division, 37, 44, 71, 92, 99, 163/4, 207
Army, First, 138, 149, 163
Army (US) Fifth, 81/2, 211, 217, 234, 242
Army, (British) 8th, 88/90, 99/100, 111, 119, 134, 150, 163, 172, 176, 183, 217, 227, 233/4, *et seq.*

248   *The Struggle for the Mediterranean*

Army, (German) 10th., 208, 218, 243
Army, (German) 14th., 208, 218, 242
Arnim, Colonel General Jurgen von, 149, 160, 165
Arnold, General H.M., 166
Arzeu, 141
Athenia, SS, 14
Athens, 41, 50, 175, 237
Atlantic, 15
Attacker, HMS, 179
Auchinleck, General Sir Claude, 74, 78, 84, 89/90, 100, 119, *et seq.*
Augusta, 22, 174
Aurora, HMS, 84, 97, 169/170, 192, 196
Australian, No. 8 Division, 38, 44
Australian, No. 9 Division, 44, 119
Ausonia, M/V, 233
Australian pilots, 216
Austria, 10, 229
Australian troops, 60
Avondale, HMS, 103

Badoglio, Marshal Pietro, 177/8
Badsworth, HMS, 114
Baede, General, 212
Balaeric Islands, 3, 123
Balance of naval power, 10
Balkan Air Force, 216
Balkan Air Terminal Services, 216
Balkan front, 31, 51
Ball, Captain, (later Admiral) Alexander, 6
Baltimore aircraft, 190, 216
Baqqush, 134
Barbary corsairs, 1
Barchini, 78
Bardia, 22, 39, 95
Barham, HMS, 11, 40, 46, 48, 66, 75, 82, 91
Bari, 183, 217
Basuto, 171
Battipaglia, 182

Battle of Britain, 91
Battle of Matapan, 47/9
Battle of Sirte, 103/6
Battler, HMS, 179
Beaufighters, 199, 197
Beaufort, HMS, 103, 198
Beda Fomm, 43, 94
Bedell-Smith, General, 178
Bedouin, HMS, 114
Belgium, 17, 55
Belvoir, HMS, 201
Benghazi, 24, 42, 49, 94, 100, 150
Beresford-Pierce, General, 37, 72
Bessarabia, 236
Bethouart, (French) General, 137
Bideford, HMS, 15
Biferno airfield, 216
Bir-el-Gubi, 86, 92
Bir Hacheim, 112
Birmingham, HMS, 114
Bizerta, 146, 161/2, 165
Blankney, HMS, 114
Blenheim, Bristol bomber, 21,34
Blitzkrieg, 14
Blockade, 113
Blunders, 35
Boer War, 8
Bologna, 242
Bonaparte, Napoleon, 4
Bonaventure, HMS, 40
Bone, 146
Borde, Admiral de la, 145, 148
Bordeaux, 233
Boston aircraft, 216
Bradley, General Omar, 162
Bramham, HMS, 126
Brauchitsch, General von, 38
Breconshire, M/V, 83, 96, 106
Bretagne, (French) battleship, 23
Brigade, 5th New Zealand, 64
Brigade, 22nd, 86
Brigade, 231st Infantry, 170, 188
Brigade Group, 36th Infantry, 147
Briggs, Major-General Raymond, 161
Brindisi, 183

Index

Brisbane Star, M/V, 124/5
Britain, 1, 7, 13, 27, *et seq.*
British Cabinet, 35, 67, 122, et seq.
British Expeditionary Force, 17, 44
British Intelligence Service, 167
British Navy, 5, 7, 23, et seq.
British troops, 171, 217, et seq.
Brittorous, Major-General, 197
Broadhurst, Air Vice-Marshal, Harry, 160, 215
Brooke, General Alan, 101, 120, 151, 166
Bruce, Captain Sir Henry, 2
Bruneval, 204
Brunskill, Brigadier, 45
Buerat, 150
Buffs, the, 189, 199
Bulgaria, M/W, 194
Burma, 79,. 101, 188
Burns, (Canadian) General, 222
Burrough, Rear-Admiral H, 123, 138

Caballero, (Italian) General, 122
Cachalot, HMS, 75
Cagliari, 3
Caio Diulio, (Italian battleship), 181
Cairo, 41, 43, 117
Cairo, HMS, 114, 124
Calabria, 24
Calchi, 196
Calcutta, HMS, 26, 40, 62, 64
Caledon, HMS, 19
Calypso, HMS, 19, 21
Campoleone, 211
Canadian, 1st Division, 171/2, 178
Canadian troops, 217, 222, 234
Canaris, Admiral, 35
Canea, 55, 59, 62
Cannes, 233
Cape Matapan, 24
Cape Passero, 172
Cape Pillaro, 178
Cape Town, HMS, 19
Capuzzo, Fort, 22, 73
Caracciolo (italian submarine), 96

Carducci, (italian destroyer), 49
Carlisle, HMS, 62, 103, 194
Casablanca, 137, 150
Casablanca Conference, 150, 177
Cassibile, 174
Cassino, Monastery, 212
Cassino, Mount, 206, 212, 222
Castelforte, 209, 220
Castellano (italian) General, 178
Casteloriso, island of, 185, 188
Castiglione, 142
Castle Hill, 199
Catania, 174, 176
Caunter, Brigadier J.A.C., 22, 42
Cavour, (italian battleship), 24, 33
Caesar Line, 215, 225, 227
Centocle airfield, 208
Central Intelligence Agency, 27
Chamberlain, Sir Neville, 11
Channel coast, 17
Charity, 20
Charles II, King, 2
Charles III, King, (of Spain) 3
Charybdis, HMS, 114
Chatillon, 233
Chevalier Paul (French) M/V, 76
Chios, 191
Churchill, Sir Winston, 8, 17, 27, 31, 35, 39, 43, 66/7, 71, 100, 120, 129, 167, 205, *et seq.*
Churchill tank, 240
Ciampino airfield, 208
Cicala, HMS, 20
Circe, (italian MTB), 20
Cisterna, 211, 225
City of Calcutta, M/V, 83
City of Lincoln, M/V, 83
Clan Campbell, M/V 106
Clan Ferguson, M/V, 83, 124
Clan Macdonald, M/V 83
Clara Pettaci, 243
Clark, General Mark, 138, 143, 179, 206, 212, 227, et seq.
Cleo, (italian) MTB, 22
Cleopatra, HMS 103/4, 114, 170
Clyde, HMS, 75

Colle Belvedere, 211
Collefano, 229
Colle Sant Angelo, 218
Comiso, 174
Commandos, 65, 180, 188
Committee for Imperial Defence, 12
Conca, 234
Convoys, 8, 28, 34, 40, 91, 103, 114, 123
Corfu, 7
Corinth Canal, 56
Cornwall, M/V, 28
Corps, 2nd (American), 150, 161/4, 209, 218, 220
Corps, 2nd (Polish), 218, 234
Corps, 6th (American), 211, 225
Corps, 9th, 164
Corps, 10th (British), 180, 208
Corps, (German) 15th Parachute, 211
Corps, 13th, 88, 92, 115, 118, 120, 183, 218, 220, 225
Corps, (German) 14th Army, 211
Corps, (German) 16th Panzer, 218
Corps (British) 30th, 88, 115/8, 120, 160, 183
Corsica, 4, 208
Cos, 188, 198, 237
Courageous, HMS, 15
Coventry, HMS, 26, 114
Credential Force, 194
Crete, 1, 21, 53, 55, 59, 67/8, 70, 114, 182, 191/2, 237, 244
Cricket, HMS, 80
Crimean War, 7
Cruewell, General Ludwig, 87
Crusader tanks, 187
Cunningham, Admiral Sir Andrew, 11, 24/5 39/40, 54, 68, 74, 82, 109, 138, 167, 171, *et seq.*
Cunningham, Rear-Admiral (later Admiral) J.H.D., 11, 162
Cunningham, Lieut. General Sir Alan, 78, 88/9
Curtiss, Admiral Sir A.T.B., 114
Cyclades Islands, 191

Cyprus, 1, 7, 185
Cyprenaica, 43, 71, 95, *et seq.*

Daba, 132
Dakar, 136
D'Albiac, Air Vice-Marshal J.H., 51
Dardanelles, battle of, 8
Darlan, Admiral J.F., 139, 141/3, 145, 151
Decima Flotilla Mas, 54, 77, 97
Decoy, HMS 21, 68
Defender, HMS, 65, 80
De Gaulle, General Charles, 133, 151
Deichman, Air Marshal, 102
Delhi, HMS, 12, 19
Dempsey, General Miles, 178
Derbyshire Yeomanry, 165
Derna, 94
Desert Air Force, 128, 160, 172, 241
Desert Army, 58
Desert Rats, 163
Deucalion, M/V, 124
Deutschland, 15
Devonshire, HMS, 11
Dickson, Air-Vice Marshal, 215
Dido, HMS, 62, 68, 103, 114, 170, 182
Dieppe, 204
Dill, General Sir John, 43, 79
Division, 1st Airborne, 183
Division, 1st (American) Infantry, 171, 173
Division, 1st (American) Armoured, 210
Division, 1st (British) Infantry, 210
Division, 1st (German) Parachute, 222
Division, 2nd (New Zealand), 212
Division, 3rd (American) Infantry, 210
Division, 4th (German) Parachute, 218
Division, 4th (British) Infantry, 164, 221

Index

Division, 5th (British) Infantry, 171, 178
Division, 8th (Indian) Infantry, 187, 222
Division, 34th (American), 212
Division, 45th (American), 182, 210
Division 46th Infantry, 182, 184
Division 50th Infantry, 160, 162, 171
Division 56th Infantry, 182, 184
Division, 65th (German) Infantry, 218
Division, 78th Infantry, 147
Division, 82nd (American) Parachute, 183, 207
Division, 305th (German) Infantry, 218
Division, 362 (German) Infantry, 218
Division 715 (German) Infantry, 218
Djededda airfield, 147
Dobbie, Maj. General Sir William, 20, 107, 121
Dodecanese Islands, 185
Donovan, Big Bill, 27
Doolittle, Lieut. General James, 138
Dorman-Smith, Brigadier (later Maj. General) Eric, 367
Dorset, M/V, 125/6
Dreadnought, HMS, 8
Duca degli Abruzzi, (italian cruiser), 83
Duguay, (french cruiser), 22
Duke of York, HMS, 143
Dulles, Allen W., 240
Dulverton, HMS, 103, 201
Dundas, Maj. General David, 4
Dunedin Star, M/V, 83
Dunkerque, (french battleship), 23
Dunkirk, 17, 71
Dunphie, Brigadier Charles, 155
Durham Light Infantry, 160, 189

Eagle, HMS, 21, 28, 40, 103, 109, 114, 124
Eaker, General Ira, 207
East Africa, 15
E Boats, 78, 123, 125
Echo, HMS, 201,
Eclipse, HMS, 189, 192, 196
Eden, Sir Anthony, 31, 43
Edinburgh, HMS, 83
Egypt, 4, 7, 13, 16, 36, 58, 108, 117
Egyptian army, mutiny in, 7
Eisenhower, General Dwight, 138, 150, 167, 171, 182, 208, 233
El Alamein, 117
ELAS, 238
Elba, 208, 230
Elencathra, HMS, 202
Eleusis, 192
El Hasciat, 95
Eliott, Air-Vice Marshal W., 216
Empire Hope, SS, 55
Enfidaville, 161
England, 4, *et seq.*
Enhait Hase Parachute Division, 200
Eridge, HMS, 103
Escapade, HMS, 114
Eskimo, HMS, 169
Esperia, 222
Espero, (italian destroyer), 24
Esteva, General & Admiral, 146
Euryalus, HMS, 86, 103.4, 110/111, 114, 179
Evelegh, Maj. General V., 147
Evette, Maj. General J.B., 68

Faid, 153
Faith, 20
Far East, 11, 80
Farndale, HMS, 96
Fascists, 9
Faulknor, HMS, 189, 192, 194, 198
Fedala, 141
Fermoy, HMS, 20

Ferrana, 243
Ferranc, 153
Fiat CR.42 (italian) fighters, 15
Fighter squadrons, 13
Fiji, HMS, 58, 64
Fiume, (italian cruiser), 49
Flamingo, HMS 80
Fliegerkorps VII, 55
Fliegerkorps X, 40
Foggia, 227
Force N, 103
Force R, 123
Force X, 123
Force Z, 123
Force 292, 196
Ford, Vice-Admiral William T.R., 20
Formidable, HMS, 49, 61, 66, 74, 143, 170
Fourstein, General, 219
France, 1, 14, 17, 23, 176, *et seq.*
Fredendall, Maj. General Lloyd, 137
Free French Brigade, 112
French, 3, 72, 216, *et. seq.*
French Expediationary Force, 218/9
French navy, 21, 23
French troops, 212, 230
Freyberg, Lieut, General Bernard, 57, 63/4, 67, 160, 212
Fricks, Admiral, 187
Fries, General, 209
Fuka, 132
Fulmar, Fairey fighters, 26, 40, 57, 66, 123
Frosinone, 227
Furious, HMS, 16, 123/4 143
Fury, HMS, 192, 194

Gafsa, 58
Galatas, 65/6
Galatea, HMS 12, 96
Gambut, 112
Garigliano river, 205, 209
Garda, Lake, 175
Gavodo island, 46

Gazala, 93/4, 100, 111, 127
Gela, 172
Genoa, 1, 81
Gensoul, French admiral, 23
George Cross, 108/9, 170
George, King of Greece, 42
George VI, King of England, 108, 169
Georgic, SS, 80
German navy, 15
Germany, 8, 35, 43, 56, *et seq.*
Gibraltar, 1/3, 24, 123
Giraud, General Henri, 139, 142, 145, 151
Giulio Cesare, (italian) battleship, 24, 181
Gladiator, Gloster fighters, 17, 25, 57
Gladstone, W.E., Prime Minister, 7
Glennie, Rear-Admiral, 62/64
Glenorcky, SS, 126
Glorious, HMS, 12, 15/17
Gloucester HMS, 12, 29, 40, 46, 64
Godfroy, (french) Admiral, 23
Godwin-Austen, Lieut, General A.R., 78, 84, 93, 100
Goering, Herman, Division, 151, 173, 209, 224
Gop, 233
Gori, 225
Gorizia, (italian cruiser) 83
Gort, General Lord, 109, 121, 125
Gothic Line, 230
Gott, Brigadier (later General) W.H.E., 71, 101, 115, 118, 120 225
Gozo, 171
Grampus, HMS, 22
Grand Harbour, 41, 107, 126
Grant, tanks, 111
Grantham, Captain (later Admiral) Guy, 84
Graser, General Fritz-Hubert, 218
Graziani, Marshal, 20
Great War, 8
Greece, 30, 35, 43, 56, 71, 168,

175, 182, 217, 236, 238
Greiner, General Heinz, 239
Grenadier (German) Division, 150
Grenoble, 233
Greyhound, HMS, 46, 64
Griffin, HMS, 46
Grifo Bay, 199
Group, Army 21st, 207
Guards, 22nd Motor Brigade, 84
Guards, 201 Brigade, 164
Guerard, french warship, 74/5
Guillaume, (french) General, 219
Gurna, 193, 198
Gustav Line, 205, 212
Haifa, 26, 187
Halagh Eleba, 93
Halder, General F., 38
Halfaya Pass, 71
Halifax bombers, 239
Hall, Maj.-General 197
Hangman's Hill, 213
Hank, Cape A1, 142
Harcourt, Rear-Admiral, 170
Hargest, Brigadier, 61
Harwood, Admiral Sir Henry, 109, 117, 162
Hasty, HMS, 46, 62
Havock, HMS, 46, 96
Haythrop, HMS, 103
Heinkel, (German) bombers, 190
Heraklion, 54, 60, 66
Hereward, HMS, 46, 62, 68, 185
Heidrich, General, 212
Hermione, HMS, 83, 114
Highland Division, 51st, 133, 152
Hildebrand, General Hans-Georg, 218
Himmler, Heinrich, 241
Hitler, Adolf, 9/11, 30, 39, 91, 129, 144, 244
Hitler Line, 215, 224
Hobart, HMAS, 96
Holland, 55
Holmes, Lieut. General Sir William, 125
Hong Kong, 79, 97

Hood, HMS, 23
Hope, 20
Hore-Belisha, Leslie, 12
Horrocks, Lieut. General Brian, 120, 164
Hotspur, HMS, 46, 68, 75
Howe, HMS, 170, 192
Hube, General H.V., 175
Hudson aircraft, 190
Human torpedo, 77
Hunter, HMS, 179
Hurricane fighters, 25, 56, 78, 102, 123
Hursley, HMS, 103, 196
Hussars, 42, 87, 165

Iachino, (italian) Admiral, 83, 106
Icaria, 191
Icarus, HMS, 114
Ile de France 80
Ilex, HMS, 46, 75
Illustrious, HMS, 26, 28/9, 32, 40/1
Imperial, HMS, 68
Imperial Star, M/V, 83
Indian 4th Division, 37, 71, 84, 100, 133, 162/4, 212
Indian 11th Division, 92
Indian troops, 20, 217
Indomitable, HMS, 124, 170
Infanta of Portugal, 2
Intrepid, HMS, 191
Invasion, plan for Malta, 102
Ionian Islands, 32
Iran, 36
Iraq, 26, 36, 72
Ireland, 4
Irish Fusiliers, 190
Isaac Sweers, SS, 96
Isis, HMS, 75
Italia, (italian) battleship, 180
Italian air-force, 12, 25
Italian army, 37, 173
Italian navy, 11, 24, 29, 123, 181, *et seq.*
Italy, 9, 15, 17/18, 35, 167, *et seq.*

Ithuriel, HMS, 114
Jackal, HMS, 58, 68, 72, 75
Jaguar, HMS, 65
James I, 1
Jan Bart (french) battleship, 142
Janus, HMS, 46, 58, 72, 74
Japan, 34, 58, 72
Jersey, HMS, 58
Jervis, HMS 46, 58, 97, 103, 169
Jodl, Colonel-General, 85
Juin, General A.P., 134, 143, 145, 218, 219
Junker 52, troop carrier, 59, 189, 200
Junker 87, dive-bomber, 124, 173/4, 190, et seq.
Junker 88, bomber, 124, 173/4, 190, et seq.
Juno, HMS, 62

Kalymnos, 198
Kandahar, HMS, 62, 72, 96/7
Kashmir, HMS 58, 64
Kasserine Pass, 154
Kasos, 190
Kastelli, 59
Kelly, HMS, 58, 64
Kelvin, HMS, 58, 103
Kent-Hewitt, Rear-Admiral H., 137, 167
Kenya, HMS, 114, 124
Kesselring, Field Marshal, 90, 95, 122, 144, 175, 183, 207, 211, 225, 235, 241, *et seq.*
Keyes, General Geoffrey, 85, 218
Kimberley, HMS, 62, 68, 72, 92
King, Rear-Admiral E.L.S., 62, 64, 72, 84, 166
King's Own Royal Regiment, 119
King George V, HMS, 170, 192
Kingston, HMS, 62, 92, 103
Kipling, HMS, 58, 64, 103
Kirkman, General Sidney, 218
Kithira, 191

Kittyhawk, aircraft, 216
Klopper, General H.B., 112
Kluge, General von, 14
Knights of St. John, 5
Koryzis, 42
Krakowick, polish destroyer, 197
Kuchler, General von, 14
Kupresko Polje, 216
Kurjawick, polish destroyer, 114
Kythena, 236

La Difesa, Mount, 206
Lance, HMS, 84, 96
Lancers 17/21, 221
Lanuvio, 227
Larminat, (french) General, 219
La Spezia, 180, 243
Laval, Pierre, 144/5
Lavrion Gulf, 197
Laycock, Brigadier (later Maj. General) Robert, 68
Layton, Vice-Admiral Geoffrey, 11
Leake Admiral, 3
Leander, HMS, 17
Leese, Lieut, General Sir Oliver, 120, 160, 207, 217, 223, 234
Leghorn, 208
Legion, HMS, 96
Le Kefe, 154
Lemnos, 31, 191, 237
Lentini, 174
Leonforte, 174
Lepanto, Battle of, 5
Leros, 188, 193, 196/7, 203, 237, 244
Les Andalouses, 141
Levitha, 196
Liberator aircraft, 121, 188, 239
Libya, 13, *et seq.*
Licata, 172, 174
Liddell-Hart, Sir Basil, 119, 211
Lightning, HMS, 162
Lightning fighters, 194
Ligurian coast, 1

Index

Limosa Island, 169
Lipari Islands, 126
Lire River, 205
Lisbon, 178
List, General von, 14, 52
Littorio, (italian) battleship, 29, 83, 105
Lively, HMS, 84, 96, 104, 111
Liverpool, HMS, 19, 29, 114
Lohr, General, 56
Longmore, Air Chief Marshal A.M., 8, 18, 32, 58
Long Range Desert Group, 188
Lookout, HMS, 169
Lorraine, french battleship, 22
Lower Vistula river, 14
Lucas, Maj.-General John F., 210/1
Luftflotte VIII, 63
Luftwaffe, 14, 27, 38, 66, 115, 147, 174, 201, 233
Lugo 242
Lungerhausen, General, 208
Lyons, 233
Lyster, Rear-Admiral, 123
Lyttelton, Oliver, 79

Macchi, fighters, 15, 78, 181, 200
Mac Creary, General, 208
Mac Gregor, Rear-Admiral, 178
Mackay, General I.O., 39
Mackensen, General Eberhard, von, 211, 218
Magic Carpet Run, 75
Maidstone, HMS 12
Maknassy, 161
Makaga, 1
Malaya, HMS, 11, 19, 21, 24, 32, 40, 103, 114
Malborough, 3
Maleme, 54, 59, 63
Malta, 4, 6/7, 12, 16, 64, 75, 81/2, 84, 90, 101, 108, 113, 120/1, 169, 181, 190, *et seq.*
Malta dockyard, 41, *et seq.*

Manchester, HMS, 125
Mansell, Sir Robert, 1
Mantua, 243
Manxman, HMS, 81
Maori, HMS, 96
Maori, 28th Battalion, 159
Marne, HMS, 114
Maqui, 233
Marcianisi, 216
Mare Nostrum, 19
Mareth Line, 153, 159
Marmari, 191
Mars, Lieut. Commander, Alastair, 126
Marsala, 174
Marsaxlokk, 107
Mast, General, 137/8, 143
Marshal, General George, C. 117, 166
Matapan, Cape, 24, 49, 83
Matchless, HMS, 114
Matifou, Cape, 142
Matilda, 73
Matmata Hills, 159
Mauritius, HMS, 170
Mauritius troops, 171
Maynard, Air Commodore (later Air-Vice Marshal) 16, 20, 25
Mechili, 93, 100
Medenine, 158
Mediterranean, 1/2, 5, 15, 40, 113, 173, 214, *et seq.*
Medway, HMS, 16
Megara airfield, 237
Mehdia, 141
Melbourne Star, M/V, 126
Melfa river, 225
Mersa Metruh, 36, 125
Merse-Bou-Zedjar, 141
Messe, General, 160
Messina, 176
Messerchnitt, 66, 190/1, 194
Metexas, General 31, 39, 42
Miaoulis, greek destroyer, 20
Michelier, french admiral, 141/2
Middle East, 11, 39, 119, *et seq.*

Middleton, HMS, 114
Minorca, 1/3
Miraglia, italian seaplane carrier, 181
Modena 243
Mogador, (french cruiser), 23
Mohawk, HMS, 46
Mittelhauser, General, 27
Molotov, 205
Monte Cassino, 221
Montecorrino, 182
Monte Faito, 220
Montelima, 233
Monte Maggiore, 206
Monte Santa Croce, 209
Montgomery, General (later Field-Marshal) Bernard, 120/2, 128, 158, 167, 174, 178, 183, 206
Moore, Rear-Admiral, H.R., 12
Mosquito aircraft, 239
Mountain Division, 5th., 56
Mount Apetitia, 199
Mountbatten, Lord Louis, 58, 64
Mount Cazzuni, 199
Mount Clidi, 198
Mount Scumbaria, 199
Monte Trocchio, 209
Mueller, General, 192, 200
Murphy, Robert, 137
Mussolini, Benito, 9, 18, 30, 38, 113, 154, 175, 243
Mustang, aircraft, 216
Mytilene, 191
Naples, 6, 184, 205
Napoleon Bonaparte, 4
Narvik, 55
Naxos, 191, 197, 237
Neame, Lieut. General Sir Philip, 44, 50
Nehring, General Walter, 128, 146
Nelson, Admiral Horatio, 4, 6
Nelson, HMS, 76, 82/3, 123, 170, 178
Neptune, HMS, 19, 92
Nettuno, 210
Newcastle, HMS, 114

Newfoundland, HMS, 170
New Zealand pilots, 216
New Zealand troops, 20, 60, 67, 88, 115, 160, 212, 217
Niade, HMS, 58, 62/4, 103
Nibeiwa Camp, 37
Nicosia (Sicily) 174
Nigeria, HMS, 123/4
Nile Delta, 58, 98
Nogues, (french) General, 27, 141, 144/5
Norfilia, 150
Normandy, 207, 229, 233
Norrie, Lieut. General C.W.M., 79, 84, 87, 118
North Africa, 35, 38, 41, 90, 108, 122, 129, *et seq.*
North West Africa, 99
Norway, 16, 27, 55, 71
"Nostril Force", 194
Nubian, HMS, 46, 58, 62, 66, 169
Nye, Lieut. General Sir Archibald, 168

O'Connor, General Richard, 36, 41, 50
Odin, HMS, 19, 22
Ohio, SS, 124/7
Oil, 36, 70
Olympus, HMS, 19
Onslow, HMS, 114
Operation Accolade, 187
Operation Anvil, 205, 215, 229
Operation Avalanche, 179
Operation Battleaxe, 71
Operation Brassard, 230
Operation Buffalo, 225
Operation Chesterfield, 223
Operation Crusader, 79, 86, 95
Operation Diadem, 215, 217, 229
Operation Dragoon, 232/3
Operation Harpoon, 114
Operation Hats, 40
Operation Hercules, 102, 113
Operation Husky, 167
Operation Judgement, 32

Index

Operation Lightfoot, 130
Operation Microbe, 188
Operation Overlord, 204
Operation Pedestal, 123
Operation Shingle, 206
Operation Slapstick, 123
Operation Substance, 76
Operation Tiger, 58
Operation Torch, 136, 143
Oran, 23, 136/7
Order of St. John, 5
Orion, HMS, 19, 40, 46, 75, 170
Orpheus, HMS, 19, 22
Ostia, 177
Otis, HMS, 19
Ottoman Empire, 1

Pachine, 174
Pacific, 178
Padua, 243
Paestum, 180
Pakhenam, HMS, 162
Palermo, 121, 175
Palestine, 38
Palestinian troops, 171
Palma Bay, 198
Pampas, M/V, 107
Pandora, HMS, 19
Pantalleria, 40, 169, 185
Panther, HMS, 194
Panzer Divisions, 1st. 168; 3rd. 218; 15th. 88, 89, 115, 128, 160, 174; 21st. 88/9, 115; 26th. 222; 29th 175 224; 76th. 211; 218; 90th 209.
Park, Air Vice Marshal Sir Keith; 121
Parthian, HMS, 19, 76
Partisans (Italian), 230/1
Partridge, HMS, 114
Passero, Cape, 6
Patton, General George B. 137, 161, 167, 172, 233
Pearl Harbour, 34, 92
Penelope, HMS, 12, 84, 96, 104, 170, 192/4
Penn, HMS, 126, 192, 202
Pericles, SS, 54
Perseus, HMS, 19
Perth, HMAS, 40, 62
Petty, Captain 29
Petard, HMS, 192, 194, 197
Pfeiffer, General Hellmuth, 230
Phoebe, HMS, 72, 78, 201
Phoenix, HMS, 19
Pico, 224
Piedimonte, 214, 223
Pindos, greek destroyer, 198
Piombino, 208
Pireaus, 50
Pirgos, 60
Pitt, Prime Minister William, 4
Ploesti, 36
Pohl, General von, 211
Pola, italian cruiser, 49
Poland, 11, 13/4,
Polish pilots, 216
Polish troops 217, 223
Portal, Air Chief Marshal, Sir Charles, 166
Port Chalmers, M/V, 125/7
Portugal, 2,4
Potenza, 192
Pridham Wippell, Vice-Admiral, 46, 58
Prince of Wales, HMS, 82, 93
Pound, Admiral Sir Dudley, 30, 83, 108, 166
Proteus, HMS, 19
Provence, french battleship, 23
Puttick, General, 64, 67

Qattara Depression, 127
Queen Elizabeth, HMS, 58, 66, 82, 91, 97
Queen Elizabeth, SS, 80
Queen Mary, SS, 80
Queen Olga, greek destroyer, 189, 191

Rachi ridge, 201/2
RAF, 8/9, 34, 80, 95, 111, 119, 121, 128, 147 *et seq.*
RAF Malta Group, 8
RAF Regiment, 190
Rainbow, HMS, 19
Ramillies, HMS, 11, 16, 19, 32, 40
Ramsay, Admiral Sir Bertram, 167, 171
Ramsden, Lieut. General W.H., 119
Rangers, 180
Rapido river, 205, 209
Ravenna, 238
Rawlings, Rear-Admiral, 58, 69, 91
Red Sea, 11, 117
Regent, HMS, 20
Reggio, 178
Regiment, 1st Coast, RMA, 78
Regulus, HMS, 20
Reichenan, General von, 14
Renown, HMS, 40, 76, 143
Repulse, HMS, 93
Resolution, HMS, 23
Retimo, 54, 60
Rhineland, 9
Rhodes, 28, 40, 185, 188, 192, 237
Ribbentrop, Joachim von, 13
Richtofen, Air General Freihen von, 63
Ridgeway, General Matthew, 182
Riete airfield, 208
Rimini, 205, 235
Ritchie, General Neil, 90, 100, 113
Rochester Castle, M/V, 126
Rockwood, HMS, 197, 202
Rodney, HMS, 123, 143, 170, 178
Roma, italian battleship, 180
Rome, 204, 214, 225, 227
Rommel, Field Marshal Erwin, 44, 50, 70, 87, 103/4, 110, 117, 127/9, 134, 150, 155/6, 175, *et seq.*
Rooks, Sir George, 2
Roosevelt, President Franklin D., 109, 117, 140, 205, 242
Rorqual, HMS, 19, 75

Rowallan Castle, M/V, 83
Royal Irish Fusiliers, 190, 199
Royalist government, 25
Royal Malta Artillery, 17, 78, 95
Royal Navy, 66, 80, 83, 194, *et seq.*
Royal Oak, HMS, 15
Royal Sovereign, HMS, 7, 19, 24
Royal Tank Regiment, 7th., 37
Royal West Kent Regiment, 190, 200
Rumania, 36, 56
Runstedt, Field Marshal C.R.G., von, 204, 243
Russia, 13, 70, 76
Russian armies, 14, 236
Ryder, Maj. General Charles, 138

Safi, 141
Sagona, SS, 97
Sahib, HMS, 162
Saint Nazaire, 204
Saint Tropez, 233
Salerno, 179/80, 182
Salonica, 192
Samos, 188, 192
Sandwich, Admiral Lord, 2
Santa Eliza, SS 125
Santa Maria Convoy, 127
Santori, 237
San Vittore, 209
Sardinia, 3, 40, 167/8, 182, 207
Straits of Scarpanto, 191, 194, 237
Schlemm, General Alfred, 218
Scoglietti, 172
Scoular, General, 67
Semmering, 130, 175
Senger-Etterlin, General von, 208, 218
Senger Line, 224
Seraph, HMS, 140
Seven Year War, 3
Sheffield, HMS, 83
Shelters, 17
Sherman tanks, 187, 240
Short Sunbeam, 320 float planes, 9

Index

Shropshire, HMS, 12
Sicilian Narrows, 58, 123, 178
Sicily, 6, 38, 40, 166, 173
Sidi Breghiac, 93
Sidi Ferruch, Cape, 142
Sidi Rezegh, 86/7
Sikh, HMS, 96
Simeto River, 174
Simi, 191/3
Simovic, General, 51
Singapore, 79
Sirius, HMS, 170, 192, 194, 196
Sirte, 106
Slessor, Air Marshal John, 207
Souk-el-Aiba, 146
Sfax, 150
Sousse, 161
Somerville, Admiral Sir James, 24, 58, 76, 82
South African Air Force, 216
South African troops, 217
South African 1st Division, 86
South African 2nd Division, 84
Southampton, HMS, 40
Southern France, 232
Southwold, HMS, 103, 107
Spain, 1
Special Boat Section, 188
Spitfire fighters, 102/3, 121/2, 126, 173/4, 189/90, 216
Splendid, HMS, 162
Sporades Islands, 191
Squadron No. 38, Wellingtons, 190
Squadron No. 162, 174
Squadron No. 267 Seaplane, 8
Squadron No. 268, 8
Stalink, President Joseph, 13, 205
Stalker, HMS, 179
Stalos, 66
Stampalia, 191
Stewart, General I.M.D.G., 65
Strait of Messina, 22
Strale, Italian destroyer, 22
Strasbourg, French battleship, 23
Strategic Air Force, 192, 216
Strong, Brigadier Kenneth, 178

Stuart, HMS, 46
Student, General Karl, 55, 63, 70, 168, 174, 177
Stuka, dive bomber, 66, 107, 124, 194
Suda Bay, 54, 59, 66
Sudan, 37
Suez, 27, 70, 81
Suez Canal, 7/8, 80, 117
Suffrein, french cruiser, 22
Surcouf, french submarine, 76
Sussex, HMS, 11
Swordfish aircraft, 29, 33/4, 40
Sydney, HMAS, 16, 19, 28
Syfret, Vice-Admiral E.W., 123/4
Syracuse, 174/5
Syria, 26, 72, 76
Syros, 237

Tabourka, 146/7
Tafaroud airfield, 142
Talabot, M/V 107
Tangier, 2
Taranto 29, 32, 109, 192
Tebesa, 153
Tedder, Air Chief Marshal, 65, 68, 130, 167, 207
Teheran, 205
Terracina, 224
Terello, 211
Terror, HMS, 20
Thela, 154
Thelepta, 153
Themistocles, greek destroyer, 20, 194
Thira, 237
Thoma, General von, 38, 134
Thomas, Captain, 198
Thrasher, HMS, 75
Thunderbolt, HMS, 162
Tigris, HMS, 162
Tilney, Brigadier, 197, 200
Tithbury, Brigadier, 53
Tito, Marshal Josef, 216
Tobruk, 22, 41, 71, 81, 86, 88, 92,

107, 113, 4, 23, 137, 143, 148
Tovey, Rear-Admiral J.C., 12
Trasimere Line, 230
Traugott-Herr, General, 218
Trento, italian cruiser, 83
Trettner, General Heinrich, 218
Tribune, italian destroyer, 22
Trigh el Abd, 86
Trigh Capuzzo, 87
Tripoli, 43, 82, 114, 152
Tripolitania, 41, 150
Trouin, french cruiser, 22
Troubridge, Commodore Thomas, 137
Truscott, General Lucian K., 213, 217, 225
Tuker, General Francis, 106
Tunis, 99, 144, 146, 164
Tunisia, 144, 149, 165
Turbulent, HMS, 162
Turin, 244
Turkey, 31, 186

U Boats, 15, 123
Uganda, HMS, 170
Utmost, HMS, 96, 121
Ultra, 56
Unbroken, HMS, 121, 126
Unicorn, HMS, 179
United, HMS, 121
United States Army Air Force, 147, 216
Unruly, HMS, 194
Upright, HMS, 96
Urge, HMS, 96
Utrecht, Treaty of, 3

Valiant, HMS, 23, 32, 40, 48, 64, 91, 97, 170, 178, 181
Valletta, 5
Valmonte, 224
Valmy, HMS, 74
Vanguard, HMS, 6
Vedette, HMS, 114

Velletri, 227
Vendetta, HMS, 46
Venetian gun-ships, 4
Venice 243
Vian, Rear-Admiral Philip, 84, 96, 103, 114, 179
Vichy, 27
Victorious, HMS 124, 143
Victory Kitchens, 102
Vietinghoff, General, 179, 218, 235
Viterbo airfield, 208
Vittorio Veneto, italian battleship, 29, 47, 83, 96, 180/1
Volturno river, 205
Voroshilov, Marshal, 205

Wadi Akarit, 160/1
Wadi Zigzou, 160
Wagener, Maj-General, 244
Warrior, HMS, 7
Warrangi, M/V, 125
Warsaw, 15
Warspite, HMS, 11,15/17, 24, 32, 40, 46, 58, 64, 75, 170, 178, 181
Wasp, U.S. aircraft carrier, 121
Waterhen, HMS, 80
Wavell, General Sir Archibald, 13, 26, 28, 35/7, 57, 67, 71, 74, *et seq.*

Weich, General von, 52
Wellington bomber, 21, 24
Welsh, Air Marshal William, 138
Welshman, HMS, 109
Westcott, HMS, 114
Western Desert, 34, 36, 41, *et seq.*
Western Front, 10
Western Mediterranean, 3, 21, *et seq.*
West Kent Regiment, 189, 200
Weston, Maj. General E.C., 54, 67/8
Westrick, Gerhard, 27
Weygand, General, 17

Willis, Vice-Admiral, 170, 194
Wilson, General Sir Henry Maitland, 72, 187, 207, 215
Wishart, HMS, 114
Wolff, General Karl, 240
Wolseley, Sir Garnet, 8
Woolwich, HMS, 12
Wrestler, HMS, 114

Yalta Conference, 238
York, HMS, 40, 54, 77
Yugoslavia, 31, 35, 51/2, 216 236

Zara, italian cruiser, 49
Ziegler, General von, 153

Bleach
Juice
Milk
plums
Dates